Faith at Suicide

Also published by Kenneth Cragg

Semitism: The Whence and Whither
"How dear are your counsels"

The Weight in the Word
Prophethood: Biblical and Quranic

With God in Human Trust
Christian Faith and Contemporary Humanism
A meeting of minds

The Christian Jesus
Faith in the Finding

Faiths in Their Pronouns
Websites of Identity

Readings in the Qur'an
Selected and translated by Kenneth Cragg

A Certain Sympathy of Scriptures
Biblical and Quranic

Faith at Suicide

LIVES FORFEIT

Violent Religion – Human Despair

KENNETH CRAGG

sussex
ACADEMIC
PRESS

BRIGHTON • PORTLAND

2 4 6 8 10 9 7 5 3

First published 2005 in Great Britain by
SUSSEX ACADEMIC PRESS
PO Box 2950
Brighton BN2 5SP

and in the United States of America by
SUSSEX ACADEMIC PRESS
920 NE 58th Ave   Suite 300
Portland, Oregon 97213–3786

British Library Cataloguing in Publication Data
A CIP catalogue record for this book is available from the British Library.

Library of Congress Cataloging-in-Publication Data
Cragg, Kenneth.
  Faith at suicide : lives forfeit : violent religion – human
  despair/ Kenneth Cragg.
    p. cm.
  Includes bibliographical references and index.
  ISBN 1-84519-110-2 (pbk. : alk. paper)
  1. Suicide—Religious aspects—Islam. 2. Suicide—Religious
aspects—Judaism. 3. Suicide—Religious aspects—
Christianity. 4. Martyrdom—Islam. 5. Suicide bombers.
  I. Title.

BP190.5.S94C73 2005
297.2′3—dc22

                                                      2005010129

Typeset and designed by G&G Editorial, Brighton
Printed by TJ International, Padstow, Cornwall
This book is printed on acid-free paper.

Contents

Preface

These chapters are not debating about euthanasia, the turning off of life-supporting machines or assisted dying in the anguished circumstances of terminal disease. They have to do with deliberate self-homicide as the decision of persons in full or proximate control of themselves.

Purposeful suicide in contemporary Islam and the deep pathos in its frequency for religious ends is the main impulse to the topic of *Faith at Suicide*. 'At' is meant in the double sense of deed and time, as in 'men at work' and 'life at sixty'. But the Islamic phenomenon needs to be set in a wider context which reckons with its incidence elsewhere, with its uneasy associations in martyrdom and with how it interrogates – or is interrogated by – the ethics of religious faith. The enigma in wilful suicide is no less a challenge to our sanity or our compassion when such faith is absent from the deed or dimly yearned for by it.

'I am pregnant with my cause', orators may boast. But they were never pregnant with themselves. All births are unsolicited on the part of the 'who' they usher into life. The will to the intercourse that duly led to their initiation was not their own. It follows that at some point we have all to reach some philosophy about our birth. For one is perpetually at stake in living. The time-length it bestows is one we are free to curtail. Dark cynics have said that life is no more than forebearing to do so. The sheer mystery of birth demands we disavow all such self-refusal and summons us steadily to greet its laden invitation. What then of those who resolve to make it forfeit for an end they must also abdicate in doing do?

With how many terms can selfhood be hyphenated! Such is the compass of mortality. Places of self-storage stand ready for our property. They are no harbour for self-fulfilment. Selves are 'banished and betrayed' when weary despair registers what ill-fate itself has done to them. It is more darkly so when the precious human frame, the body's wonder, by 'self-bombing' encases lethal death in and for and from itself.

The issue belongs with the conscience of Islam today, but also for the mind of all, we whose common human birth has 'involved us in mankind'.

The main concern of these chapters is the horror and perplexity kindled by the grim prodigality of Muslim suicides and the negative malignity of their vengefulness. However, the phenomenon is here deliberately set in the wider context of a suiciding human despair and other violent occasions. Only so could perspective be true and compassionate.

Hence, too, the inter-association in a cover design which features the Biblical tradition of 'the hill of evil counsel' and its Akeldama, or 'field of blood', for ever symbolizing the suicide of Judas Iscariot. The place is usually located across the Valley of Hinnom and south of the city. Centuries earlier, it had seen the suicide of Achitophel – 'the fondly foolish' advisor of Absalom in uprising against his father David. Achitopel seems to have been something of a Judean Polonius undone by his own busybody role at court. Was it injured pride or the sad miscarriage of his 'counsel' that prompted demise at his own hand?

Jesus' Zealot disciple, Judas, died on the same hillside, more grievously still the victim of his own misguided and misguiding mind. His 'thirty pieces of silver' purchased 'the potter's field to bury strangers in'. These would often be the suiciders who could never properly find graves among honest folk.

Long practice in Judeo, Christian and Muslim tradition has kept that apartheid of the dead whose dying has too sharply flouted the trust of our mortality. That Judas story is worlds away from the current Muslim tragedy of multiplied self-immolation. Yet there is poetic – not to say human – justice in a study that relates them. For, beyond all disparity, whether in violence or despair, they brought untimely pathos to the ever common liability of human dying,

'I think there are committed fighters out there who want to die in Fallujah. We are in the process of allowing them to self-actualize.'
US Lieutenant-Colonel, Reportedly, Iraq, November, 2004

'To die is to be banished from myself.'
William Shakespeare

'Suicide, so to speak, is the elementary sin.'
Ludwig Wittgenstein

'There is only one serious philosophical problem – the problem of suicide,'
Albert Camus

'Here the significance of life is conceived as a moment not as a succession.'
Søren Kierkegaard

'There never was a prophet yet who drew a pension.'
Akbar Ilahabadi

'It may be that death is to be your ultimate gift to life: it must not be an act of treachery against it.'
Dag Hammarskjöld

Faith at Suicide

LIVES FORFEIT

Violent Religion – Human Despair

Introduction

Body-Tenancy/Soul-Tenure

There is a strange irony in the recent emergence in the popular image of Islam as a suiciding religion, sadly disproportionate as the perception is. For, while the factors involved do find occasion from reasons deep in Islamic story, their current expression turns on factors only coming to present measure in the 20th century. 'Faith at Suicide' – as we must argue – is a theme-title that must embrace the whole universe of religions and of the despair, as here in Chapter 9, which belongs with the sundry lengths of human travail that are essentially a religious protest against what is, and ought not such to be.[1]

Meaning by 'Faith at Suicide' a deed such faith performs in the when and how of its own decision, 'selves at suicide' are parties to the deed. Hence the triple sub-title – Lives Forfeit: Violent Religion: Human Despair – in immediate but not inclusively Muslim terms.[2] Whatever the means employed in self-homicide, they call into a final radical question the authenticity of being human. Such authenticity has peculiar resonance for Islamic faith thanks to its traditional reading of human birth itself, inaugurating life.

There are two reasons why this is so. It is not always realized that the Arabic terms Islam and Muslim are only capitalized by English (and languages similarly employing capital letters). In their native Arabic they lack initial capital 'i's and 'm's so that *islam* and *muslim* are genuine descriptives clearly differentiated from the Islam and Muslim of historic, institutional, formal and ritually official status. The distinction Arabic does not indicate is crucially important to the understanding of either in their double currency.

With this first reason goes the second, namely that in an expressive way *islam* has always held that *muslim* is the proper term for all humanity at large. There is a long tradition that it is parents who make children 'non-*muslim*' in diverting them from their natural *islam*. This born-as-*muslim* status inherently theirs should attach them to Islam. It is a situation partially resembling that in Jewry and Judaism, in that birth ensures participation.

In neither faith does one have to 'become', as the Christian Gospel enjoins for being 'Christian'. In the Judaic birth-belonging is inalienable, being ethnic by virtue of the mother. In Islam it is diverted and suspended by parental circumstance and wilfulness but ever retrievable by dint of post-forfeiture 'conversion'. Hence the vital thrust of *Jihad* and *Daʿwah* in Islam to promote and ensure this.

Since 'religion with Allah is Islam' (Surah 3.19), there is this essential identity between being human and being *muslim* prior to the compromise of either from the other in the living post-natal sequel to its ideal beginning. Given this perception in long tradition, it seems the more paradoxical that devoted Muslims are found ardently forfeiting their life in the name of the faith birth essentially conferred in its very incidence.[3] They curtail the human span on which birth had set their feet, renouncing it in its full mortal measure, in the name of the faith the measure ought to own as only living can. Thus Muslim self-homicide commits a faith-homicide also if *islam* and birth are by the Qur'an synonymous.

Of course, there is the problem of deviance from *islam* which Islam must strive to correct, assuming there can be a correct alignment of the two 'islams'. That, however, leaves us with the question whether the doctrine *per se* does not force inter-religious thinking back to the human equation itself, contentious as it must always remain what 'nature' and 'natural' can truly mean in identifying what is 'human' and what, in truth, birth inaugurates and biography shapes. Are we 'naturally' amenable' or 'perverse', 'surrendered' (*muslim*) or deviant? What discernibly is the point of the prayer in the *Fatihah* 'guide us . . . the straight path'[4] if right Muslim parents have not obscured it in turning us astray?

Perplexities remain but for the moment we stay with the alleged identity at birth of 'human' and '*muslim*' defining each other. In being rightly the one we are truly the other. That will take us far from Primo Levi's motto, drawn from Ulysses in Chapter 9, *polla plankte*, 'driven to wander far and wide'.

This leads the course of thought towards two further considerations, the one positive, the other negative. The concept in Islam we have examined holds a deep truth. Birth, conferring mortal span, means a liability to be. Yet, as such, it holds latent a constant issue. It cannot – and it can – be undone. It inaugurates what is not 'naturally' self-rejecting. As an event out of expectation into expectation, it has self-intending life-duration ahead. Such is its critical quality.

Despite the Muslim/confidence in a human/*muslim* equation, or perhaps because of it, traditional folk-Islam has long been anxious also for its ensuring. Birth ceremonies whisper the *Adhan* into the new-born's right ear, the *iqamah* (second call) in the left. They are witness to how prized procreation is in minds taught by the Qur'an. Infertility in women is socially a stigma, while deliberate avoidance of progeny is reprehensible in all normal practice. One would rarely find a Muslim echoing the words of W. B. Yeats:

> How could a passion run so deep? Had I never thought
> That the crime of being born, Blackens all our lot?
> But where the crime's committed the crime can be forgot.[5]

Tradition required that birth took place on *kursi al-wiladah*, 'the birth-throne', and be followed by a salute of festivity that left no doubt of the 'welcome' of the child, the more so in the event of a son.[6]

However modified by modern conditions overtaking old midwifery, this greeting of procreation lies deep in the Qur'an, as do the rights and exigencies of orphans. The *Iqra'* Surah (96) saluting as it were the Qur'an itself, rhymes *al-khalaq* with *al-'alaq*, creating at large with the 'sperm' from human loins that so holds the text in awe. Creation befriends procreation. The *'alaq* term is rich in connotation, from the 'leech' that clings and draws blood, to the love that likewise 'clings' and yields potential birth into wombs, and that which tells and transacts it.[7] This generative perpetuation of the race is a prime dimension of the over-all human *khilafah* or 'empire' the Creator vested in the creature within the intention of creation. Hence the guilt of infanticide and the deep, positive trusteeship of parenthood in the Qur'an's esteem.

'Undoing birth', then, as the suicide does – if we allow that birth is life-long-meant – violates the whole ethos of Islam. That verdict is only confirmed by the further truth that, for the true Muslim, its length is only and ever in divine disposal. The point recurs throughout the present argument but its ground is not mere 'fatalist' resignation to what will be. It is rather a law of 'unlimited liability' for the business of living which will never say, with the homeless King Lear, 'age is unnecessary'.[8] Suicide must be read in active life as like abortion in the womb, a casting out that should have been a ripening in.

From these criteria, rooted in Islam itself and its Quranic self-perception, introductory thoughts do well to turn to more general aspects in which at least Semitic faiths might broadly agree, despite the Judaic insistence on the exceptionality of Jewish birth and the Christian decision for a necessary decisiveness in the faith-issue in life and its living. All alike need the basic concept of bodily tenure and life-tenancy in place and time. Literature, so often akin to theology, can afford us a clue to these.

A crucial test of drama or the novel is how to begin. Shakespeare contrived it superbly with two guards on the battlements in *Hamlet*, the one challenging the other with: 'Who goes there?' – and the question reverberates through the whole play with its focus on the Prince in the toils of the enigma he must resolve, the anguish of love and the riddle of revenge.[9] Herman Melville, in *Moby Dick*, launched his saga of 'the watery part of the world' with a no less evocative: 'Call me Ishmael', its inner witness and its sole survivor.[10] Charles Dickens, for reasons needed here in Chapter 9, was no less masterly in site-ing *Our Mutual Friend* in the corpse-hiding mud-flats of the River Thames.

Once embarked on the flood of a story the other problem is how to end. Dickens' readers were prone to quarrel with endings that displeased them. For they took his personae to heart with sentiments less honest than his own.[11] The art of the end is no less exacting than the skill of the first *mise en scène*. Writer and reader alike might protest:

> I don't like this cobbling sort of business . . . I like to take in hand none but clean, virgin, fair-and-square, mathematical jobs, some that regularly begins at the beginning, and is at the middle when midway, and comes to an end at the conclusion: not a cobbler's job, that's at an end in the middle, and at the beginning at the end.[12]

A novelist's preference is one he can indulge. How many personal lives are 'clean, virgin, fair-and-square mathematical jobs'? So many are of 'the cobbling sort' fated, as the poet had it, 'to broken off careers'.[13] Presiding over a story is the narrator's prerogative, wielding the imperialism of the pen as master of what it may unfold. Not so the lived tale of mortal years. These cannot plead, as authors may, for suspension of disbelief. Plots are all too concrete and sequences existential. Biography is not a historical novel which knows where it is going and has in hand where it must end.

Persons however have the advantage of the dramatist in being exempt from the task of a beginning, sound or sorry. Birth takes care of the outset and does so with a biological finality over which we have no writ. It is well, therefore, not to say reverent, to begin with the positives of birth, as we do here in Chapter 1. It would be fair to say that there is a Biblical 'positivism' about the stature and dignity of the human condition from which all our study takes its cue. That it is also deeply Quranic we have already explored. The more tragic then the current frequency of Muslim self-homicide as the prime concern of all these chapters.

Hence the 'body-tenancy/soul tenure' language in the heading disowns the Comtean 'positivism' of the late 19th century, the philosophy that banished imagination from the business of mind and language and had its heirs in 20th century logic-masters of the A. J. Ayer kindred. Those minds conjured a minimalist view of the human privilege measured by the Semitic reckoning of the Bible and the Qur'an. This perceives and receives a human responsibility in and to a responsive universe and an intelligibility yielding a genuine *imperium*, over which significant human personhood 'reigns by a servanthood' which is called a 'caliphate', a 'dominion', where to 'exploit' is to 'belong' via 'body tenancy' that 'mortalizes a soul tenure'.

This reading of a 'liability to be' under-writes the sundry bans on murder and self-homicide we review in Chapter 1. It traces their provenance in the concept of creation and of a creaturehood in us humans within it. In its own different way Socratic Greece agrees. A destiny of the free comes inside the constraints of the indebted – and these within the purview of a divine intention that willed it so.[14] The veto on suicide could stand on no surer ground. No version of Islam has warrant to overturn it. No Muslim Hamlet, did we surmise one, 'sicklied o'er with the wild case of thought', could contest that same 'canon fixed'. Nor do suicide-bombers in Islam attempt to rationalize their dying. They invoke some grim mandate believed to be theirs beyond all sacred scruple, all mental veto.

For 'something after death' brings them enticingly to think the warrant entirely theirs. It comes in the Paradise-seeking of the suiciding mind of Islam noted in Chapter 8. There are, however devious notions of the 'veto rescinded' and of self-immolating logics elsewhere in history. Immediately to hand for Chapter 2 are the casuistries of none other than the Christian John Donne, whose 17th century treatise *Biathanatos* teasingly argues them. If a man can be the 'magistrate' in the 'law-court' of his own 'body tenancy' is he not the arbiter of his 'soul-tenure'? Ample reasons can be found for an expedited exit from an intolerable world. Grief, anger, envy, shame, jealousy, defiance, despair, the private irreconcilability of the public scene – all might 'justify' untimely exit and outweigh regret for all that a grisly end could imply in the reaction of the surviving world. Unsolicited birth, ruminating on the tally of the years, might find – as many poets have done – legitimate escape from its burden by the very writ of its mortality. Might not its quietus be as privately arbitrary as had been its origin? If birth proved to have willed the unwilling, might not death undo it by proving life no longer willed?

Yet we would have to say, by warrant of any Biblical/Quranic light, that the 'unwilled-ness' of life on any conscious part of ours never cancelled the meaning of the ex-wombing we received. For it ushered us into the privilege of being which its incidence immediately inaugurated and which its sequel steadily confirmed. For, unwitting, we found things reciprocal to us as the only and the sure reality of infancy and youth. These ministries might darkly go by default. Their absence could only prove how elemental they were. In this sense, and thanks to its finality, there is no undoing of the mystery of birth. Thus it follows, in the language of Ludwig Wittgenstein, that 'suicide . . . is the cardinal sin', or – in the opening words of Albert Camus' *The Myth of Sisyphus*, 'the only serious philosophical problem'.[15] Birth, and therefore life, have a given-ness about them that must make their willed undoing a haunted paradox of contradiction and only not a crime if exonerations can suffice.

Through and after all 'Yes' and 'No' around vetoes on self-homicide, that must be the Christian conclusion. It may also claim to be Quranic. Other sources might counter it, but only by disowning the reading of birth and time and life on which those faiths rely, inside a perceived creature-hood as the human stature. Some theorists have speculated on enwombment and its pre-natal memories as dark and sinister, a trauma with which suicidal impulses might later be associated. To such misgivings around nativity a Christian 'positivism' would respond by reading all sexuality, and intercourse therein, as altogether within the sacramental order of its faith in the declared goodness of creation. There the Bible and – in its own idiom – the Qur'an firmly locate them. 'The seed we spill' (Surah 56.58) and the physicality in which we do so, are among the 'signs for a people who reflect'. The explicit trust in parenthood, all too evident after birth in infancy, belongs no less with a theology of the operative intercourse that was prior and which has full place in the *imperium* we studied as being alike our dignity and our test.[16] The Islamic version of parenthood we noted will not gainsay that trust.

Introduction turns from these basics of a 'canon fixed' or unfixed, to two salient episodes (Chapters 3 and 4) in Judaic tradition. Was Samson the first celebrated suicide on behalf of YAHWEH? Should we rank him among death-dealing sacrificers of the self? His Gaza theatre became the potent inspiration, the goad, of many of his emulators in costly immolations – their own and their victims. How ought we to weigh the careful approval of Samson as *agonistes* by John Milton's Christianity, where the avenging hero emerges as altogether praiseworthy? Does the plain opportunism of his prowess lift him into a different category above the 'mill of slaves' in Gaza's present tragedy? What of the survival of his legend in the literature of a recovered Zion? What survives of him is certainly the enmity with Philistia. He was a fascinating figure for the Zionist Jabotinsky.

The Zionist mind has shown itself liable to link itself with an epic of suiciders a millennium and more after the feats of Samson. There was, according to Josephus, the grim pact of mutual homicide among the defenders of Masada in the final stronghold of the Jewish Revolt three years after the fateful Fall of their Jerusalem. We might take refuge in dismissing the credentials of a 'biased' historian and suppose the horror never happened, but for the role its ardent archaeologist destined it to play in the counsels and the morale of the newborn State of Israel, while still in the throes of self-ensuring. The narrative of Masada, its lessons old and new, in the mind of Yigael Yadin are the theme of Chapter 4.

At the heart of the passion in the Zealot catastrophe on the height of Masada was the ardour of their refusal to live under Rome. Religious passion made the essence of religion political, in that it required a national independence in being spiritual at all. Faith forfeited all licence to life in being denied statehood of its own. Leaving in their corporate suicide ample provisions of food, they meant to demonstrate that they had not died of starvation. They had died with equal deliberateness because there were political factors under which they could never will to live, perishing for a cause in repudiation of the will to live for it.

That dire quality of options, perceived or framed within a mind-set, belongs differently to the entire theme of martyrdom both in Christianity and Islam. Chapter 5 concentrates on the Christian version in the early centuries when sundry factors conduced to things darkly dubious between honest martyrdom and wilful suicide. The reasons were many, in that a right readiness to suffer, in the ultimate measure, could subvert into self-slaughter under unworthy pressures, whether psychic or societal. Pondering these in the Christendom context can serve us well when coming to the heavy contemporary burden of suicidal zealotry besetting the tragic mind of self-forfeiture among Muslims. When and where is martyrdom authentic or self-homicide worthy? What 'cause' was T. S. Eliot's Thomas of Canterbury 'serving'? Whose 'cause' was it in so grievously being his?[17]

In that dubiety around martyrdom/suicide in Christendom there were puzzling elements arising from emulation of the crucified Jesus himself. 'The imitation of Christ' could be invoked in settings far removed from the reality of Gethsemane. Scrutiny of how it could happen so has to take us further into the founding event of Christian theology as to 'God in Christ'. While the Creeds have immortalized Pontius Pilate, is it not remarkable that the popular Christian mind has taken scant care of the fact that Jesus was 'betrayed *with a kiss*' by Judas named Iscariot? This is the more to be deplored in that Judas Iscariot has been so malign, if untoward, occasion of Christian anti-Semitism as a contrived but potent factor in its instigation.

On both counts, it is vital to get in true focus that a close disciple's suicide followed so hard upon the immediate antecedents of the Cross. No study of religious suicide could sanely ignore the tragic exit of Judas ensuing – as we now locate it – on that 'hill of evil counsel' by Jerusalem. How could it be that a 'kiss' could possibly enshrine and symbolize that story? Suiciding religion has to live with Judas, whether as the deep enigma of the New Testament or as the tool of anti-Semitic guile. These are the pre-occupations of Chapter 6.

But what of the Gethsemane of Jesus himself? Was Jesus 'suicidal' in discerning 'a cup that he must drink', 'an exodus he must accomplish'? Was there a fatedness about his Passion, given how steadfastly he foresaw and reached it? To exclude that impossible temptation we must know the measure of its presence in its absence. This means a careful reckoning with his sense of Messianic destiny, insofar as we can identify it from the Gospels. It further means that, through those Gospels, we must heed the emerging faith of the Church, educating itself in the Epistles inside its pastoral cares and its growing world community astride the Mediterranean. For such emerging community-*cum*-conviction must be a surer guide to where retro-actively it belongs than the academic conjectures of an external scholarship, whether secular, Judaic or Christian.[18] Christian faith has no suiciding origins but it is important to appreciate the terms in which it is otherwise. For unless we do so we forfeit all right measures of what genuine martyrdom will be and we learn why – to quote Paul the apostle – 'abiding in the flesh is more needful'.

Understanding aright the 'kiss and suicide' of Judas and having the sure measure of Gethsemane and the Passion will leave the course of thought more ready for the suicidings of Chapter 9 that have endlessly ensued in the confusion, or the absence, or the atrophy of Christian faith. Such faith may not neglect those tragedies that, in their perplexity and pain, are 'believing only in an unbelief'. It can want no immunity from a like honesty, nor from a common kinship with all that is human.

Only oddly do the figures we ponder in Chapter 9 consort with those of the central concern, in Chapter 8, of the whole book. Their self-homicide is of a different order – assured in its resolve, ardent in its fervour and expectant of its reward. With these, there is no 'shuffling off this mortal coil', but a self-fulfilling destiny to die in an ultimate throw of mortal dice.

The constraints we must examine are deep in the ethos of Islam, but they are also drawn from the world scene as perceived inside that ethos as they inter-act. The suicide is thereby countering the imbalance he perceives in the military equation he confronts, as well as the economic imbalance of the hemispheres. These are further embittered by impulses psychic and emotional, given resentment, exploitation, dis-appreciation, 'envy, hatred and malice, and all uncharitableness'.[19] For these and their sources in the West, the West has every reason to learn a conscience and a sane response. 'Why do they hate us?' may well be a question to alert the United States: it is hardly one that should amaze them.

The sinister reality, however, of the Muslim suicide-bomber is not merely a tactic on the part of the outgunned and the out-mastered militarily, resorting to guerilla-style tactics of surprise and cunning. It has roots in the original ethos of Islam *qua* faith and culture – depending on where one sees such 'original' to be. Decision on this score underlies all the concerns of Chapter 8. Does Islam genuinely date, like its Calendar, from the Prophet's decision for Hijrah, or 'emigration' to Yathrib which, in year 1 AH would become Medina? For then his faith first assumed a posture of physical belligerence of which, earlier, it had been signally free. With that stance it developed a theme of 'faith via power' duly confirmed by its ensuing Meccan success and its ongoing subjugation of the entire Middle East and beyond. Was it, therefore, stamped for ever by the imprint of its Hijri centuries, its 'founding' dating from the first?

Being so far a fact, that can hardly be a question. Yet there was a prior 'original' dating from around 609 CE (i.e. Hijri 1 minus thirteen) when Islam was only and solely a *balagh*, a spiritual message, a meaning preached, a religious call sounded. To those, then, Muhammad had been rigorously confined by divine decree.

Moreover, when it transpired, that Hijrah with its empowered sequel had been on behalf of that 'preached religion'. If we are seeking 'originals' in any debate between them, there can be no doubt that the Meccan one was prior. The issue that Islam now has to resolve, and with which all suiciding has to do, concerns adapting that Hijrah meaning to a 21st century and a global scene urgent for a co-existence, rather than a conflict, of religions.

This, more than any idealism about virtuous democracy, is the inner crisis within contemporary Islam and the theme here of Chapter 8. It is one which only Muslims can resolve, but one to which a western world may – at due distance – contribute – by educating its mis-comprehensions and assisting all it may the wiser counsels of Islam both in diaspora and in its heartlands. It requires on all hands an unhardening of the heart. The suiciders serve a desperate aggravation of the Medinan mind-set, an Islam that prevails by bringing the world under its sway. In its first Meccan terms, it availed in the world by an uncoercive persuasion with its religious meanings, a religion that might now be within the comity of nations in quality of conscience and mind.[20] 'Bringing them to justice', if they mean to die cause-wise, is a barren formula. Bringing them to sanity and self-awareness of that first order would be the wiser aim. In those terms, too, the West has everything to gain.

The grimly purposeful suicides within Islam are in stark contrast to the miscellany of self-exitings to which we come in Chapter 9 but the balance of the book requires that we do so. If we say that 'biology is destiny', where violent acts against themselves and others arise from deep manic depression, does the theme of suicide to which Islam brings us in the here and now have the same strange aura of 'fatedness', as a mystery with which we must wrestle? We must ask, not only because 'sanity' and 'self-forfeiture' are comparably at stake, but also because religious faith ought to have redeeming work in either case. Acts of self-homicide will always be its grimmest point of saving relevance or of dire failure. Where, in zealotry, it actually connives with suiciding souls, how shall it ever redeem unwanted living anywhere? Its own capacity to care and retrieve, to atone and redeem, is forfeit in total treachery to humankind and to itself as duly 'religious'.

It is for this reason that we must take stock of figures whose literature made them articulate in the deep waters of their tragedy. Chapter 9 then can fitly lead into the final question life sets us, the question which so variously suiciders spurn or silence: Why continue living? Old Simeon in the Gospel prayed his *Nunc Dimittis*, leaving the timing and ruling with his Lord. The Greek verb had to do with the manumission, not of a 'hireling' but of a duly indentured servant, an onus he had never found onerous.[21]

I

'Canon Fixed 'Gainst Self-Slaughter'

I

Shakespeare's Hamlet brooded over 'to be or not to be'. Only because the first had never been a personal option had it transpired that the second could propose itself to him. Perhaps there in the mystery of being at all is the sure clue we need when the Hamlet question presents itself to us. Only inside the positive can the negative be faced.

No birth was ever preceded by consultation within the womb. Ought we to ponder, still less to claim, exemption when it is too late? Yet, if what birth inaugurated proved unsustainable, how should we respond? If, at the first, there had been no option, what of any option of its undoing in where potentially it led? Birth had ushered us into liability to life. Could life unthink, to undo its liability. Linked with 'to be', 'or not to be' was not a question.

Yet, in the very yearning of a Hamlet, question it remained. Hence the plea against conviction in his anguished cry:

> Or that the Everlasting had not fixed
> His canon 'gainst self-slaughter . . .

The playwright repeated the ruling in *Cymbeline*: 'Against self-slaughter; There is a provision so divine.'[1] Our liability in life must abjure the notion that it might curtail itself, until divinely relieved of the onus it conferred. The self realized at birth was duly realized in the life-span of the same 'natural causes'. For these, in their purely physical incidence, were the context of a spiritual hospitality.

The logic which faith might formulate to tell more surely this natal mystery, by dint of far wider perspectives on our 'letting be', was somehow instinctive to the piety of Shakespeare's world. Life was naturally self-cherishing and morally ought so to be. 'A canon fixed' only enjoined what

10

instinct and impulse knew. 'To be or not to be' was not a question. 'Being' is no theme for abdication. If, however, questions refuse to be discounted no 'canon' can exclude them. 'Being' contains them and demands they be allowed. The 'no abdication' rule itself keeps them in place, if they are part of what 'being' brings. 'No one ever lacks a good reason for suicide,' wrote the 20th century Italian novelist, Cesare Pavese, and acted out his own at the age of 41.[2] 'All the uses of this world,' as Hamlet knew them, seemed 'pestilential vapours' where 'we strut and fret'. There might even be something brave as well as sane in breathing them no more, when mere breath is all that prolongs their nuisance. Those impulses apart, there have always been casuists who could 'unfix' that daunting 'canon' of the allegedly 'Almighty'. Their wiles and wisdom belong to Chapter 2.

Midwives, from time to time in days less furnished with pre-natal care, have needed to decide between birth and still-birth or wonder if the offspring can survive. The poet Thomas Hardy recalled that he was one such and the image of his doubtfulness remained with him through length of years.[3] But normally, it is otherwise. Life initially affirms itself in clamant noise and claim and takes to the world as owing it the debts its long dependence must require. Being is somehow instinctively self-announcing, self-awaiting, self-proposing. What transpired without consenting ensues in fervent self-assenting. It has a 'here-and-now-ness' embarked towards a future for which both it and its world are meant. Thus one might say:

> Time let me play and be
> Golden in the mercy of his means,
> And green and golden, I was huntsman and herdman . . . [4]

'Canon fixed 'gainst' is a harsh if valid rubric only in the setting of the truly positive, the conviction of Semitic theology as also the Semitic humanism concerning the 'giftedness' of the human in the 'given-ness' of things and both as the privilege of mortality – the Biblical/Quranic theme of creation and a created order. Our 'here-and-now-ness' all philosophy has to explore and any faith interpret as the purposive intent that recruits us humans to its plot and narrative. This perception of a created order is entirely congenial to sophisticated, scientific explorations into the question how? because it is living with the reason why? The distinction between the two is manifest. The second lives confidently with the researches of the astronomers and the conjectures of cosmology and the caveats of micro-biology. 'Mercy in his means' is the reverence by which we greet the given-ness of being in its conscious tuition of the heart into a sacramental acceptance of all physical occasions they mortally sustain, equip and verify.

Faith about creation is just this sense of an 'intendedness' in things and in their being reciprocal to our human cognizance. Are we not presented in all rational experience with a realm of the intelligible, responsive to the art and focus of intelligence? Both ways there would seem to be an evident wantedness about the world we register – a wantedness that might be ascribed to a presiding will yet also reciprocated by receiving and perceiving minds that grasped its meantness to their employ in joy and sanity. Far from being 'on our own', we might assess and fulfill ourselves as recipients of a cosmic realm of mutuality in which will kindled to will, mind answered to mind and soul breathed with soul. These, then, would be our 'theology' only because they were our human definition. The world had been meant just as art is by the artist meant, in intention for fulfilment of a theme which moved through will to act.

Discerning theological faith this way by living relevance to reverent perception of ourselves would in no way be pretentious – something that ought to be discounted, laughed out of court, by reference to the vast unimaginable spaces of time and the hazards of incredible chances through which it had ensued. For those chilling immensities do not know themselves as such, had no course but to wait for the consciousness that might inform them of their daunting character. Such power of comprehension has no reason to be intimidated by vastnesses that must stay for the science that might give them identity. The only autonomy would belong with sentient selves in whom alone purpose could be read and that only because, there, it could be fulfilled.

Such Semitic theism, far from being nonplussed by widening, daunting and revising perceptions of the universe, warrants itself the more by its awareness of a given-ness about all things as credibly meant for recognition as a vocation, even a hospitality and certainly an empire, anticipating trust and duly greeted by wonder. Had not the Qur'an insisted that the world was not a celestial jest, a plaything of omnipotence, a thing of taunting vanity.[5] Banishing futility, with occasion for cynicism for ever scouted, the Qur'an renewed the Biblical theme of human 'dominion', which it termed *khilafah*. We had been appointed Allah's *khulafa'*, His 'deputies', in managerial trust over the created order as tenants, organizers, peasants, engineers, with all our 'sciences' tending to cultures and economies for whose fruits we were liable, and all under the divine accounting.

In total corroboration of that calling, Bible and Qur'an alike affirmed the mission of 'messengers' by whom the trust would be guided, monitored and kept in view, against the vagaries of our human waywardness, forgetfulness or sheer perversity. These faithful prophethoods, and Muhammad's supremely, the Qur'an affirmed as the ultimate tribute to the seriousness and authenticity of the human calling. The God who 'presided' did so with us 'associates' with Him in the autonomy He bestowed, over us in sovereignty, for us in guidance and through us in strategy.[6]

The pursuits of human sciences have astonishingly re-informed the mind-set of those far-off days of scriptural formation, but they have only confirmed the essential fact of the human autonomy by which their exploits have attained their present feats of knowledge and devising. Moreover, those feats have darkly intensified in global menace the urgent risk-quality of the autonomy by which they have encompassed them. The divine stake in the human has never been more critically at risk than in the current scene. Theology finds its authenticity in the very sense of things where, otherwise, we might find our despair.

It is, therefore, in this perception of a cosmos intended for the autonomous tenure of humankind, at once scientific and God-aware, that we locate the 'canon' 'gainst self-slaughter'. It could derive from nowhere else. Its negative for craven or hopeless exit from life is from the clear positive of our meantness legible in the meantness for us. 'Not to be' is not a question 'to be' can ever contemplate, unless by logics we leave to Chapter 2. The self-receiving to which birth conveyed us deserves and claims to be a sustaining self-obtaining through all the reaches and occasions of mortality. *Kun fayakun* 'Be and so be' was in the Qur'an the creative formula, alike for the earth and the human, habitat and inhabitant. 'Go your way into his gates with thanksgiving and into His courts with praise.' For the earth is 'the Temple of the Lord'. Being in a self, for Bible and Qur'an alike, is of that order, a summons into gratitude, an essay into the text of life, a cherishing that can be mutual between what thinks and what engages thought. The clue we have within ourselves is the key to why and who we are.

'Whether we would be grateful or whether churlish,' was how the Qur'an contrasted our 'Yes' or 'No', to 'being', where 'churlish' renders that *Kafir* Arabic of wilful 'God negation',[7] as a sort of self-negation also. The 'Yes' is one of full perception as of 'one who notices (such) things'.[8] It is, for the Qur'an, the 'significant' and in Christian vocabulary the 'sacramental'. All that is 'signifies', not merely as words do conveying meanings, but as housing them for sense-awareness and, thence, for articulate appreciation and employ. These *Ayat* of the Qur'an on every hand around us are the *material* of scientific enterprise. They also alert us to religious gratitude and aesthetic delight. They bind sentient being into one with the non-sentient and minister to the pursuits of the autonomous will, whereby cultures happen and cities stand and civilizations pass. Thus nature and economy alike present to us a sacramental situation, in which – more than physically – 'we live and move and have our being'.

The Anglican George Herbert told it all in his celebration of 'Man', meaning by the word, as we surely still must, all humans in one humanness:

> Man is all symmetrie,
> Full of proportions, one limbe to another,
> And all to all the world besides:
> Each part may call the farthest, brother:

> For head with foot hath private amitie,
> And both with winds and tides.
>
> The stars have us to bed;
> Night draws the curtain, which the sunne withdraws;
> Musick and light attend our head.
> All things unto our flesh are kinde
> In their descent and being: to our minds
> In their ascent and cause.
>
> More servants wait on Man,
> Than he'll take notice of: in ev'ry path
> He treads down that which doth befriend him,
> When sicknesse makes him pale and wan.
> Oh mightie love! Man is one world and hath
> Another to attend him.

The 17th century might be naïve about medicinal herbs in country grasses but the final logic is celebratory and sound:

> Since then, my God, thou hast
> So brave a Palace built: O dwell in it,
> That it may dwell with thee at last!
> Till then, afford us so much wit:
> That, as the world serves us, we may serve thee,
> And both they servants be.[9]

'How are all things neat?' another line enquires in the archaic sense of 'luminous' rhyming with 'our meat', the diet of his reflective acceptance to be and be in terms that serve in a serving world. 'All things unto our flesh are kinde' our following chapter has to query but the due reach of scepticism may not, does not, counter the positive from which alone with umbrage it argues.

Such, in aptly poetic measure, is the great affirmative from which any imperative canon against suicide should proceed. There are sundry other aspects of the Biblical and Quranic worlds by which the argument could be further made – the given 'imperialism' of the lowly plough, the colonizing remit of a good earth to man, the recruitment of the human to divine employ in prophethood, the host/guest situation at nature's table.[10]

Then when the Decalogue enjoins 'Thou shalt not kill,' or Surah 4.29: 'O believers' . . . kill not one another' the prohibitions are not mere orders from on high, but these as also the human sanctity *per se*. To be sure, there are ways around their veto ruling but only by also violating what we have positively studied. Did that *anfusakum* 'yourselves', mean fellow-humans or only fellow-Muslims? How did it ride with the rest of the verse about not squandering or wantonly handling one's possessions as if life was no more than a chattel? The Hebrew Bible had no compunction about warmongering, the Qur'an still less, so that forbidding murder could have tragic rescinding. The negative veto would prove far less categorical than the positive 'Let there be . . . ' where its case must always dwell.

Even so it is well that the ethical order should be as strong as it may, in clear reliance on its positive sanction in the preciousness of human life and in the ever private, inalienable shape that mortally conditions it. For the preciousness marries with the ever precarious privacy in its 'this-only' self.

II

Hence that 'Canon fixed' that gave such pause to Hamlet's 'resolution' – its 'native hue' 'sicklied o'er with the pale cast of thought'. The notion of suicide could only come from a diseased mind. Hence the trend in many cultures to read some tragic loss of sanity in the antecedents to 'self-slaughter'. How could one ever be 'self-possessed' in the very act of 'self-dispossession?' Wisdom in the Socratic garden had every reason to rule out suicide.

> Any man who has the spirit of philosophy will be willing to die: but he will not take his own life, for that is held to be unlawful.

Questioned further, Socrates went on, purportedly only to repeat what he had heard:

> There is a doctrine whispered in secret that man is a prisoner who has no right to open the door and run away: this is a great mystery which I do not quite understand. Yet I too believe that the gods are our guardians, and that we men are a possession of theirs.

On the strange analogy of some ox or ass having 'no liberty to put himself out of the way', he went on:

> There may be reason in saying that a man should wait, and not take his own life until God summons him . . . [11]

In Plato's *Laws*, IX, para 873 we read:

> And what shall he suffer who of all men, as they say, is his own best friend? I mean the suicide who deprives himself by violence of his appointed share of life . . . from sloth or want of manliness imposes upon himself an unjust penalty. . . . They who meet their death this way should be buried alone, and none shall be laid by their side . . . buried ingloriously . . . in such places as are uncultivated and nameless, and no column or inscription shall mark the place of their interment.[12]

Evidently the Greeks had their version of the Christian 'unconsecrated ground', which for long was the due resting place of such 'renegades'.

Either way, the studied isolation, akin to some wilderness 'scape-goating', tells a puzzled revulsion or maybe a dark perplexity.

The sense of the body as a prison was made familiar in the Greek tradition by the famous *soma/sema* formula. Had we not been tributary to 'the gods', it might be thought fair warrant for a suicidal self-emancipation, defying the chagrin of those mentors of our bars. The contrast is eloquent between this and the New Testament's 'self-in-the body' as a 'temple' and an instrument of divine/human purpose staked in the gift of selfhood whose span was meant 'to make the sacrifice complete'.[13] Death might then be somehow thought of as 'escape' but only in terms of such completion, the body being a tenancy, not as 'prisons' might be viewed, but as postings in an embassy. Its ending would be partner to its constant end and suicide would be false, not for the chagrin of the gods but from fidelity with God.

Maybe then, 'canon' is too hard and legal a term ''gainst self-slaughter', yet the sense of one has been prevalent among the religions as something instinctive to the possession of life. The impulse to self-preservation was seen as implicit in the very fact of self-awareness. Was it society that grimly made it reprehensible as a further measure of collective defence against the vagaries of individual forebodings or the sundry distresses of the living scene?

Certainly the Deuteronomist might be read in that sense, when (4.9) the injunction was:

> Only take heed to thyself and keep thy soul diligently, lest thou forget the things which thine eyes have seen, and lest they depart from thy heart all the days of thy life.

It could hardly be obeyed if 'the days of life' were wantonly curtailed. They would be needed for ensuring, as the verse went on, the continuity of the generations in the tuition of identity.

While it can be claimed that there is no direct prohibition of suicide in the Bible, it is clear that there were several seemingly commendable self-contrived suicides there, as of Abimelech (Judges 9.54), Saul (1 Samuel 31.5 and his armour-bearer), Achitophel (2 Samuel 17.23), and Zimri (1 Kings 16.18). Did these have the precedent of Samson in mind in their still more desperate plight of ignominy by their Hebrew codes of honour? That would hardly give licence to his emulation.

More puzzling is the passion of Job's remonstrance with God in 7.15–16.

> My soul chooses strangling and death rather than my life. I loathe it: I would not live always.

Earlier, in Chapter 2, he had reproved his wife's words about giving such thoughts place but even she had asked: 'Dost though still retain thine integrity?' as if her proposal would have him forfeit it. Retain it he did and the Book of Job as his (or its other master-author's) abides as the sublime vindication of the will to survive, abjuring exit by his own hand.[14] Staying the course through the allotted span would be the shape of a true fidelity. The Book which so powerfully depicts the case for suicide becomes the most eloquent witness for its repudiation. Yet the repudiation only happens as a strenuous struggle for the integrity it told.

In their Talmudic or midrashic exegesis the Fathers read a 'canon 'gainst self-slaughter' in the words of Genesis 9.5:

> Surely the blood of your lives will I require . . . at the hand of every man's brother will I require the life of man.

That principle of the *lex talionis* in the case of homicide could hardly admit exoneration of the act of self-homicide even when the 'murderer' was beyond mortal reach (*Midrash Rabbah* 34). Hence, no doubt, the denial of normal burial, the leaving of a suicide's remains exposed to all hazards.[15] When Elijah and Jonah requested to die their pleas were disallowed.

Surely the most 'canonical' directives of all against suicide must be the injunction in *Mishnah, Sanhedrin* 4.5, which comes also in the Qur'an's Surah 5.32:

> He who slays a single soul is as if he slew all humankind, and he who saves a single life is as if he saved the whole race of humans.

In either case there is the proviso 'unless it be in due revenge' or because of 'corrupting in the earth'. These in either authority have dire implications for any outright 'canon' against the taking of life but they are not of the order to qualify the guilt of self-homicide. Potentially, the core principle of these words, in the context of Cain's fratricide, is one with John Donne's words about the tolling bell of some village funeral. 'I am involved in mankind.' Therefore, 'any man's death diminishes me'. The corollary must be that 'my death diminishes mankind' and the more heinously in being my own doing. If, as Shakespeare's Feeble had it: 'We owe God a death,' then we owe humankind a life.[16]

Pirke Aboth (4.21) is of that same mind. It reads:

> Despite yourself you were fashioned, Despite yourself you were born and despite yourself you live. Despite yourself you die and despite yourself with hereafter have account and reckoning before the King of kings, the Holy One, blessed be He.[17]

Is this more than finding divine sanction for the sanctity of kin and kind in the collective apprehension of society? The private person should not exempt that selfhood from the matrix that alone gave it to itself as only so 'his/her own'. Divine forbidding might be known as the other side of social depriving.

It is well to realize around the Biblical and Quranic narratives of the first fratricide that Abel's was the first corpse human eyes had seen. Was the subsequent outlawing of the guilty brother the measure of the horror the deed evoked? The Talmudic/Quranic principle whereby 'all humankind' were present in that first life-forfeiture, even as they were present had it stayed undone, indicated the inherent sanctity of life itself. There was then no call to inflict on Cain/Habil his brother's fate. Even when later a *lex talionis* appeared, it could be seen, by its strict limiting of vengeance, to vindicate the preciousness of life even where it had been most criminally flouted. The old 'cities of refuge' generated the medieval right of sanctuary. In none of this was there any licence to suicide even in the most desperate predicament. The theme of Surah 4.29 could be taken as categorical, read alongside 5.32, as veto-ing any notion of Muslim suicide. The exemptions in the latter could in no way obtain in the case of suicide, while the former was followed (in v. 30) by words grimly retributive about homicide in pursuit of aggression and injustice. If the suicides we must come to in Chapters 2 and 8 to follow are not in that category, those of that September 11 certainly are.

Is there not also a clear anathema on Muslim suicide in 4.93?

> Anyone killing a believer deliberately (of set purpose) *Jahannam* is his requital, where he will stay eternally with the wrath of God upon him and His curse. Allah prepares for an awful retribution.

There is also a continuous emphasis in the Qur'an that the length of human days is determined only in the will of God and is not, therefore, to be self-contrived by any device of suicide. For example, Surah 16.61:

> He defers (the judgement He must otherwise require) for a time decreed but when due term arrives they can in no way postpone it, not even for a single hour, nor can they bring it forward.

Further, in the same Surah (v. 70): 'God created you and He calls you to your account.'[18] All deliberate suicide is thus what, in his own different context, the psalmist (19.13) thought 'presumptuous sin'.[19] Hence in Islam as elsewhere, the habit of withholding due burial from those who died by their own hand.

III

The Biblical tradition is of the same mind in this root conviction of the inherent sanctity of human life. The forbidding in the Decalogue of murder is assumed to include self-homicide. More positively, the ban must belong essentially with the human 'caliphate' as both trust and task. Thanks to being 'let be', by our being created in and for this cosmos, the option of a *nunc dimitto* is present. The ability is ours. *'Alaikum anfusukum*: 'Upon you your souls' as the Qur'an has it (5.105). Psalm 119.109 captures this Biblical personhood exactly: 'My soul is ever in my hand, yet do I not forget Your Law.' Being has the capacity for 'not-being' but there is a 'law' against such wilfulness that ever arbiters against it, since the privilege to be is a trust bestowed, in which divine claim can obtain only inside a human acknowledgement of its authority.

That double truth of things is at the heart of the Christian sense of self which Hamlet so faithfully echoed. In his *Pilgrim's Progress*, John Bunyan was equally sure of it. Suicide could only propose itself as a 'temptation', since plainly it was an eminently feasible act, by all kinds of devices, yet something sublime told forbiddingly against it. His 'Giant Despair'

> told them that since they were never likely to come out of that place, their only way would be forthwith to make an end of themselves, either with knife, halter or poison. 'For why?' said he, 'should you choose life seeing it is attended by so much bitterness?'

Whereupon, while 'Giant Despair threw one of his epileptic fits, Christian asked 'Why not die out of hand. My soul chooseth strangling rather than life,' only to have Hopeful concede that such a logic might hold, but counselled:

> Yet let us consider, the Lord of the country to which we are going has said 'Thou shalt do no murder', no not to another man's person, much more then are we forbidden to take his (the 'giant's') counsel to kill ourselves. Besides, he that kills another can but commit murder upon his body but for one to kill himself is to kill both soul and body at once.[20]

And to ruminate on 'ease in the grave', is to forget the nemesis of Hell. 'Giant Despair' is mortal anyway and might die first.

It is clear that Bunyan's boast about 'Who would valiant be' was dearly made and soundly reached. Bunyan, for all his 'tinker' status in the scales of lore and learning, knew the classic Christian mind here, the more so for the intense pathos he also measured in his much harassed 'pilgrim'. For his text was wholly biographical and came in prolonged 'prison-spent' adversity, where 'Giant Despair' was no fiction. 'Blessed are they that mourn, for they will be fortified' was truism for his day-to-day faith.

In line with those Beatitudes, the teaching of Jesus about non-restrictive greeting in Matthew 5.47 argued implicitly – as he indeed did explicitly – against the *lex talionis* of the old law. There was an *a fortiori* case against suicide, if retaliation for murder in one's own clan was to be forbidden. For such avenging murder meant that the victim-member of the other breed incurred a sort of involuntary suicide by the sheer fact of his membership, unless the *lex talionis* was transcended and nullified. The sanctity of personal life was thus upheld against that bitter loop-hole in the 'Thou shalt not kill' command. Islam as well as Jewry has long been tenacious about 'greeting brethren only'.[21] The social solidarity that made suicide so reprehensible in the popular mind could yet exonerate homicide when, in pursuance of that tribal worship, it took its toll elsewhere. There was something of the same collective constraint at work in the deeply seated attitude to the deceased by their own hand, in treatment of corpses, disinheritance, and implied reproach over the distress of relatives as if in betrayal. Of the same order was the will for the fact or fiction of insanity in the legal and social verdict on 'self-slaughter'. It was not only that 'the Almighty had fixed His canon' but that society, in its own insistent particularity, had done the same.

All the pros – and cons we must come to in the next chapter – around the anathema on suicide must be seen to bear on the issue of individuality, especially in the Qur'an's terms of 'no burden-bearers bearing any burden but their own'. In one of his more plaintive lyrics, the Urdu poet Mir asks: 'Did we have no one present when they wrote their record down?' 'The angels write and we are seized.'[22]

He is referring to the Islamic *kitab*-of-the-soul, written pro and con about us during life for final reckoning eternally.

Is Mir hinting at some measure of collective liability in life's wayfaring and its toll? So much of what may be posing the private question: 'Why not kill myself?' derives from more than private deeds or only from these as inexorably immersed in public scenes and forces. Mir's own 'My being has defeated me' could never be true without the circumstances publicly contrived by which he reached it.[23] While no deed can be more reprehensible than self-homicide as being the violation of our individual 'existent', its wilfulness becomes also a verdict on the world the world must heed, incriminated in some measure, not only 'diminished' by 'every man's death', death of this order, but accused.

These perspectives of death by suicide, as somehow a 'law of retaliation' against the world at large, merge into Chapters 2 and 9. They also lead into the great positive antithesis to suicide, the steadfast logic of the will to be. For contrived departure from the mortal scene brings to drastic termination all possibility of further relevance to it. The suicide – and indeed the martyr – mortgage entirely whatever concern they ever prized or served to its ongoing fortunes in the world. They forfeit any continuing contribution to its destiny, or may even jettison its life-expectancy with their own. Doubtless, the martyr does so with a confidence death cannot shatter and despite the duress that disallows the years that might otherwise remain. It is not so, however, with the suicide, who forecloses the business of living and invokes the past of biography to cancel its still latent and potential future. What that future might have held, whether of ministry and apt occasion or even of suffering, is conclusively eliminated. To decide that 'Time must have a stop' is a verdict against the nature of time itself. Or it is to read a negativity akin to that of the speaker in Feodor Dostoevsky's *Notes from the Underground*, who in suicide observes:

> I have only after all in my life carried to an extreme what you have not dared to carry half-way.[24]

By contrast, is the sort of Churchillian zest which thanked the high gods for the gift of existence, though clearly the very impulse to suicide is beyond such logic. Hence the urge for compassion to be argued in the next chapter. Yet such compassion, too, can only make its case from the sense of loss it has to include, since it cannot bring the solace of approval. In his own different idiom, Paul read 'abiding in the flesh' as 'more needful', despite his, therefore, non-suicidal 'desire to depart'.[25]

We might capture the point by noting how, in 1994, the régime in Cuba denounced suicide as 'a non-revolutionary position'. The Communist destiny could allow no self-forfeit of selfhood so urgently required for the programme in hand. The New Testament Church, for its proper reasons, showed the same cast of mind. Ministry was too vital a business to tolerate being exempt from life, least of all by one's own hand. When Hamlet pondered 'not to be', he described it as 'his quietus', his 'quittance' would be the apter word with that paternal 'Remember me' tormenting his mind. Or in the academic prose of Wittgenstein:

> This throws a light on the nature of ethics . . . Suicide, so to speak, is the elementary sin.[26]

Is it here that we reach the possibility, to be explored later in Chapters 4 and 8, that the negative will not to live longer, used as a fact, or as an ideal, in a religio/political cause, tends towards the ultimate atrophy of that cause itself. There is a sort of 'self-denial' of what is thus served in the denying-of-self that purports to be pursuing it. The near absurdity of no longer *living* for it lets a sort of death overtake its theme also. Something of what the suicide cherished in forsaking it as life's task dies with his demise. He takes his purpose with him in his own discouragement. He cannot say, with Bunyan's 'Valiant': 'My sword I gave to him that shall succeed me in my pilgrimage'. For he has fallen upon it himself. The 'Canon' is 'fixed' for more positive reasons than mere prohibition. And yet, and yet . . . ?

2

The Veto Rescinded

I

Shakespeare's Macbeth had much to do with death and knew how life's 'lighted candle' could be readily extinguished. Means were so amply to hand then in his grimly twilight world. Selves are easily self-ended despite the urgent onus to that 'present continuous' with which the previous Chapter closed. As Albert Camus had it in his *The Myth of Sisyphus*:

> There is only one serious philosophical problem – the problem of suicide.[1]

The phenomenon we are studying of 'suicidal faith' means that it no longer stays 'philosophical'. Its being 'serious' translates into the recruitment of the suicidal into the counsels and the strategies of religion. The present century, to a degree never before manifest, is burdened like none other by its impact.[2] The sanctity of selfhood is violated precisely where it could be assumed to be most devoutly cherished, if self-valuing was the sure corollary of God-affirming. 'Curse God and die' Job's wife had recommended to her long suffering husband, perhaps only in an irresponsible despair . . . 'Curse life in God's Name' is of another order. It bypasses all the other pleas by which life might re-assess its own tenacity and explicitly rescinds them, engrossing all other motives into a single final forfeiture of all. It may help to measure how dire the second is, if we look briefly at the first.

The preacher poet John Donne, among advocates of a 'canon' against death, was ready to find it *less* than 'fixed'. In one of his 'Holy Sonnets', he had counselled: 'Death be not proud.' Some years later he wrote *Biathanatos*. Prudently perhaps, it was not published until 1634, years after Donne himself had died. The Greek word means 'death by violence self-inflicted'. His advocacy used many familiar arguments in extenuation of self homicide – extreme adversities, the need for 'charitableness' before condemning, the case for some onset of mental imbalance. While his Sonnet had cried to the great ogre: 'Death, thou shalt die' the treatise revised it to '"Death". I can die.' Death had no just cause to lord it over folk as inexorably its prey. Individuals could take its writ into their own hands and – as it were – 'cock a snoop' at its prestige. The suicide, far from shrinking before death's tyranny, could enlist it as a deliberate ally.

Donne's was a pointed casuistry. Contrary to the case made in Chapter 1, from 'Thou shalt not kill' as obviously inclusive of the self, he said that this was no part of its range. 'Love to God and others' was all that should be pleaded as due from it. It was a strange gloss to make on his part, seeing that 'he is as you are' was ever the meaning of 'as thyself', since self-love was never paradigm for love of the neighbour. It was the logic of being 'involved in mankind', to quote against Donne his own sermon. This aberration was only a measure of how adept he was in making the case he wanted – perhaps with 'tongue in cheek'. For he went counter to all that piety might assume.

'Whether self-homicide is so naturally a sin as it may not be otherwise,' he wrote, had a too legal cast of mind. 'Many learned and subtle men who have traveled in this point,' he went on, 'lacked all compassion in condemning suicide outright'. While disavowing those 'hungry for an imagined martyrdom', he argued:

> Whensoever any affliction assails me, methinks I have the keyes of my prison in mine owne hand. No remedy presents itself so soon to my heart as mine owne sword.

This spurred him to opt for the kindly view. To be sure, 'conscience should disapprove rebellious grudging at God's gifts', yet 'peremptory judgements' should not so promptly damn the tragic victims. The dead ought always to be a theme of pity, while we 'corrected in ourselves this easiness of being scandalized', and be more alert to our own sins.[3]

This 17th century Christian argument would have little relevance to suicidal bombers. Nearer to our present concern around them is when Donne continues:

> So may any man be the Bishop and Magistrate to himselfe and dispense with his conscience, when it can appeare that the reason, which is the soule and form of the law, is ceased . . . What is profitable and honest becomes no longer so by reason of some event, requiring the dispensation.[4]

He is anxious to leave no loopholes here for false coveting of martyrdom which he deplores as a disease.[5] He insists that:

> No law is so primary and simple, but it fore-imagines a reason upon which it was founded, and scarce any reason is so constant but that circumstances alter it. In which case a private man is Emperor to himselfe.[6]

Our being 'made in the image of God' is, for John Donne, the warrant of this God-like aegis over the self – a sophistry that could even make him the strange bed-fellow of those September bombers.

Though these might be already too self-assured to invoke it, might not this 'Emperors to ourselves' be argued, by more alert Muslims exegetically, from the central Quranic theme of human *khilafah*? If our personal being, our mortal span, are a divine entrustment set in our very own hands, could not that privilege of 'self-possession' claim – as proper to it – some deliberate self 'dis-possession' in God's Name? Do we not take the Donor at His word? – 'On you are your own souls' (5.105). We had given no consent when we were embryonic, but life had brought its own liability to be in intrinsically personal terms. Could the option for exit lie in the implied non-obligation of birth itself, the more so if we have positive faith-reason?

Certainly the deed remains feasible enough even if the sanction were not compelling, as a *Jihad*-style faith might see it. In his poem 'The Man and the Echo' W. B. Yeats has his 'man' addressing a rocky cliff-face which gives back its chilling answer to his yearning words. A weary 'why not?' is ever present.

> He shouts a secret to the stone.
> All that I have said and done
> Now that I am old and ill
> Turns into a question till . . .

Awake all night, he ponders the tally of his doings.

> And all seems evil until I
> Sleepless would lie down and die.[7]

Whereat 'Echo' answers: 'Lie down and die', to which the man replies that to do so would be to 'shirk the intellect's great work'. 'From life's task there is no release in a bodkin or disease.' For 'body gone, he sleeps no more' but 'stands in judgement on his soul'.

All such scruples, suicidal faith is ready to over-rule, if they have register at all. For 'life's task' is courting 'release' in zealotry's 'great work'.

II

We might leave Donne so oddly with his 'bed-fellows', given his final counsel:

> If the reason for self-preservation ceases in him (a man) may also presume that the law ceases too and may do that then which otherwise were against the law.[8]

Our Dean of St. Paul's comes uncannily close to what religious self-destruction means and does. By such pleading are we to equate the 'good fruit' of conscience with the 'bad fruit' of a doctrinaire religion? The deed may be at utter private cost but it belongs in an inhuman public cause. Any virtue it may claim as self-forfeiture is hostage to the malignity it serves and cannot redeem its criminality. The wilful suicide in deliberate action concerted as the price of it, or the soul that wills to end all because that 'all' spells what he cannot abide – these flout the very nature of mortality. Thanks to the singularity of death, corollary to the singularity of birth, they do violence to the irrepeatability of life, foreclosing all the options it could otherwise contain, including the gains it visualizes in the act. These it consigns to an imagined eternity or invests in a religio/political future it wills not to see. In both there lies the paradox of despair, since life here and now is betrayed from within if it ceases to esteem the trust of it. As we must see anon, the sages who withdrew to Yavneh on the Palestinian shore, with their Torah and their synagogues, after the ruin of the Jerusalem Temple, had a saner esteem of life than the fanatics ending themselves on the height of Masada. The *Desperanda* of the latter needed the *Nil* of the former in no less a despair over their tribulation.

This self-dispensing with the self, as elements of the Semitic tradition have approved it, has a sort of *de jure* or 'by divine right' quality that makes it a far cry from the *de facto* drift or drive into suicide discussed by Donne in *Biathanatos*. Such hapless ones in their 'escapades of escape' were aptly portrayed in Robert Browning's poem celebrating the 'old morgue' in Paris where he imagined their bodies lay – 'the three men who did most abhor their life in Paris yesterday, so killed themselves'.

> Sacred from touch, each had his berth,
> His bounds, his proper place of rest,
> Who last night tenanted on earth
> Some arch . . .

Browning speculates on their stories and concludes with a generous 'charitableness' that bettered Donne's. One could not think of the heroics on Masada in those terms nor of the corpses of conspirators mangled in the debris of their handiwork.

Their suicide *de jure* was no case of Browning's 'Apparent Failure' over which to cry: 'Poor men, God made and all for that!' It contrived itself as eminently 'do-able' by divine mandate. Life foregone would be taking others with it in its own disastrous disesteem. It presumed to transact Allah's supreme decree in the magisterial dispensation of its own religious mind. So doing it gave ultimate – and perverted – expression to its hallowed concept in the Quranic notion of *Jihad*. It is necessary to study *Jihad* with due care. For, in controversial measure, it underwrites the contemporary fulfilment to which we must come in Chapter 8. It means that the *mujahid* Muslim, invoking *Jihad* violently, is not saying, like some doomed

Oedipus, 'O Zeus, what have you planned to do with me?'[10] Rather he is crying: 'Ya Allah, this for You I am doing with You ordaining me.' May not such have been also the dying thoughts of Samson clinging to the falling pillars?

When John Donne claimed a self might be 'magistrate of his own soul', flouting by his own leave the very law he should obey, he may have been indulging a certain anti-Catholic prejudice.[11] For the plea was that Papal Bulls and edicts were subject to 'dispensation'. The authority that promulgated had authority to suspend its own decrees. Thus laws had within themselves their undoing. Everything was eminently revisable from within its own warrant. Ordaining could have interior dis-ordaining by the same token implicit in its origin. Law could never be immune from its own inherent mind. Private 'dispensing' would only be doing the same.

Why then, Donne argued, could we not 'dispense' ourselves from obedience to laws which were themselves so far in fee to themselves as to be revisable? His idea was mischievous and its casuistry familiar in ecclesiastical debate. While the Qur'an tells of *naskh*, or 'abrogation', whereby Allah 'changes' what He has decreed in order to 'bring something better',[12] no Muslim could sanely argue along Donne's line. What is divine can only be 'immutable', and immune from human 'dispensation'. Its status is sacrosanct.

Even so, has immutability ever been assured or inviolate or guaranteed in Islam? Could such ever be in a world of time and flux? Is not the Qur'an, on its own showing, given into the ken of readership, bringing circumstance and setting into its possession? Is not a certain flexibility thereby implicit in its reception, albeit reverent and loyally deferential? Precisely in caring with those qualities, readership becomes more duly custodial in discerning relevance for situations never changeless. Thus there has always been room and occasion – with due restraint – for the formula: 'The Qur'an means what Muslims find it to mean.'[13] Those so minded, could as cogently 'read' as sanctioning their self-homicide as others could for utterly disowning it. Suicidal zealotry could not be banned from claiming its Qur'an against gentler readers convinced that those excesses were quite forbidden there. No religious text, however assertive of its standing, can ensure either immunity from false interpretation or from dubiety about the right one.

There is a comparable situation around divine *Shari'ah*. Only a modicum of its content especially in the political sphere is directly from the Qur'an alone. For the Qur'an is remarkably silent on many issues that belong there. Much of the *Shari'ah* has historically stemmed from 'human' factors, however divinely supervised. Among them *Hadith*, Tradition humanly collected, edited, vetted and sifted, to draw on the Prophet's example as a due source of guidance, supplementing the sacred Scripture; analogy or *Qiyas*, extending a given law to cover an arguably kindred situation; and Consensus of the community, or *Ijma'*, whereby much customary law or approved practice came to be part of the whole *Shari'ah*. Shi'ah Islam had its own distinctive means for kindred needs and aptitudes. The story is familiar enough and witness to that 'divine via the human, the human for the divine' pattern that belongs to theism.

Given this shape of things in the alternatives around 'the Muslim mind', those who would anathematize the suicidal in Islam have no surer mandate than those who would glorify and invoke it. A divided mind between the two there can only be, however disparate the spread of either mind-set in the vast 'household of Islam'. There are those who abhor the violation of Allah's 'canon fixed': there are others convinced of their possession of His warrant to ignore it.

This issue concerning human discernment of the divine will in matters of life and death waits all the time on the exegesis of sacred textual authority whatever the faith. It also haunts the vocabulary, the familiar terminology by which institutions of religion operate. What Judaism meant by 'covenant' and 'Torah', or Islam by *Jihad* and *Ummah*, or Christianity by 'Church' and 'grace', were all, like their Scriptures, somehow within the purview of their common/uncommon mind and always precariously at stake in the flux of their story. The meanings to which believers were subject were also strangely mastered by them. What Donne called *biathanatos*, being so dire an act and so wild a concept, could not escape this situation. All faiths live in some measure with the open question of themselves.

How this stand is exemplified in Jewry belongs with Chapters 3 and 4 to follow: the Islamic with Chapter 8. The Christian shape of the issue is reached in Chapter 5. The reason why Chapters 6 and 7 intervene is that they carry the implications of the whole theme in its wide diversity into the central story of New Testament Christianity, as vital to what is set here to follow them.

III

In all three religions the 'to be or not to be' question becoming 'the be as not to be' answer is closely tied into the common theme of 'martyrdom'. The theisms are strong on martyrologies. Their languages love the kinship between 'one who witnesses' and 'one who dies'. Examples abound in each tradition of a deep instinct about needing to die (faith-wise) and wanting to die. The readiness in either case can well also argue an ambition to die which may then approximate almost to a suicidal intent. The sacred urge in the sad duty to suffer in the name of faith can deepen into the very yearning to do so. The bitter centuries of Christian persecution under Rome, prior to Constantine, saw many occasions of martyrdoms deliberate, among martyrdoms undergone. They were not acts akin to Masada, nor to the suicidal in Islamic retaliation, but they came close to comparable 'zeal for God', primed to disdain further to live, in a world with which your passion can no longer deal otherwise. All three faiths revere martyrs of genuine sincerity whose lives were yielded in the goodness of good faith. Each has the many others who covet to die in the badness of bad faith – 'bad' in its 'unselfing self's' lust after fantasy, or status, or eternal recompense. Their veto on their living 'caliphate' was the deed of their own hand out of the lure in their own minds. They were virtual suicides. 'Faith' had made them 'unfaithful' contrasting darkly with the 'faithful unto death'.

There is one concluding concern in this chapter as to lives rescinding the divine canon. It has to do with the collective factor. We note that Donne's *biathanatos* is a singular noun. Thus far we have pondered suicidal event in the singular, whether of the *de facto* kind as in Browning's morgue, lying dead from despair or folly or revolt, or of the *de jure* kind of suicidal 'believers'. And, indeed, suicide is eminently singular. It was right to study it as such, seeing that 'it remaineth unto man once (and once only) to die' and as '*one* dying'.[14]

Yet what we observe about religious suicidings is how far they belong with community, not as mass action on a Masada, but thanks to a shared incentive, as with zealots and anarchists, and often the more likely by the sanction of numbers in the thrust of mutual emulation, if not in one instance then over extended time – witness the long seasons of the Maccabees and of the Jewish Revolt. Personal suicide in religious cause is – it seems fair to say – rarely private. The impulse finds, or is found by, community.

It is not difficult to discern how it comes to be so. Faiths – being always, in theism, verbally expressive and even in witness terms aggressive – are also physically belligerent and invasive. They come to be involved in killing others. Their forcible intrusion breeds resistance. Perhaps laws of retaliation supervene. Any rubric they may have against killing is over-ridden by necessities of aggression and of countering aggression. Killings become reciprocal, as in Joshua's campaigns against 'the land of Canaan', or Jewish rebels against the Roman power, or Islam in its post-Hijrah, Medinan terms in battle against Mecca and its Quraish. It was the mark and salvation of three founding centuries of Christianity that it was never of this order. It had no militancy, neither in the set of its soul or the context of its world, all power belonging elsewhere. It was an entity for ever only engaged in word of witness and evidence of life.

When killing 'in the Name' begins the risk of having oneself killed in the process at once arises and demands to be faced.[15] The faith concerned is then liable to a process of arms in which death, either way, becomes axiomatic. In letting – and getting – oneself killed the temptation lurks of esteeming death as a deed of faith. For death adds to the stakes beyond mere words for the faith and thus does despite to what wording of itself was meant to say. Once death is then squarely 'in the frame', the thought will not be far away that there can be deliberate self-homicide, especially if – as on Masada – all else seems futile, or as in our immediate decade, it contrives the element of surprise or otherwise ensures the desired end. The only way out of this quagmire is to renounce the way of force and return to the original, purely verbal, meaning of *marturos* and *shahid*.[16] Where belligerence is in the field, it is likely that at some further point a will to suicide will ensue, whether recourse to force is failing or the will to prevail prefers the paradox of sheer defiance, or – as with the ever memorable Samson – circumstance proposes it, induces it dramatically.

Two famous symbols of Jewish faith in the act of suicide in Jewish history follow. They are the more eloquent for the place they hold in communal memory and admiration. There are far grimmer ones in this fifteenth century of Islam, the analysis of which in Muslim rationale takes us into the sharp crisis between two Islams at the heart of its origins and implicit through its history.

That the rubric ''gainst self-slaughter' is indeed 'unfixed', the veto rescinded, happens – perhaps only deviously but none the less surely – when a faith resorts to what opts to deal death to others in risk to its own mortality, in the pursuance of its existence in the human scene. Its invocation of armed conflict may be in corroboration of its ethnic self-understanding or of its religious witness. Either way, it ceases to be satisfied with a vocal presence in its possession of 'the divine Name'. Or it may assume that its vocal presence is in a jeopardy that requires the conflictual form to which it has recourse. Or mutuality has somehow been assumed to be inherently conflictual, enmity-bred and enmity-borne.

Either way, it is where religious faith entails its truth in some power equation that no longer relies on the worth of its witness, that 'self-slaughter' may also make its dread claim on a combative fervour. We might say that suicidal witness is a contradiction in terms.[17]

3

Eyeless in Gaza

I

There was a strange irony in the phrase John Milton coined concerning the quintessential 'suicide' – the famed Samson of early Biblical tradition. Being 'eyeless' indeed gave him the impulse of revenge against those who had put out his eyes lest the omen of his regrown hair should threaten a renewal of his deadly feats. But they had also sharpened the hearing in his ears, as his sightless eyes wandered uselessly around the theatre where the pride of their society were festively assembled. Eyelessly, he sensed the hint of destiny, the presence of a season in the economy of YAHWEH, his presiding Genius, by which 'all things might seasoned be' – the blissful avenging of his wrongs, the dire attainment of his triumph, the ultimate of his anti-Philistine vocation. He had once carried off the city's massive gates on his own shoulders. He knew the pattern of the arena to which they had led him from 'grinding at the mill'. His respite would be brief, contrived only by their will to make sport of him and sure to condemn him anew to that bitter degradation. *In extremis* could give way to *in excelsis* if he could bring the structure crashing down upon his tormentors by one valiant tug his straining muscles might achieve where its construction made it vulnerable. 'Years of mourning to the sons of Caphtor' passed across his mind. His victors could lie about him as heaps of victims.

And he immortally among them. That was the price. He could not save himself in dooming them. He was prepared to lie among them in a final proximity he had always disdained. Survivors would find his corpse mangled among the dead by his own solitary hand. In devising his ultimate vindication he would engage his own grim demise. He would be the paradigm of suicides with their dire versions of the ancient prayer: 'God be in my understanding . . . and at my departing.' For in the crudest way they wed the two together, disdaining the always richly potential vocation in survival.[1] Only the darkest casuistry underwrites this *biathanatos* with a Judaic Samson its long celebrated exemplar.

The fact that he had so much extenuating if not roundly justifying his deed only makes him the more representative of 'faith at suicide'. For all occasions fit his scenario if many lack the pathos of his provocation. Even so, he is representative of the suicidal avenger in every tradition. Whether or not aware of him as a model or a symbol, they read their situations by like emotions, pitting their own 'justice' against their woes. They move and die inside the same system of patron deities or 'causes', sanctifying the enmities they patronize. What is between Samson and these 'lords of the Philistines' is between his YAHWEH and their Dagon.[2] The rival passions are the creatures of the divinized aegis by which both are governed. Their ethnic strife has the warrant of tribal worships. The encounter deepens into murderous suicide.

There is a graphic simplicity about the Biblical narrative in Judges 16.21–31. Its hero undergoes the bitterest humiliation: 'he did grind in the prison house', set to the task of the ass or the slave, on the treadmill of futility. His captors are at the festal height of their exultant taunting of him, playing on his legendary skill as jesting performer, though as Milton notes they had such clowns of their own folk.[3] The whole *mise-en-scène* is a calculated defiance of Samson's whole license-to-be – this Nazirite of consecrating birth, the child of divine theophany, the butt of raucous ridicule on the high day of his people's pagan adversary, a figure of fun and shame from follies and fantasies of his own devising. Should he not make his own self-destruction complete? Was there not a logic for suicide in the very climax of his woes?

There is no such hint in the narrative. Rather the nadir of despair holds a secret of triumph. If a suicide there must be, let it take victory in its stride. Let it take off its enemy in the thrust of its enmity and go to death with a retinue in train. Samson senses in his intensity of mind an impulse, intimated by mental impressions of the theatre, that the setting may be ripe for a condign revenge. The very drama of his self-awareness in that scene, heightened by his audial alertness to the crowd, seeks answer in the architecture he can guess from the pillar on which he pleads to lean. It may be in his 'arm-ed' power to bring down upon his persecutors in one last climax of sacrifice the shrine of their Dagon and the medley of his celebrants. Is he not still his 'Lord's anointed'? Are not his muscles the seat of his sanctity, the pledge as well as the weapon of his call to kill and so prevail in YAHWEH's Name? He is the very text of suicidal faith.

Was the *mise-en-scène* a sort of 'globe theatre' audience with Samson fronting on the elite of the assembly while lesser folk stood on the fringes, as Milton suggests,[4] or hung on galleries or awnings? Whatever light archaeology may throw upon such detail the theological lesson is clear. Samson can propose his act of vengeance only at the price of his own death. The cost in his case is not that of the element of surprise alone, as with any modern counterpart. There was no suspicious vigilance to overcome. He did not have to contrive his opportunity. For unwittingly, his enemies had done so. He only had to seize it, but seizing it he would destroy himself. Faith, in this drama, could only be suicidal. Suicidal were precisely the terms of its inner obedience, but only because these were the terms of its reading of the world and of its bond with deity.

This willingness to destroy the self was the condition on which the will to destroy others could be fulfilled. Samson, like all other such suicides, is the victim of his own hate. It is the utmost of irony that he, and they, can only be vicarious in their negativity, whereas there is – at the heart of all redemption – a positive vicariousness which undergoes its dying for the sake of, and not out of spite for, those it takes to heart. Thus suicide distorts and perverts the whole meaning of sacrifice, to bring a wretched ambivalence into its connotation.[5]

Hence the entail of grief and hence the callousness in which the tragedy is held. 'Nothing is here for tears', sings in Milton like a cracked bell around 'years of mourning and lamentation' only for 'the sons of Caphtor'.[6] The narrative in the Book of Judges is happily responsive to the devastation in lively terms of celebration. 'The dead which he slew at his death were more than they which he slew in his life' (16.30). Samson left to his people a mangled corpse for tearful burial and utter satisfaction at a feat of heroism. There had been enough attraction in the Philistines, if only of their women, for Samson in his amours; now only this inveterate enmity to their identity. 'Faith at suicide' eliminates compassion alike in action and in ideology and both for the same reason, the burden in its own logic.

It may seem idle to assess the story this way rather than to plead, as many would, the 'values' of the time, the mind-set of a distant age. The Book of Judges – oddly so named – is not a book of values and we should concede the patterns of time and place and remember that the progress of religion has required the denunciation of gods enjoining enmities to human neighbourhood. Yet, with suicidal faith still among us, there is no escape on that score from the legacy of Samson's story.

Nor is there rescue in surmising that this Biblical scenario bears comparison with the legend of Beowulf or the Epic of Gilgamesh where some echoes are discernible. It is true that Semes, our Samson's name, links him with the sun, a luminary of majestic course and setting in a resplendent end. 'Thy heart is in evil case', the Epic tells Gilgamesh. 'When thou arrivest at the waters of death, what wilt thou do?' It may well be that Samson is a kind of Semitic Hercules around whom legend built fantasies of heroic valour or prodigious physique, whose actual history is irrecoverable. The Biblical chronicler in Judges is naïve to conclude that Samson 'judged Israel twenty years' yet he is alert enough to omit the usual comment: 'And the land had rest "x" years.'

So the moral dilemma in unrelieved for our minds today, given that suicidal faith is still around with means availing for its opportunism or even its targets unknowingly giving it occasion by behaviours that could provoke it. The sage of Samson is not irrelevant because it belongs with far antiquity and the morals of a bygone age. Horrors inflicted and satisfactions found persist independently of times.

Nor is the admiration that can approve them necessarily lacking in unexpected places. It is dismaying to find the Letter to the Hebrews in the New Testament listing Samson among its gallery of those who 'wrought righteousness' (11.32) in the company of such as Jephthah and Barak. Perhaps it was that the writer, as elsewhere in his logic, was at pains to make his Judaic loyalty plain to his Jewish readers. Neither he nor they needed scruple about the credentials of their Samson. The writer helped father a cast of mind that persisted to the great Augustine and Doctor Aquinas. No theology, or Christology, that had understood the Garden of Gethsemane could have misread the deed of Samson or extenuated its xenophobic anger.

To pass to John Milton's classic *Samson Agonistes* is to encounter the same astigmatism in yet more striking terms. The 17th century English poet had every reason to be drawn towards the Biblical figure. There was the mutual circumstance of a despairing blindness ensuing darkly upon years of divine vocation. For Milton had long been aware of 'that gift in me', now at length unused as 'light denied' in double sense. He too had known some youthful prowess as 'the lady of Christ's', the focus of ardent hopes and duties, entangled in the toils of destiny. He too was caught in dubious adversity, the champion of republican liberties in the age of Restoration. While the price on his head had been lifted, he lived in a sort of limbo, in the harsh retrospect of his loves and the burden of his age.

Presenting his Biblical 'agonistes' in the shape of a Greek drama, with an interpreting chorus and the central personality engaged in a series of interviews with others in the drama – his father, his temptress, Harapha the Philistine and the chorus also – Milton was able to absorb, or ignore, the moral problem of avengeful suicide in the classical morale of Greek tragedy and so reach Aristotle's goal to purge the souls of spectators of all unworthy thoughts in the presence of such exemplary heroism. Hence the poet's 'all passion spent' when the drama ends. The 'antagonistes' emerges as the sublime retriever of his own frailties, having fulfilled himself in the patient endurance of his woes and the final redemption of his destiny.

The occasion Samson takes of enemy slaughter at the price of self-destruction is prompted, for Milton, by the hero's inspired decision to accept the demand that he 'make sport', which he had first rejected in scorn. His will to submit thus becomes his vindication, in the event which takes advantage from the very humiliation the Philistines intend. Samson will, indeed, 'make sport' for them. Divine fates are with him. He only seems to be beguiled into a situation of which he had rightly been utterly contemptuous. It is set to prove the seal of his victory. The tables are completely turned. Samson is not being lured into ever deeper degradation. That appearance of things is over-ruled by a divine mandate which will take his life only because it achieves his soul. In true Greek idiom the audience is left to wonder at the paradox of greatness and the tuition in emotions of pity and fear. Compunction about the Philistines and their grievings would be superfluous. Samson proves a suiciding avenger almost in spite of himself but that suicide is required of him is the logic of his cause. He was no secular martyr. His occasion was the offer of his enemies: his grasping of it was the will of his religion to their doom.

The precedent is both remote from Muslim 'suicidals' yet not irrelevant. Samson finds no mention in the Qur'an. What he brought to pass was opportune and not contrived as the crucial circumstance. It simply played into his hands. Yet that his hands played with it to such dire effect was akin to the same opportunism in contemporary suicidings 'making sport' of those they incriminate in also incriminating themselves. The precedent is blurred as all such *in situ* has to be but the art of outwitting the foe is one, and that also of exploiting the off-guardedness where he is most vulnerable.

Certainly the legend of Samson lingered long in the Judaic mind. That he 'judged Israel' meant that – perhaps – the land had rest forty years – a 'rest' denied the Philistines. Broadly Christian tradition, too, has its celebratory salutes to the famous name. What of that powerful music of Handel: 'Let the Bright Seraphim' telling Samson's last triumph on 'immortal harps'. The 18th century oratorio puts Milton's 'Samson' to the stage as an ideal saga for a music's genius. It memorably recites those strangely pregnant words of the forlorn Samson to his father:

> To what can I be useful? . . .
> My genial spirits droop, my hopes are fled.
> Nature in me seems weary of herself:
> My race of glory run, my race of shame,
> Death, invoked oft, shall end my pains
> And lay me gently down with them that rest.

It is precisely out of such private register of personal despair that the death-seeking wish is born which public angers will translate, by Islam's contrivance from its long tradition, into the invocation of a death of duly violent order, given and received.

Such parallels apart, it is the Hebrew resonances of the great Samson that are most evident. They echo in the saga of the Maccabees and the awesome legend of Masada. They belong more recently with certain moods of nascent Zionism, the one that named itself 'the catastrophic' version.[8] To these we must come. For they point to the strange irony that belongs with causes that take to suicidal means, namely that something akin to suicidal may, by that very decision, do the same violence to the cause itself. Those who take to death for living ends may find a death attending on those ends. Hosea's cry: 'Thou hast destroyed thyself' is then no bare telling of fact but a verdict on the issue.[9]

That the Samson saga is no mere bygone of Hebraic story but a spur in its modern tasks was evident enough in the writing and career of Vladimir Jabotinsky (1880–1940). Born in Odessa, he was the most articulate and realist about the inherent 'violence' of the Zionist venture. In his eloquent evidence before the Peel Commission in 1937, he passionately invoked the 'catastrophic' case in double sense. He pleaded with the Commission adequately to register – and to heed from Jewish lips – the deep tribulation of perennial Jewish experience at the hands of the non-Jewish world. Though retrospective over centuries, and over more recent decades of Russian Jewry, his plea carried prophetically the shadow of the Holocaust yet to bring down night upon the soul.

His very ardour and his urgent 'nationalist' intent made him aware that the Zionist purpose would have to be implacable in its perception of the Palestinians and their reaction. Not for him the irenic 'dream' of a feasible compatibility. He had no truck with the notion – useful in other quarters as a tactic of presentation – that Zionism was engaged in a quest for 'hospitality' sought and afforded. It had to be honestly invasive and, therefore, harshly confrontational. Its mission meant displacement for which conflict, leading to capitulation, was inherent. He realized that Zionism as 'nationalism' about the same territory would confront a Palestinian counterpart – the one which other Zionists would later dismiss as a pseudo-thing, born only of the umbrage around Jewry wanting the same land.[10]

Jabotinsky knew it for a valid antagonism. In the House of Lords, London, on February 11, 1937, he told his hearers:

> Our demand for a Jewish majority is not our 'maximum'. It is our minimum
> . . . When the Arab claim is confronted with our Jewish demand to be saved,
> it is like the claims of appetite versus the claims of starvation. No tribunal
> has ever had the luck of trying a case where all the justice was on the side of
> one party and the other party had no case whatsoever.[10]

Palestinians, he insisted, had their numerous 'national states' across an Arab world and, in any event 'Palestine' also covered the east side of the Jordan where they could belong. He urged the Commission to look at what he called 'the Jewish hell', and realize the unassailable legitimacy of an uncompromising and uncompromised Zionism. His was a Zionism that claimed Transjordan, but – in case only an Israel west of the Jordan it had to be – he wrote:

> As long as the Arabs feel that there is the least hope of getting rid of us, they
> will refuse to give up this hope . . . because they are not a rabble but a living
> people. And when a living people yields in matters of such a vital character

it is only when there is no longer any hope . . . because they can make no breach in the iron wall.[11]

A conclusion could be 'negotiated' when the power factor was utterly decisive. The victor would come to his own terms with the subdued. It had long been a Zionist resolve that the indomitable purpose could not fail ('We are only defeated if we think we are'). Palestinianism must not be allowed such dogged fortitude. As Jabotinsky affirmed elsewhere:

> It is impossible to dream of a voluntary agreement between us and the Arabs of Eretz Israel . . . Every nation (sic) civilized or primitive, sees its land as its national home, where it wants to stay as the sole landlord for ever.[12]

Jabotinsky was the candid voice of that grim comment on the gentle ideal of mere 'lovers of the soil' in innocent settlements which comes in the Negev Lullaby:

> Without weapons no furrow will run deep.[13]

It is therefore no surprise that so forthright and ardent a Zionist as this son of Odessa should have turned to the hero Samson when he told his soul in a novel. His legend fitted well the novelist's version of 'champions' of 'the land of the championship of God'.[14] Samson's feats in life had been one, if also less drastic, with his feat in death. The narrator in Judges 16.30 had been prompt to note it so. The novel's choice of Samson is akin to the long fascination of Israelis with the fame of Masada (deferred to Chapter 4). It chimes with how Samson, in Milton's setting of converse with Manoah, his father, had hinted at suicide. 'Act not in thy own affliction . . . son, self-preservation bids . . . '

> And let another hand, not thine, exact
> Thy penal forfeit from thyself . . .
> Than who self-rigorous chooses death as due . . . [15]

Old Manoah's Jewish piety argues that his son's morbid death-wish should leave all to God, all unaware that such death-wish could have sublime fulfilment at the 'let' of 'other hands' – the hands that bring him derisively between those fatal pillars of their set of scene.

Jabotinsky, as remorseless about 'Philistines' as Samson in his heyday, admires the opportunism his novel celebrates. He sees it not as once the gift in miscalculation of 'the enemy', but as the resolute contriving of the Zionist will. Unlike some of his contemporaries, he was not averse to journalism in non-Jewish publishing. Something of Samson's dying quality to see and seize the moment has always been crucial to the Zionist enterprise, while recruiting the foibles of potential allies or the follies of resisters.

He practiced that art superbly in his presentation in 1937 with the members of the Peel Commission. Because the cause is sacred, no advocate can fail to strain every nerve and retrieve every chance to further it, the more so when they can speak or act out of a case so forthright as Samson's in the depth of his humiliation in his Philistine theatre. The enormity of the Holocaust lay below a near horizon in 1937 but its omens were discernible. In any event, as Zionists have always urged, the Holocaust underlined but did not originate the demand Herzl had first made categorical long decades earlier as to the inveterate hostility of the 'Gentile' world. Jabotinsky spared no pains in bringing that urgency home to his British hearers, nor in courting the likely sympathies he knew their traditions might cherish.

Such, in strange terms, was his kinship with his Samson and with Milton's Samson, in sensing the moment and drawing on access of strength, feeling for the oratorical 'pillars' on which his pleas could stand and stay. Partition was far from the conclusion his logic sought but the mind for it would prove a vital waymark in the ongoing story in making the case from which in due course a (the) State of Israel could come to pass.[16]

It is a most tragic of ironies that the restitution of dignity and salvation, of soul-identity, which Zionism sought in political form should have aligned exorably with ancient enmities long implicit in the territory on which its heart was set.[17] That strange fate aligned the likes of Jabotinsky with the likes of Samson.[18] Even Gaza with its 'gates' and borders, its tanks and bulldozers, its gun battles and slaughters, would be witness to the new–old enmities. Samson's eyes would have no sight for the wild chaos and affright his arms devised.

It would, therefore, be idle to enquire whether, as he sensed his latent strength and 'bowed himself' to bring the pillars down, he stayed to wonder whether his destiny was righteous. It was no Gethsemane. 'Only this once, O God, that I may be avenged . . . ' (16.28). There would be no need for any second chance. His enmity was rational, his calamity dire – degraded, mocked and long manacled in slavery. These evils claimed to be requited. But his foes, no less, had reason for their malice. Theirs also was the logic of revenge. Had he not ravished their fields, taunted their villagers, violated their women and single-handedly bereaved their society of numerous male members, making play with their lives in more grim 'sporting' than the 'game' they played on him in the theatre? Given this vexing Philistines/Palestinians equation, was political Zionism somehow fated to be inevitably combative in the psyche no less than in the land? Inevitably there was an element of 'being avenged' on the 'Gentile' world in the very thrust of Zionism, urged as its case had to be, on a centuries-long malignity and then on the Shoah as its unquestioned warrant, ground and logic. 'Only this once, O God' as Samson's prayer would then have echoed tragically long long after among other mourners in other mourning, among whom would then be those of Samson's kin and kind.[18]

'Quitting himself like Samson,' as John Milton saw it, Samson was only partially an exponent of 'faith at suicide', not quintessentially. For his was a spur of the moment opportunism that did not 'look its gift-horse in the mouth'. It is the dastardly self-devising exemplars of the art we have to reach in their betrayal, yet presenting, of Islam. But Samson's saga stands as a defining symbol of a suicidal faith that 'takes mortal time by the fore-lock' and forfeits life as 'the perfect sacrifice' in YAHWEH's Name. The celebration of his legend perpetuates his lesson. It had resounding echo in the feats of the Maccabees and the suicides of Masada.

4

The Masada Mind

I

The mind that belongs with the massive fortress in the Judean wilderness has a saga with a history in two centuries of the AD/CE calendar – the first and the twentieth. If we can rely on the drama exclusively narrated by the renegade Jewish historian, Flavius Josephus, Masada was the scene of a mass suicide on the part of 960 zealots there, finally yielding in defeat to the forces of the Roman Empire but resolved to die in doing so by their own hand, rather than submit their persons to its will.

Whether or not such reliance is justified, there was such mythic power in the event (or legend) that seemed eminently apt for liturgical celebration by the soldier/scholar Yigael Yadin, for the 20th century psychic needs and aspirations of a renewed Zion. During the nineteen-sixties he led an archaeological exploration and ardent repossession of the site in a widely sponsored venture amid strong publicity.[1] Whether his logic was always convincing, there was no mistaking the power of the tradition he identified as urgent to be revived for the still embattled State. His lavish publication *Masada*: *Herod's Fortress and the Zealot's Last Stand*, gave wide currency to the story and served to enshrine the Zionist/zealot ardour as a valour across the long centuries, a single heritage of godly fervour.[2]

So captivating for his mind and that of many was the theme of Masada heroism ''gainst all disaster' that, in his other capacity beyond archaeology, he inaugurated and for a period sustained the ritual of initiation of recruits into the Israeli 'Defence Forces' on the summit of Masada, so that commitment to the parable would be engraved upon the mind in whatever necessary conflict the years might bring. 'Palestinians' in their resistance (always reminiscent of the age-old 'Philistines') would be countered as if they were some Rome *redivivus*. The ritual and the oath came to seem to many in 'secular' Israel – and indeed later to Yadin himself[3] – as somehow embarrassing. The inter-association, even so, proved a decisive dimension of a necessarily armed, and perhaps defiant, citizenship.

Masada in Yadin terms is no more than a salient example of the role of archaeology in the Israeli story, especially since the rooting in the land of successive *aliyahs* physically asserting and fulfilling the right of 'presence'. The intimate bond, in any event, between place and people, soil and soul, required this 'digging' nexus. But, given an immigrant identity, gathering itself from a wide diversity of long diaspora, archaeology fulfilled a psychological need, going backward into history. David Ben-Gurion's interest in the Bible was kindled most by Joshua's campaigns. The heartening parallel stood in two warrior images. The soldier/politician Moshe Dayan found great fascination in disclosing and museumizing the past, with Moses, Samson and David his mentors, though it was observed that he evinced no interest in the great prophets, in Isaiah and Jeremiah. The story to be ransacked like a treasure house below the present landscape proved the readiest solace and stimulus of the Zionist enterprise. Recoveries of history long hidden suitably partnered the strenuous repossessions of a present task. Israeli coins and stamps commemorated both at once.

As for Masada, whatever might be the factual truth, the new State by the nineteen-sixties knew it for a deeply mythic reality. Yigael Yadin may have been too liable to find what he sought but his excavations had real power in confirming several features of the Josephus story. He could read a female martyr in the plaited hair and skull located near the western wall, where the last stand reportedly had been, perhaps also the tablets on which the lots had been cast to decide the order of the suiciders in mutual pledge to complete the serial killing until no survivor remained, and only 'a frightful silence' and heaps of corpses would greet the Romans breaking in to complete their triumph.

There can be no doubt that the famous speech of the leader Eleazar, reviewing the loaded story of the years, 66–73 and summoning his hearers to one common mind for defiant self-homicide, can only be Josephus' composition. As a historian, he wrote somewhat in the tradition of Thucydides and believed he could capture the meaning of high event by setting it on the lips of the very actors in the drama and be surer historian thereby. If the grim drama had been told by two (?) surviving women who had hidden themselves, they could not have retained a vocal text. While search for the truth of Josephus' narrative and its famous oratory can never be foreclosed from query and surmise, there is no question of its being in zealot's character in the light of the passionate intensity of the grim Revolt, its long antecedents with the Maccabees, and its smouldering re-eruption sixty years later under Bar Kokhbah. Josephus may be a suspect historian but there was much sanity in his perception of the Romans, as enshrined in his defection after being himself a commander of the Jewish faithful. The historical question about Masada involves some careful analysis of the things at stake between its zealotry and their historian's biography of disavowal, alike of their passion and their policy – a disavowal he had reached by personal assessment of the stakes between Jewry and Rome.

It is possible for a discerning reader, familiar with the antecedents of Biblical story and with the biography of Josephus, to realize how authentic the oration was and yet how and where an alert scepticism was proper – and neither conclusion without the other. It surely spoke the mind of Eleazar and of his comrades' zealotry. Yet it incorporated a judgement on it, hardly credible on his lips but in full accord with the mind-set of Josephus. Thus he was a true historian, in that all history is 'judgemental', while anchoring its non-neutrality in the event which cannot be truly understood such 'duality' apart.[4] Thus we 'have' Eleazar through the 'reservations' about him which the entire Jewish Revolt necessarily prompted when gauged in and with the immediate Roman reality within which alone it transpired. It is fair to conclude that the very 'partiality' of Josephus, as kindled by a relevant perspective, effectively told its meaning in the true proportions of the zealotry, as sheer admiration could not. Yet a sober admiration was not lacking. It is well to have his text in view on both counts.

The speech has all the zealot pride and defiance:

> We resolved never to be servants to the Romans, nor than to any other than to God Himself, who is the true and just Lord of mankind, the time is now come for us to make that resolution true in practice . . . We were the first that revolted against them . . . God hath granted us that it is still in our power to die bravely and in a state of freedom . . .

Eleazar acknowledged that 'the game was up'.[5]

> . . . but it is still an eligible thing to die after a glorious manner . . . That is what our enemies cannot by any means hinder . . . For the nature of this fortress, which was in itself unconquerable, hath not proved the means of our deliverance . . . and while we still have great abundance of food, and a great quantity of arms and other necessaries more than we want, we are openly deprived by God Himself of all hope of deliverance.

The conviction of being mutually championed by YAHWEH, His theirs and theirs His, could thus bow to a secularly realist reckoning with dire events, whereby inexplicably the sacred nexus had been from the one side divinely abandoned. The zealot partnership was vivid enough to concede its own factual breakdown. Yet it must still hold in a will to sustain that sole worship by the way of corporate suicide, letting their death maintain its logic of non-slavery to Rome. What life had failed to render death might for ever perpetuate – the Jewish anathema on Rome. Punishment must be borne, but never at the enemy's hand.

> Let our wives die before they are abused, and our children before they have tasted of slavery and after we have slain them let us bestow that glorious

benefit upon one another mutually, and preserve ourselves in freedom as an excellent funeral monument for us. But let us first destroy our money and our fortress by fire . . . for . . . the Romans shall not be able to seize upon our bodies . . . Let us spare them nothing but our provisions: for that will be a testimonial when we are dead that we were not subdued by want of necessities, but that, according to our original resolution, we have preferred death before slavery.

There can be little doubt that authenticity is here, however phrased by authorship. Here the long recollection, the persuasion on the congenial ground of visual evidence, but the dying/undying defiance of an enemy found to be implacable. There is that sense of what the future may tell, of what 'the foe' may muse, that has seldom been lacking in the mind of suicides as in many martyred scenes.

Yet, by inherent paradox, there is urgent query about Josephus having Eleazar say:

It had been proper indeed for us to have conjectured the purpose of God much sooner, and at the very first, when we were so desirous of preserving our liberty . . . and to have been sensible that the same God, which had of old taken the Jewish nation into His favour, had now condemned them to destruction.[6]

Here surely the Jewish Flavius is speaking in his Roman voice. Zealotry had never 'conjectured the purpose of God'. 'At the very first' it had been sure of it and that divine 'purpose' lay with its arms and valour. 'The voice is the voice of Eleazar but the hands are the scribe Josephus.' Such had been his self-interrogation during his embassy to Rome from the field in Galilee, the misgivings that assailed him about the wisdom of the path the zealots were taking with such resolute intent.[7]

Whatever the verdict – if reckoning can reach it – about them and about Josephus' *volte-face*, it seems clear that among Eleazar's hearers on Masada, there were those who did not share his dread analysis of the decision demanded of them. Desperate fears, gnawing doubts, the sheer human horror of witnessing serial killing by a community sworn to leave no member alive, had to be overcome. Josephus has Eleazar 'stirring up himself and recollecting proper arguments for raising their courage'. He reproached their fear of dying and made his case for suicide by common resolve, by turning their very extremity into proof that God Himself 'had now condemned them to destruction'. The evidences were all around on every hand.

We are openly deprived by God Himself of all hopes of deliverance . . . the punishment of which let us not receive from the Romans but from God Himself as executed by our own hands, for these will be more moderate than the other. (After the killing of wives and children) let us bestow that glorious benefit upon one another mutually and preserve ourselves in freedom, as an excellent funeral monument for us.[8]

Could there be clearer, firmer case for 'faith at suicide' than this by which Josephus 'reads' the zealotry of his Eleazar? Still, however, the fatal Chapter 8 of his Book 7 lingers over its own urgency. The leader recounts atrocities already committed by the Romans and sure to be renewed. He ponders the immortal soul freed from the burdening body as in the gift of sleep. He covets the glory of their fame, the utter amazement of the Romans. He broods on the actual pursuance of the common oath as numbers dwindle but 'certainly our hands are still at liberty and have a sword in them, let them be subservient to us in our glorious design'.[9] But the supreme note is falling into the hands of God as now manifestly denying them the occasion of success.

Could it be that Josephus has well understood the mind-set because he could not share it? This will to die rather than survive has the Judaic ring of paradox, if all things Judeo-Semitic are *sui generis*.[10] It is as if Eleazar's faith in the act of suicide is the other side of his faith in covenant and given destiny. Once it is concluded that the 'author of destiny' has inexplicably but manifestly 'unwilled' it here and now, suicide seems a proper surrender to that realism. The very conviction by which resolution holds becomes the despair to which it yields the very life it owes. Life disowns itself when God rescinds the terms on which we lived it. So intimate is the bond between the human and the divine. The one renounces survival in the quandary about the other.[11] Eleazar's zealotry proved able to reach an empirical conclusion about the will of God as adverse to their hopes. Was there not then a case for assessing, with a similar realism, how God's positive will might be in authentic Jewish survival even under Rome? Only too late did he concede the duty to let circumstance into his counsels and keep fidelity intact, if only in those suicidal terms.

The evidences were there for all eyes to see. Their Masada retreat was surrounded by a circumvallant wall with several watch-towers to prevent escape. There were eight base camps and, on the western side a massive ramp of earth and stones, atop which stood a siege-tower equipped with battering ram and catapults. Then there were the mocking vagaries of the winds that first seemed to aid the besiegers' strategy to fire the stronghold, then changed dramatically if briefly, to blow back upon the Romans, until they veered again to deny the glimpse of hope.[12] The Tenth Legion, under Flavius Silva, had Jewish prisoners labouring on the erection of the ramp.

Buoyed they might be as grim defenders by the memory that Jonathan, brother of Judas the Maccabee, had occupied Masada in the middle 2nd century BC and by the élan of being in possession of a great monument of the hated Herod, his luxury, savagery and pride. They were in physical, if precarious, possession of a supreme symbol of those whom in their story they most yearned to disown and vilify.

That consolation, moreover, was fortified by the sheer location of their stand, if last it should prove to be. They were on the very edge of the land to which the eternal 'promise' belonged – assuming they took the same view of its border as Joshua had defined it by his entry over Jordan. That river-line was the last surety so much more solidly based than in the central highlands and the lynch-pin of sacred Jerusalem. Even on Masada their territorial awareness could still hold.

Furthermore, Masada was a bastion of the desert. Herod had appreci-ated the asset of its precipitous remoteness, its sheer defensibility against all plotting enemies. For Eleazar and his men, however, the desert was the place of trial, the terrain of penitence, the haven of godly expectation where, those miles to the north of Masada, the dedicated souls of Qumran had braved the travails of their piety, their lustrations and their vigils. The zealots sought their goals in their other terms of armed revolt and violent insurrection but these were their alternative form of godly repentance, their godly sorrow over the defilements that had fired their will to fight. Theirs was sincerely 'holy war', and their physical context reinforced their will to know it so.

Further yet, as Eleazar stressed in his alleged words, the Temple – for all the tensions the zealots had about its priesthood – already lay in ruins. The hallowed invulnerability of Jerusalem had been shattered in tragic decisiveness. Masada was not merely remote and desert-placed, it was the last remaining tenure the ideology of Jewry could cling to unless they yielded their very soul to those renegades who, having advised against revolt, conceded the crucial issue to allow that the sole sovereignty due to YAHWEH was compatible with passive allowance of Roman rule. What, therefore, took the circumstantial as it plainly was, unless Masada could be held, had no remaining option, short of ignominious capitulation, than to forego the very will to live. For such surviving would not leave the true self of Jewishness alive but disallowed the shape in which alone it knew itself. There was a self-disowning logic in events, unless Masada could stay defiant.

And even if it could, and thwarted Romans lifted the failing siege as bootless, what could exultant Masadans do to make good the heartening symbol in any foray against the Roman occupation at large? Might they somehow have renounced themselves sufficiently to follow the sages down to the western shore to succour that other Jewishness at Yavneh around the Torah, by implicit leave of that still enduring pagan Rome? Their zealotry had long made that a spiritually suicidal option, giving the lie to their passionate reading of themselves. They were of the rugged Maccabean order, whose Hasmonean heyday, in its impermanence, had no legacy wherewith to counter Rome. If Zealotry had to concede defeat how could zealots survive? As Eleazar read it, the dilemma was implicit. Faith could not live with its own explicit denial. Death by circumstance argued death by decision in one self-forfeiture. We may assume that they were spared in their anguish any knowledge of the final irony, namely that the story of their heroism should have its resounding echo in Jewish history thanks to the pen and narrative skill of one, Flavius, sharing the Latin name of Masada's siege commander, the Josephus whose biography enshrined all that was grotesque to them. This bitterness the defenders were surely spared, though Eleazar, it is clear, had a certain sense of things ironical, when he argued how their very 'advantages' *ex eventu* only served to heighten their foes' satisfaction in victory.

> We had arms and walls and fortresses so prepared as not to be easily taken, and courage not to be moved by any dangers in the cause of liberty . . . but then these advantages sufficed but for a short time and only raised our hopes, while they really appeared to be the very origin of our miseries: For all we had hath been taken from us, and all hath fallen under our enemies, as if these advantages were only to render their victory over us the more glorious, and were not disposed for the preservation of those by whom these preparations were made.[13]

It is not difficult to imagine counsels of suicide coming from a soul so perceptive of an enemy's way of making your very assets tell against you. For all that horrifies the imagination, whenever it dwells on the taking and executing of those lots on serial death-dealing on the height of Masada, there was a mythic poetic justice about that consummation and its bitter antecedents in the Revolt. The last mortal self-abrogation was of heroic piece with a zealot reading of the lot of the Jew in the Roman world.[14]

II

The Roman astonishment at the defiant capitulation of only corpses, neither cowed, nor starved nor slain at Roman hands but still well-provisioned, still unbroken, lived on as a legend but in no material terms. A Roman camp was continued there until 111. About a decade later, Flavius Josephus, high in Roman favour, would have composed his *Wars of the Jews*, which, if it immortalized the heroism (with his *The Antiquities* about another decade on) also ensured a critical measure of its heroics and the reckonings of a different Jewishness.

The extreme gesture of corporate suicide at Masada could be seen as the apex point of Judaic tenacity, a literal self-abnegation, defying what was perceived to be a self-abnegation demanded by the politics of Rome.[15] Lesser only by that comparison were the valours of the Maccabees against the Seleucids during the second century BC and grimly recorded in their

Books. 1 Maccabees 2.29–38 records how a group of their devotees died refusing to make war on the Sabbath. When the Maccabean insurrection began under the famous Mattathias the priest and then his succession of sons, Judas, Jonathan and Simon, there was heroism and martyrdom aplenty. But with their internal tensions the Seleucids lacked the firmness of imperial control the Romans would later bring and there were vacillations around the 'policy' of Hellenization (when such it was) they contrived to follow, as well as chronic contentions about the authentic destiny of Jewry *vis-à-vis* the post-Alexander infusion of Greek culture despite 'the fence around the Torah'.[16]

At length in the reign of Antiochus VII, John Hyrcarnus, son of Simon the Maccabee, and grandson of the great Mattathias, attained the independent Jewish Kingdom for which his ancestry had yearned and strived. He and his successor, Alexander Jannaeus, led the Hasmonean dynasty from 135 to 76 BC, holding the kingship and priesthood in one and warring to re-establish the aura, and the territorial spread, of the old Davidic monarchy. Their brief and inglorious successors succumbed to the Romans under Pompey in 64 BC when Rome finally ousted the Seleucid elements from the mid-eastern power equation. From the perspective of the men of Masada the Hasmonean power had only betrayed the genius of Jewry and defiled the martyr legacy of the valiant Maccabees. Yet the moral of its story as the Jewish theme of armed revolt and its dubious sequel in a short-lived Jewish kingship, seems to have been lost upon them in their even sterner encounter with the superiority of Rome.

Could those self-martyring Masadans have pondered the Psalms of Solomon, those eighteen hymns that lamented the destruction of the Hasmonean power and the subsequent accession of Herod the Great to Roman recruitment? The second Psalm almost told a Masada tale.

> When the sinner waxed proud, with a battering ram he cast down fortified walls, and Thou didst not restrain (him). Alien nations ascended Thine altar and trampled it proudly with their sandals . . . [17]

The soldiery of Pompey committed their sacrilege in the context of open war, whereas the notorious Antiochus IV (Epiphanes) had set his 'abomination' in the very 'Holy of Holies'. The Hasmonean history had not dissuaded the zealots from their commitment to a politics for YAHWEH that held implacable hostility to Rome. As Masada would so grimly signify, the insistent ambition for a Jewish 'theocracy' by violent, political means would find the Romans a still more formidable factor in its denial than the Seleucids had proved. The Hasmonean decades of dubious attainment would come to seem a sad mirage of short-lived and ever contentious success.

In that retrospect and in the immediate context of the Fall of Jerusalem and the loss of the Temple, 'the Masada mind' represents the emotional quintessence of a high and futile zeal. Nor could its sequel retrieve or salvage its desperate yearnings. The passion its pattern had dramatically bequeathed could not merely lapse into history and be resolved into the mythical. The impulse in those lots cast and daggers wielded on Masada lived was paralleled in zealous dedication to death on the part of those who married their own demise with the death throes of the Temple.[18] Death in those defiant terms persisted until its mind-set some sixty years later in the rising under the Messianic claimant, Bar Kokhbah (Bar Koseba), drew down upon Jerusalem and the Jewish story a far more devastating penalty under Hadrian, than even the dire tragedy under Vespasian and Titus. With the earlier loss of the Temple came total banishment from Jerusalem and its pagan re-naming as Aelia Capitolina. Cynics and aliens might read a 'death-wish' into the history of the land between the collapse of the Hasmonean saga, the arrival of Pompey and the finale under Hadrian. If so, the suicide on Masada as an apex in that narrative grimly captured its entire significance and, so doing, merited the salute a recovered Zion was moved to accord it.

> If this struggle is viewed as a whole, it can be regarded as a first attempt to establish by violent means an unrestricted theocracy in the earthly and polit-ical sphere . . . Failure to achieve this goal forced rabbinic Judaism to move . . . in a fundamentally new direction.[19]

There is a poetic justice in the fact that the narrator of that history also personified, in his own Jewishness, the logic by which the will-to-death, whether in the drama on Masada or the drama at large, might have been undone.[20]

That logic was highly auto-biographical

III

Flavius Josephus has always remained a suspect figure in Jewish eyes. What were the motives and the precise circumstances of his defection to Rome, if – indeed – such it must be termed? What of the many privileges he received from Vespasian and Titus, arguably giving this erstwhile Jewish soldier-leader the status of a hireling? He wrote *The Antiquities of the Jewish People* as for at least twelve years the recipient of an imperial pension. Yet he was eagerly and industrially concerned to be the historian of his people and took deep pride in his own priestly ancestry and lineage. Assessments of such biographies are caught in the criteria with which we come to them.

Will it not be sane to see in the career and talent of Josephus a genuine Jewish effort after compatibility with Rome, one which sought to hold Judaic exceptionality as viably present and carefully articulate within, and not against, the reality that was Rome? There is no mistaking the dismay and abhorrence he came to feel for zealotry, as a tragically distorted direction for Jewish identity to take. The Jewish diaspora through which he moved was already vigorous and tested. The mind of the Maccabees, the vagaries of the Hasmoneans, were no necessary or arguable expressions of authentic Israel, whom prophets had envisioned with neither priest nor king.[21] As he wrote, the Temple, in any event, was laid waste and the future must lie with the rabbis and the synagogue. The rabid perpetuation of zealotry could only further imperil all survival and present to Rome only a barren belligerence, betraying the co-existent possibilities that might be searched for and fulfilled in both parties. Accommodation could uphold the exclusive covenantal bond between YAHWEH and His people and read the pagan deities of Rome as 'worshipped' only as symbols of the State and its claim on loyal citizens and subjects. If intelligent Romans took them that way, why not also sensible Jews?

Perhaps we push the mind of Josephus too far into a territory towards which he only meant to point. But, if the two realities, as he saw them to be, were thus – the one uniquely spiritual, the other supremely political – obliged to co-exist, ought not 'the people of YAHWEH' to tell themselves in better, truer light than ever Zealots did? If so, what better way than to trace their long and noble history and to interpret its dignity to Roman minds? Hence his prolonged and earnest labours, pursuing for Israel's sake the models of historiography Greece and Rome employed. Vision might fail exactitude but could still 'mean' without it. Either way, the just balance between them would always be elusive.

It is surely in this context we can appreciate his effort to mediate Jewish history and ethos to Roman minds. He presented his Biblical patriarchs and leaders from Noah to Nehemiah and beyond as akin to great figures in the classical world. Taking pains to master his Greek language and sources, he stressed that 'Gentiles' were not 'Jew-hating'. Haman, for example, was no example being an Amalekite and so no Roman. Josephus gave large reference to the Septuagint as well as to Aramaic Targums. A non-Jew, Epaphroditus was his patron as he wrote, and if he took some liberties with his sources, so also did the Books of Chronicles.

The effort was to serve some minding between diaspora Jewry and the Graeco-Roman culture. Could not some elements of the Greek tragedians' human studies be detected in the pathos and passion of Hebrew counterparts, or exemplars of Biblical virtues appeal to Stoic admiration of unflinching courage? Elijah might be embarrassing in his zealotry against the baalim but Elisha restored the art of gentleness. The essence of Jewishness was not to be cantankerous but happy and to practice *philanthropia*, the bond of human-ness.[22]

There were, of course, tensions and contrarities. But what apologist does not have to negotiate them? Jews could well be vindicated in Roman eyes and the worlds of Sophocles, Socrates and Augustus interpreted to the heirs of Hezekiah who had faced a Sennacherib not a Marcus Aurelius. Old Balaam had rightly discerned how Jews and their specialness should be perceived. Their 'messianic' hopes did not spell the need for revolt against Rome nor necessitate a Jewish state. While it was true that Jews (or proselytes) disavowing pagan gods called in question how these – as Rome's patrons – served to under-write her victories, but Rome had shown a capacity to concede that Yahwism meant nothing derogatory to Rome if it duly refrained from its barbarous zealotry.

Of his long labours in *The Antiquities*, he wrote, after citing instances of Roman decrees of tolerance:

> I have hereby demonstrated . . . that we have formerly been held in great esteem . . . while we followed our own religion and the worship we paid to God, and I have frequently made mention of these decrees, in order to recon-cile other people to us, and to take away the causes of that hatred which unreasonable men bear to us . . . Natural justice is most agreeable to the advantage of all men equally, both Greeks and barbarians, to which our laws have the greatest regard . . . on which account we have reason to expect the like return from others, and to inform them that they ought not to esteem difference of positive institutions a sufficient cause of alienation but (rather) the pursuit of virtue and probity. For this belongs to all men in common, and of itself alone is sufficient for the preservation of human life. I now return to the thread of my history. (Book 16, Chap. 6, 174–8)

In returning to it as a chronicler, he had never left it as an apologist. 'The thread of my history' betrays a double sense. For it clearly reveals the inner motif in his biography and the clue to a seeming renegade, acceding to Rome to become more aptly Jewish.

IV

In it not in this light that we wisely assess his narrative of Masada? The climax of zealotry is neither exaggerated nor condoned. It has been suggested that the precise statistics must derive from some official report of Flavius Silva, the Roman invader of the fortress, figures that could readily be checked.[23] As Yigael Yadin appreciated in his fascination with Masada, there was in zealot Judaism a climax to be looked for in 'zeal' that was ready to be suicidal rather than let death be passively borne. Josephus' *Wars* contained other examples (Book 1, Chap. 16, 3 11–13) while at Jocapata, with Josephus as eye-witness, some who did not die in the siege, died by their own hand 'in great numbers' (Book 3, Chap. 2, 329–31.) At Scythopolis, a certain Simon who had betrayed Jews, repenting of his perfidy, told in a speech why he was killing himself by his own hand 'so that no one of our enemies shall have it to brag of', and brutally took his aged parents, his wife and family with him (Book 2, Chap. 18, 472–6). It may well be that narratives utilize stock phrases but they indicate that a deep tradition lay behind the Masada episode. With the geography there accurate, one scholar remarks: 'We find that the Masada suicides are highly probable.'[24]

That, like Edward Gibbon and many another, Flavius Josephus was a writer of history with a slant on its interpretation is not in doubt. The charge of being a renegade was, therefore, the very price and proof of his urgent case against the Zealots, their criminal folly, and his impulse to appreciation of Rome as the sanity of the loyal Jew. We could only disavow his writings by disowning his biography. For the two are one in the reckoning of integrity. Masada, as a self-violation of Jews in the vindication of their Jewishness, symbolizes the burden that belongs with the contemporary State of Israel in its pursuit of Zionist integrity in danger of a treachery to itself.[25]

5

Suicidal Christian Martyrology

I

Archaeology may decry or establish Masada as veritably what Josephus alleged it to be, but there is no doubt that the aura of that drama belongs squarely with the Jewish tradition. Nationalist revolt against Rome gave it warrant and sanction. That political setting was the clue to its character. Entirely in contrast of setting around a century later came, powerfully in Anatolia and North Africa, a kindred bonding of the self to die during the grim years of intermittent Roman harrowing of the Church. A will to martyrdom aroused itself in the private soul, but by a communal fervour, which was virtually suicidal in its intensity. There was no casting of lots under corporate oath, as at Masada: there was an infectious mutual emulation in the passion to be sacrificed.

In the one case there was armed resistance to the Empire – armed and violent because its zealots read all allegiance to YAHWEH incompatible with physical subjection to Rome. In the Christian case, there was neither chance nor mind for martial rebellion. Insubordination would lie only in the withholding of what – for the resisters if not for sophisticated Roman pagans[1] – was 'worship' of the Emperor, Rome's form of holding its widespread authority intact. Taken in those terms by Christian ardour – heir to Judea's eager monotheism – that shape of the imperial claim denied the Lordship of Christ. Thus a totally peaceable, indeed essentially innocuous faith (as even perceptive Romans might acknowledge), was caught in the desperate tragedy of cruel slaughter by regnant political power.

The distance from Masada is complete. Yet, on the part of some, there eventuated the same determination to be rid of life, a passion to provoke this 'tyrant' into doing his worst or somehow attract and draw down its persecuting fury, when a wise discretion might, without compromise, cherish the hope and the vocation of survival. Excesses of near ecstatic impulse to covet the worst of deaths make for strange irony on the part of those who had their own Gospels' story of their Jesus in his Gethsemane and his yearning prayer about 'a cup that might pass from him'. Yet to be studied in an ensuing chapter, Jesus in that Gethsemane was no Ignatius of Antioch.

That figure of the 2nd century, thanks to his 'letter to Romans', is among the most notorious exemplars of this near suicidal fervour. Stopping in Smyrna en route to death in Rome after his arrest, he wrote there lest the faithful be tempted to plead for some stay of execution on his behalf. He was resolute about dying, fearless and reprieve-less and told it so in the most extravagant language, strangely borrowing its imagery from the Christian Eucharist. He would be 'ground by the teeth of wild beasts into the pure bread of Christ'. He boasted of anticipating the very grimness of his fate, as if revelling in its tortures.

> Come, fire and cross and encounter with wild beasts, incisions and dissections, wrenching of bones, hacking of limbs, crushing of the whole body.[2]

He made his travels an occasion for rallying the churches as though his journey to Rome was some extended theatre for its climax. At Smyrna he greeted delegates from the Churches of the region and sent letters back with them to Ephesus and elsewhere. En route at Troas he wrote back to Smyrna in the same vein and so, via Neapolis and Philippi to his last rendezvous with death. Two concepts would seem to fire him, while 'martyrdom' (in the normal sense) is not among them.[3] The Greek term *martur* still has the meaning of 'witness' rather than 'dying'. Ignatius blends the two as ever assuming the latter. 'Self-sacrifice' is taken to be implicit in 'witness' and such 'witness' seems, with him, to take over the idea of *antipsuchon* or 'substitution', as of 'one standing in for another'.

What, however, should we make of Ignatius' plea against effort by the faithful in Rome to save him from the arena, unless there was a strong instinct to do so? Clearly not all were of Ignatian fervour or – more correctly – of his pathological condition. Polycarp earlier had not suffered in Ignatian temper nor could the *Stromateis* of Clement of Alexandria possibly be reconciled with this near-suicidal zeal for death.[4] The intercessors for him in Rome whom Ignatius would silence must have been influential enough to arouse his disavowal. He stands with a suspect passion for an utter defiance of Rome, a defiance as implacable as it took Rome's own image to be.

II

To have Ignatius as a forthright exponent of that extreme dimension of the loaded situation between Roman imperialism and Christian faith is to detect a tension that goes back to the New Testament itself, as between the book of the Revelation of John on Patmos and the Epistle of Paul, the Roman citizen, to the Church in Rome. The grim imagery of the former intends only the utmost confrontation, albeit via imprisonment and bitter duress, and scorns the non-defiance of the other. Perhaps what lay between them of the active and the passive, the wild challenge and the quiet mind, can best be captured in the language from Patmos about 'the kingdom and patience of Jesus Christ' (Rev. 1.9). There is never a doubt in either case about that 'kingdom', the authentic 'sovereignty' of One 'at whose feet we fall'. But what should we understand by 'patience' in this context, of *hupomone* in what such allegiance demands? 'Long-suffering', indeed, but in what shape, 'endurance' but in what temper? All three would be entailed either way. Yet what ought they to mean, as between the defiant and the submissive? Certainly there would be no Masada-style covenant of communal self-homicide, though none could be exempt from belonging in community.

Blessedly, we have to say that it was a patient 'patience', not an Ignatian 'impatience' that prevailed through the long and grievous centuries of persecution, though the churches would be bitterly divided over 'the lapsed', the Donatists and the matter of 'once for all baptism', while the tempests raged and when they ended.

There is no point in a long rehearsal here of the tragedy from Nero to Diocletian, via Domitian, Trajan, Marcus Aurelius, Commodus, Severus, Maximin, Decius and Valerian. They were a cruel and hateful succession of powered recreants, often direly abetted by bigoted underlings, the crucial local officials on whose whims or sadism great sorrows turned. 'The kingdom of Christ' was altogether 'the kingdom of patience' during those malicious reigns. Yet there were the catacombs, the interludes of abeyance of persecuting zeal throughout innumerable instances of fortitude, out of which the very notion of 'martyrdom' as a progressive sense of 'witness' would arise. There are few examples of tenacity in faith-survival and of the ultimate defeat of tyranny more sustained than this saga of original Christianity. When Constantine perceived a potential ally in the Church rather than a nuisance a strangely different 'kingdom of power' supervened and an emerging Christendom could dispense with 'patience'.

Meanwhile, that Christian 'patience' from the days of Nero to the death of Diocletian as truly a saga of endurance, precisely in abjuring Ignatian style 'suicidal' excesses, nevertheless generated a long tradition of marty-rology for centuries, when the Church itself became its own persecutor. Ignatius might see 'the beast of Rome' in the beasts of the arena and demand they behave themselves duly. For different souls, there was always present the spur to emulation, some reading of a paragon requiring to be imitated even in quieter terms. The image of Jesus in Gethsemane might be disallowed in its yearning for 'the cup to pass' yet taken to necessitate dire letting go of life. Was not the supreme figure of Christian history and faith a cross-impaled figure who had earlier said: 'Follow me'? Or, one who according to Luke 14.26, had warned a large concourse of perhaps casual or too sanguine hearers that unless 'a man hated his own life he could not be his disciple'.[5]

There are stories of those who brought themselves forward, refusing to cringe or hide and were deterred by the sight of the beasts and reneged on their faith. Others, like the loved Polycarp of Smyrna, no rash volunteer for the worst, found the very horror kindling the due quality of courage. Once the protection of the Judaic *religio licita* Christians enjoyed as 'Jews' (even for a while after non-circumcision had been conceded) ceased, the day-to-day Christian had to live under hazardous risks around unpredictable vagaries, whether of the regime or of the mob. At the outset under Nero, it was the suddenness that stunned the mind. Thereafter the reassurance in intermissions of persecution was too often forfeit to spell any carefreeness in the soul.

That private emotions, living under such mortal risk, should have known the whole cycle of anxieties our flesh is heir to has to sober all our judgement of the ambiguities of martyrdom. How could the need of dying square with the need of living or the 'earnestness' in either with the other? Since to die is to die alone, what of the fact of 'fellowship' within the overfraught Church, its presence inside the personal soul? Living into such expectations, wrestling privately amid public vigilance, what dire searchings of heart and vacillations of will belonged with Christian allegiance through those awful centuries!

'We die in earnest' in such a milieu could not fail to take on the utmost strife of emotions. The fidelity requisite – we might almost say – by 'witness' could resolve, in the Roman context, into a self-homicide, stimulated by pride of will or the despair that demanded to bring on the inevitable. There were many occasions, as in the execution of Cyprian of Carthage, when disciples clamoured to share their leader's fate.

That sense of things was fostered by the likeness many have discerned between the role of Christian leadership in those first centuries with that of the great teachers of the Greek Sophist tradition. There are deep resemblances in the rhetoric and argumentative skill of their deliverances in either case. The official records of 'interrogation', formally held prior to sentence and its exacting, indicate how erudite and self-possessed these could be. Expositions of faith and explicit scorn of idolatrous ways had a strangely academic flavour – or seemingly so – to have happened in the grim prospect of gory demise. Corroborated as these *testimonia* were by witnesses at the trials, they excited followers in the will to emulation and gave rise to a hagiology inseparable from cumulative martyrdom which, in turn, kept the fervour towards self-immolation alive.

Moreover, that resemblance to Sophist discipleship, in distinctive context of dying rather than mere discoursing, meant that the incidence of martyrdoms in this sense made for notable public occasions calculated to arouse irrational fervour and to sway the popular mind into excess of zeal. It could prove a zeal that, from time to time, as with Cyprian, episcopal disavowal and prohibition could not deter. Such extasies of self-sacrifice suited the Roman tradition on two counts. The one was the cult of public spectacle, the other the military ethos in which, by the time of Diocletian, Christians in the Roman legions could often be overtaken.

As predominantly an urban phenomenon,[6] Christian martyrdoms provided a ready excuse for the public spectacles in which Roman officialdom excelled and the Roman populace enjoyed. An obscure victim in some village context had little publicity value, whereas the theatrical staging of death-dealing in the vast urban arena fulfilled, at one and the same time and with great public impact, the twin purposes behind it, namely – the glorification of the Roman state and the delectation of its citizens. For the Christian, withholding of his 'worship' was precisely what the Emperor's power meant to requite. Thus the cruel fate of immolated Christians advertised the grim warrant of the state to unambiguous allegiance. It did so still more effectively when, as frequently, the martyrdoms were held on high pagan festivals or imperial anniversaries.

By the same token, the contrary point could not be lost on loyal believers. They lived under a regime with which, in its worst, its unpredictable, moods and its inescapable power, they could not safely co-exist. The effect on that awareness on timid or fanatical mind alike was to create an aura of death-mindedness, at once frightening and bewildering, when so much turned on the whim of local office-holders, their leniency or their sadism. It was impossible to keep faith and live in ease of soul. The very price of fidelity was perpetual vigilance against the menace around, the unknown ahead and the frailty within.

Given the widespread incidence of believers within the Roman ranks, those monitors of peace and war, the rubric could so easily run that 'as the soldier wills to fight, so he also wills to die'. In his Latin *Scorpace*, Tertullian – so Christian in the Roman vein – even argued that God had virtually prescribed martyrdom for Christians by His prohibition of idolatry and 'vain worship'.[7] He read a destiny of death, as it were, in the very circumstance of Roman rule, given the polytheist nature of the power it imposed. For less controlled minds, that perception could well kindle a suicidal logic as somehow inseparable from one's faith-identity. Why, then, not contrive the inevitable, bring it on in its fateful character and win an early crown? If one has to live with a duty to die bravely – not, as otherwise, incidentally but inherently – might not the bravery be the more sure the less delayed?

The soldier's loyalty, however, only made the Christian civilian's situation comparable, in that Rome allowed no 'civilians' who were not ready for its 'idols', imperial and mythical. Christian exemption from that status spelled constant vulnerability of a sort that could disorder inconstant minds and find a suicidal urge in sheer jeopardy of life and limb.

III

It would take post-Constantinian time to allow the idea of *marturia* to develop, that is, of 'bloodless martyrdom' where 'witness' – as at the outset – consisted in the *apologia*, the testimony of faithful word alone. Prior to Constantine, as we have seen, the Roman ethos excluded that concept, insofar as death hovered over testimony itself. Those Christians who prompted, provoked or conjured that ethos into fulfilling their suicidal intent must be ultimately no less *its* victims than their own.

Yet it is clear that they were acting against better counsels of which there are frequent examples – bishops warning their people against excess of dying zeal, 'fathers' decrying all wilful emulation of their dying. Was it not, they argued,[8] the Roman state that coveted the gory advertisement of Christian 'unRoman-ness', by coinciding its requital with their festivals? A truly steadfast faith should not play into their hands or connive with their intentions. The cult of the dead martyr should not usurp the value of the living Christian.

Some aspects of being bonded with life come in Chapter 10. Many were anticipated in the *Stromateis*, or 'Miscellanies', of Clement of Alexandria (155–220 approx.), a mind in sharp contrast to Tertullian. Writing through scenes of persecution, Clement knew the kinship of mind a Christian could have with Plato, how Plato in *Phaedo* has Socrates say, prior to his own coming to drink the deadly hemlock:

> There may be reason in saying that a man should wait and not take his own life until God summons him, as he is summoning me now.

He agreed that he 'ought to be grieved at death', but that 'man who is a prisoner . . . has no right to open the door and run away'.[9]

Clement did not share Socrates' logic, only his Greek abhorrence of irrational despising of life and its mystery.[10] He decried the Latin vehemence of Tertullian that it could be the Lord's will to have the spectacles His evidences of Christ to pagan despisers. Witness was of a different order and must cherish the gift of life as the surest arena of ministry, of gentleness and meekness after the pattern of the Incarnate Christ, 'the Word made flesh', not 'the word made gory'. That 'law of Christ' was against all voluntary self-destruction. The self-instigator of martyrdom was 'an accomplice in sin'. Real *marturia* did not, need not, entail death at all. It was no sin to take what measures one could, not to evade duty but to conserve fidelity. Matthew 10.23 tells of Jesus counseling disciples, persecuted in one city, to flee to another. (At one point Cyprian followed that counsel.) Perhaps the 'city' word was echoing the theme of 'the cities of refuge' in the Jewish story as a provision for involuntary homicides. Even Tertullian wrestled with *Fuga in persecutione* but opted to override the Matthean passage. Clement recruited it. Perhaps it may have seemed well related to the cities, as we saw of 'public-scene' martyrdoms. These as Bowersock observes: 'could only be mustered in sufficient numbers in the big cities'.[11]

More essentially, Clement stresses *homologia*, or 'word of life', so that fidelity in deed and word witnessed most tellingly to faith and, as such, could not ride with deliberate cult of death. This note would become a large element subsequently in the thought of Augustine.[12] Origen also thought likewise. Many pagans may indeed have acquired their awareness of Christianity from the gory spectacles and admired and sometimes accepted that witness. But could it be finally the shape of the commendation of the Gospel of grace?

Clement wrote sharply against 'misapprehending' Christ on the part of those who get entangled in arguments about avoidance of dying as 'cowardice' and, therefore, of volunteering for death as proof both of bravery and fidelity. His language makes it clear that there were vigorous debates of this order within the churches and that the paradox of disproving cowardice could prompt the suicidal. Clement urged the balance of truth that courage in the prospect of death might be necessary but that to provoke the situation wilfully did despite to the gift and trust of life. Using the familiar Greek phrase for self-homicide, 'leading oneself out', he rebukes it outright and, in *Stromateis* Book IV, those who 'having leapt into death', 'throw their selves away'. Doing so, is no Christian courage. They neither reach nor gain martyrdom and the 'witness' they think to bear is a false one, having obviated any patient *homologia*. Their being publicly condemned by these means disqualifies them as witnesses.

In retrieving, in effect the meaning of 'martyr' from its acquired sense of the necessity of death, Clement brought back into vital emphasis the ruling element of 'witness', in the point of Jesus' words, according to Luke 12.8 concerning *homologia* in his name. This did not mean that he denied the term, or the authenticity, of the act of dying 'witness' but only when this was not coveted or devised. Only a genuine pagan infliction warranted the 'martyr' word in death. That matter cannot lie in our own private hands nor be concerted on our part.

Thus the defining element in valid martyrdom cannot be present in self-initiation of the event. Those who go that way, Clement argues, actually incriminate the condemning magistrate. To cry 'Me to the beasts' collaborates with persecution and denies the Church its honesty. There is no true glory in such suicide, however far a Roman mind might think it there. Clement's abhorrence of wilful self-destruction, while proof enough that suicidal acts occurred in and to the arena, eloquently repudiates any invention of warrant from the violent suffering of Jesus. His 'I lay it down of myself' (John 10.18) does not use the 'leading oneself out' verb and belongs with the idiom of 'the good shepherd' alone.[12]

Early in the argument of his *The City of God*, Augustine enshrined his debt to Clement in his rejection of suiciding martyrdoms, when the ardent Donatists were breathing the old Tertullian fire. G. W. Bowerstock remarks:

> With the ultimate exclusion of suicide from that ideology (i.e. of violently sought death) Christian martyrdom was deprived of its most militant, its most Roman feature.[13]

Perhaps the most dubious feature in its long career was its capacity to bring even laughter to its ardour. Some were capable of 'jesting' about entering into the 'eternal joy of Christ', or joking with their interrogators, while the populace was liable to watch what would grimly ensue as 'entertainment'. Rather than Seneca's concept of a virtue in bearing pain, there could even be an ironical delight. Acts of Martyrs tell of wry humour during questioning and diaries, like that of Perpetua at Carthage, tell of dreams that spelled exultation.

Plainly the three centuries of the pre-Constantinian Church were characterized in mid-stream by this sharp divide between a seeming lust for death on behalf of Christ and insistent struggle for its dissuasion and prevention. The logic of that struggle belongs with the case, to be made in Chapter 10, about 'the onus to live'. Paul knew the will to be 'with Christ' but precisely on that account understood how 'abiding alive' was more needful. After Constantine's adoption of the Church what the long scenarios of Ignatius, Perpetua and their 'gleeful' kind had meant of spiritual extravagance passed into history. The Roman ethos which had nurtured it would now be a legacy of memory.

Yet as a vivid memory it had two consequences. The demands of Empire which had set that cruel stage, and so prompted the wild extravagance and the whole anguish of the timorous, came into the realm of the Church. It brought the temptation, if not the impulse, to adapt its pattern to the monitoring or suppression of its own heresies. As the centuries passed, whether in forms of 'holy Empire', or 'state churches, the pattern of the pagan Empire showed itself anew in the rigours of Inquisition and death dealing. Defiance of the likes of Nero and Diocletian would be of a different order from defiance of Popes and Christian 'Caesars', but might kindle in the readiness to suffer the perverse urge to seek its fascination. Instances are fewer by far than in these tortured centuries but the aura of legitimacy in 'death for Christ' always concealed the danger of a covetous ardour for it.

A similar hagiology developed, for example, around *Foxe's Book of Martyrs* as around the *Acta* of pre-Constantinian ones. Interrogations were comparable. Popular 'legends' developed. There was the same cherishing of relics and narratives, the same genesis of pilgrimage. A new dimension in the medieval and early modern story of faith and martyrdom stemmed from the doctrines of divine retribution. In their light, the horrific nature of ecclesiastical punishment had some perverse warrant in official circles as meant the more to daunt the heretic into retraction and a penitent remorse. Where this failed, as with the Oxford Martyrs, veneration was the more aroused.

The other consequence of the memory of Polycarp, Justin, Cyprian, the martyrs of Lyon, Alban and all their peers, was that even the genuine martyrdoms for which Clement pleaded in his case against those self-provoked could always be attended by the subtle workings of self-will. Instigated 'quarrel' with the pagan Empire would always have a dimension different from disavowal of Church faith or order. Consciences were differently engaged, but there would be the same occasion to wilfulness and self-esteem. Or perhaps that feature would be greater, given the capacity of inter-Christian tension to be more embittered and more self-vindicated. There would seem to be no evidence that Martin Luther consulted those *Stromateis* of Clement of Alexandria. His 'I can do no other' about his convictions took his Theses outside that case-making.

Therefore the core temptation persisted and with a deeper sanction. Nowhere perhaps is the dilemma more acutely presented than in T. S. Eliot's *Murder in the Cathedral*, with its hero, Thomas the Archbishop, 'doing the right thing for the wrong reason', seeing that 'they who serve the greater cause may make the cause serve them'. Eliot has Becket envisage the nemesis his King will undergo, the reproach from popular reaction humiliating him, and the years of crowded pilgrimage to his jeweled shrine becoming the very legend of his own Cathedral.[14] How can the would-be martyr know the deviousness of his own heart, so that defending his office and his Church against its perceived despoiler beguiles him into the utmost sin of self-satisfaction.

That paradox, whether fully formulated in the mind and soul or only dimly present, is the perennial quandary of all selfhood as a 'me-ness' which needs itself to transcend itself, where there is no moral 'selflessness' that is not 'selfed' where alone it can obtain. When that predicament is intensified by the near, or ultimate, prospect of violent death, 'the cause to be served' has an anguished ambivalence. Perhaps there is something near to suicidal in the very courage summoned to resolve it. 'I am dying beyond my means' was the death-bed witticism of Oscar Wilde.[15] 'Dying within them' has ever been the vocation of the martyr.

6

The Kiss and the Suicide
of Iscariot

I

Let us not name him 'Judas', for its rhyme with Der *Jude* and the long association of the two in Christian prejudice have darkly served to embitter
Jewish feeling and engender angry repudiations of the Gospel as a *confessio
fidei* entangled in such Jewish tragedy. Was the Acts of Apostles somehow
exulting in his misery in lurid elaboration of the bare statement of the
Gospels: 'Judas went and hanged himself'?[1]

Moreover, we need the 'Iscariot' term to bring us to the clue to that dire
conclusion to his story and the 'kiss' that led to it. For though there have
been efforts to explain the word as a corruption of a place name, Kerioth,
there is little doubt that it derives from the Latin *sicar*, 'a dagger', and that
the *Sicarii* were the Jewish zealots, ready to be assassins. This antecedent
to Judas' discipleship with Jesus is crucial to our understanding of that kiss,
as loaded with a genuine affection even in being a gesture of frustration.

It is important to note that the translation of the Greek verb *paradidomi*
and of the noun *paradidous* as 'betray' and 'betrayer' mean simply 'to hand
over' and 'one who does so'. Frequently, as in John 18.30, it is used of officials in that sense, as in Jesus appearing before Pilate. There is then no
sense of 'treason' involved. There is simply an act of *habeas corpus* whereby
'x' is made present before 'y'. This was the act of Judas in the dark among
the olive trees in that 'garden into which Jesus entered'.

Knowing it so means no palliative, no exoneration. It does mean real-
izing the significance of an action born of near despair, kindling and
effectuating a desperate hope. Far from 'betraying' his Master, Judas was
willing him to be a different one. It was indeed a 'betrayal' of the Messiah
Jesus was minded to be but only in yearning for the sort Judas' loyal discipleship had steadily envisaged and which the drift of things between them
had slowly seemed to quench. The kiss was the very symbol of that
paradox. Reading it rightly, all Jewish resentment about an inimical Judas

tradition might wither away – as must also all perverted Christian 'anti-Jewishness' in false Judas-tied terms.[2]

'The kiss and the suicide' involve fuller exploration of this scenario. It is one which has to measure the deep ambivalence in all the disciples and their allegiance concerning how they anticipated or interpreted the Messianic factor always crucial there. They were not quickly or easily illusioned or disillusional, thanks to the enigmatic shape Jesus gave to his own fulfilment. That quality was inseparable both from the Messianic theme itself and from the clamorous, rumour-prone, ardent context in which it could alone come to be. It was an atmosphere in which hope could not be fulfilled except in being transformed, since the transformation was the crux of the fulfilment. Hence the 'secrecy' in which Jesus tended to move.[3]

The scholar's problem here – though not that of the disciples – is complicated by the perennial issue concerning the Gospels' *post-facto* witness to their own events.[4] Can they be trusted to present the situation as it truly was, the valid terms in which recruits to Jesus had faced it? There was relevance for them in the differentiation Jesus made between himself and John the Baptiser, the man with the followings in the wilderness, not on the highways and in the markets. Jesus was a habitué with daily society and, thus, no apocalyptic deliverer like another 'Teacher of Righteousness'.

The prayer he taught his disciples to offer spoke of 'the Kingdom of God' to 'come', and of His will to 'be done', but what did these clauses imply as to discipled action there and then? 'On earth as it is in heaven' must surely argue for an inward deed not for violent revolt – of which there was none in heaven. Other issues here belong with the next chapter, where all that Jesus took with him and them into Gethsemane brought them to a head, in respect of Jesus and the rest. Here the concern is with their place in the kiss and the suicide of the one Iscariot.

II

Yet, by that designation, he was not a man alone. It follows from the foregoing about elusive Messiahship – and, therefore about perplexed discipleship – that Jesus was ready and able to seek and find following from two opposing camps. He certainly invited tax-gatherers, stooges of Rome, into his fellowship, neglected as the fact is by 'zealot' scholars. Scenes and parables leave that dimension in no doubt.[5] It did not, however, collide with a like apparent compatibility with *sicarii*. How Simon the Zealot – so explicitly dubbed – consorted with Matthew, once that chief of Rome's local revenue-gathering, is hard to imagine, apart from the reconciling aegis of Jesus in charge. There *were* tensions among them about 'who should be chief' and these could well have been clashes of vested interest more than of personality. Simon the Zealot may have only incidental mention but of Judas Iscariot's major role, as of his 'zealot' motives, there is no doubt.

Were James and John, the fiery 'sons of Zebedee', of the same vintage? There is a broad and positive hint in their nicknamed status as 'Boanerges'. If not a reference to an irascible temper, its translation as 'sons of wrath' suggests association with political activism.[6] In any event, their generation belonged with the ferment aroused in their Galilee by the likes of Judas the Galilean (so named) which under Menahem, a Messianic pretender, erupted in the years preceding the Jewish Revolt in 66. There is no doubt that the Jesus movement lived inside a passionate context of incipient revolt and of fevered expectation of divine deliverance to reward an ardent nationalism. The word *lestes*, used to describe Barabbas, spelled all Jesus' pained anguish that they should come with 'an armed band' to his arrest, he who was 'daily with them preaching in the Temple', where he would have been far easier quarry to waylay (Luke 22.53). That protest is eloquent enough as to the misread credentials of Jesus in every quarter, eager or adverse. Judas had his part to play in why, in the event, Jesus was arrested in a manner so incongruous.[7]

And what, in the same context, should we say of the reference to 'men of violence' in Matthew 11.12, forcibly 'seizing the kingdom'? The language concedes the presence of what it in no way condones. It hints at how disciples too might be caught between contrasted moods. The verb in question always has a sinister sense (cf. Luke 16.16) and cannot, therefore, be read about an over-wrought ardour for loving discipleship.[8] And what of 'until now'? Were there political activists wanting to divert John's mission by word into insurrection, as translating his own likeness to Elijah into Elijah-like terms? Or there may be in Jesus' mind a general reference to the ever present temptation to force God's hand in the interests of 'the Kingdom of heaven'. Or again, is there a deep paradox about that Kingdom making its gentle, tireless way, while 'suffering' what violent men make it undergo of false 'seizure' as 'plunderers' would?

However we read an enigmatic passage, it is witness enough to the whole context of Gethsemane as the place of ultimate climaxing of these issues, alike for Judas and by Jesus.

III

Given this inherent tension inside the 'zealot'/quisling duality in Jesus' discipleship, and given how deeply it pressed on the ever latent Messianic question, it is not surprising that, at least for one of their number, it should prove unbearable. If only Judas has the 'Iscariot' label was he perhaps the most ardent of their kind and, therefore, the more distressed at the sort of

Jesus he discovered he was following? Given sincere ardour, may that disillusion have been cumulative as, hoping against hope for the incidence of what he looked for, he grew more and more inwardly distraught? If that made him more urgent than his fellow 'zealots' like Simon and those Boanerges, would not that fact make him the more intensely Jesus' disciple, albeit of the wrong mind?

But who should say what 'the right mind' was? It is implicit throughout that the issue was there, indeterminate, ambivalent and gnawing at the heart-strings of anticipation. At near mid-point in the ministry came the withdrawal to Caesarea-Philippi and the otherwise strange interrogation of the disciples by Jesus as to his identity, both with the masses and among themselves. Judas assumedly was present to brood on the answer, to hear Simon Peter, (not of his mind?) that ex-fisherman, reproached for a right confession with the wrong reading, the theme without its narrative.

Peter's not 'minding rightly the things of God' must have pained and puzzled them all, hearing the severity of the rebuke. Yet in their private hearing Jesus had conceded his Messianic status and spoken enigmatically about its 'prevailing over the gates of Hell' – a thoroughly Messianic form of words.[9] How should Judas read the subtle balance between the hope this seemed to hold and the ominous threat it held for Judas' shape of it? The confused in mind are not seldom dogged in cherishing their dream – the more so when the pursuit of it has been so costly. A disciple will not cheaply forego the fruition of his sacrifice or think to forsake the logic of his life.

Moreover, Jesus was so eminently 'featous'[10] for the ends Judas coveted him, if only he would be also amenable. What might that charisma achieve if only rightly directed into the channels that could harness it! What might his wide repute attain if only he would set himself at the head of a 'zealot' style mission to accomplish the nationalist Messianism for which Judas yearned, and for which – *ex hypothesi* – he had become his follower! Why did he still forebear to be the avowed Christ and behave accordingly in Judas terms? When might the turning moment arrive and the die be cast? After months and anxieties in suspense it was worth waiting for. The point had not yet come at which Judas would cut his losses and renege altogether on discipleship.

Then came the decisive journey to Jerusalem – and with a retinue of vulgar Galileans, a mixed company of erstwhile beneficiaries of his compassion, but at least a throng that might augur a popular uprising, slowly toiling its upward way from Jericho.

The direction was right and the omens looked good. For the Temple and Jerusalem were the place where action must be. Was something of the Judas mind about to happen, scouting at long last all habitual despair? But then another more dramatic version of the same miscarriage. There were plaudits and celebratory ardours, but only to end at nightfall with near fugitives on the Mount of Olives. Palm Sunday, as the later Church would know it, proved a total anti-climax. Jesus had fumbled his opportunity or worse he had deliberately mistaken the real task, which was to galvanize not dissipate emotion, precipitate not disown violence. The seemingly barren gesture had only alerted established priestly authority to conspire more urgently against him.

That enemies had a conspiracy against Jesus, far other than zealous would-be conspirators with him, could only deepen the frustration in minds akin to Judas, as the very reversal of their dreams – and all the sorry fruit of the Master's evasion of the true 'zealot' option. According to the chronology of the Fourth Gospel, it was at the opening of the final week that Jesus had supper with the family at Bethany. It was there that Mary of Bethany gave the disciples the most provocatively 'un-zealot' reading of Jesus, in the extravagance of her costly ointment of anointing on his feet and her effeminate wiping of his feet with her hair. 'How beautiful are the feet of them that preach the Gospel of peace.' She seemed to be acting out the utmost negation of 'zealotry' and the ways its feet were meant to tread with the courage of the brave.

This – and maybe the unnerving presence of that Lazarus – brought Judas to his Rubicon. There was mere petulance in the murmur about what those shekels spent might otherwise have done. It merely concealed the final resolution of the Judas crisis, the last forfeiture of hope and the compensating access of antipathy, a surge of wretched miscalculation far more radical than any petty larceny.[11] Jesus had warned his disciples about 'enduring to the end'. Judas had done so and 'the end', when he saw it, had a form he could no longer gainsay, the form in which he had yearned from the start it would never prove to be.[12]

Yet, in the bitterness of his disillusion about Jesus, was there perhaps, for Judas, a final throw that might retrieve everything and so redeem from complete fiasco the long devotion he had brought to one, in misreading, he had loved with zeal? It would be a dire scenario but suppose it might succeed? This 'Messiah-figure' who had so far tantalizingly refused the essentials of the role, suppose he were confronted with what must compel him to them or, in a final crisis, spell his doom and the end also of the sort of mission on which, it madly seemed, his mind was set? The imminent danger of arrest by a band of armed men might rouse him to resist. Their 'swords and staves' would show how, as the broadest hint of what might supervene. Even then, Jesus might be launched upon the duty he had always refused, the proper task of Messianic zealotry, as the only option short of ignominy and the grim demise of all.

Jewish authority would certainly be amenable. They were eager for Jesus' arrest and might appreciate[13] one who might facilitate it. If so, a retaining fee might be desirable to them, though leaving him open to the charge of mercenary intent. Either way, 'thirty pieces of silver' were merely incidental to this plot-making, if we read the signs aright. They could be conveniently shown where: he could ensure how. If a final desperate act of hope should founder, it would carry the irony of a seeming revenge for wasted devotion.

IV

That hope and that irony are all in 'the kiss' of Judas. 'He whom I shall kiss, that same is he' (Mark 14.44). Luke 22.48 has Jesus asking: 'Are you handing over the Son of Man with a kiss?' The kiss, not least in that time and culture, was the age-long sacrament of friendship. Could it be also *in situ* the necessary sign of identity? Many have questioned how it need be, unless the gloom of night in a dark olive-grove explains it. What does mere detail matter in the terrible pathos of the moment? The sure expression of personal love, the kiss was also a Semitic sign of homage, as an allusion to the strange language of Psalm 2 would show.[14] Was Judas' kiss on the cheek of Jesus the last eloquent token of the Iscariot he had been in his steady loyalty, at once despairing of Jesus and giving him the Messianic submission he had always yearned to bring had Jesus only sought it well? If so, the very same gesture with which Judas relinquished Jesus to what would be his Cross was his supreme tribute to what might have been. 'Kiss the Son lest he stay unrealized . . . ' was a Judas reading of the psalm.[15] Jesus was arrested and led away.

After the arrest 'all the disciples forsook him and fled' – not, surely out of mere cowardice, for they were utterly devoted, but from being totally at a loss about how to belong with a Master who deterred them from being loyal in the only terms they knew how. Their ability to rally and to belong came when at length they understood the making of 'the Son of Man'. Not so Judas. The miscarriage of his devisings could only end in deadly remorse, the shattering of all he lived by, the atrophy at one and the same time of his life-investment in Jesus and his yearning to have that Jesus implement his 'zealot' reading of their world.

'He repented himself', writes the evangelist. The reaction of Jesus to his strategy had killed it and there could be no sequel with which he Judas could live. The authorities with whom he had connived had no room for his tragedy. He had needed them no less than they had needed him and their ends had been served. Judas' recourse to them was a futile kind of expiation, as if what had ensued could be reversed. Their scorn of him could only sharpen his own despair by engraving it more bitterly in his soul. 'Judas went and hanged himself.' The 'field of blood', where tradition has it now he did so, has a clear view across the landscape to Gethsemane. He could see in his dying anguish the place to which his biography had led. He would always carry that epitaph – ' . . . Iscariot who also betrayed him'.

How well deserved the long centuries would say. How ill-deserved a more imaginative perception might reply.[16] The Church, as we must note later, would always have difficulty coping with the Judas story. But – we must ask – is the version followed here credible or merely one to obviate the worst forms of Jewish reproach of Christian vilification of Jewry via the Judas one? It is well to remove all that can minister to human hate in the reading of history and doctrine, but the case made here has its own different *bona fides* and stands, all inter-relational concerns apart. Believing so makes it the more urgent to ask whether we can really think that Iscariot, and others of his mind, could have stayed with Jesus so long and so hard, while under the fond illusion that he might be 'zealotized'? Were not all the portents and the evidences against it, the whole drift of his teaching and his practice, examined in its due place in the next chapter? It might be argued incredible he should have been deemed persuadable in their direction, fascinating as his 'assets' were for the popular propagation of their cause.

Yet their ever ambiguous discipleship can readily be understood. Consorting with tax-gatherers may have been irksome but at least those that Jesus recruited left their role behind. Matthew is recorded as decisively quitting his wayside booth, while Zaccheus left no doubt of his conscience-stricken conversion to probity of heart. When Jesus used a parable isolating one of Matthew's kindred 'tax-men' at prayer, it was to highlight a genuine penitent. Even the chief of 'zealots' could not cavil over miscreants who saw the light.

It is possible, too, that much in Jesus' teaching drew the lively interest of that fraternity compromised by 'love to Caesar' because they were yearning for deliverance from the opprobrium it brought on them and from the economic factors which had led them to it. If so, his will to reach for them, in quest of their rescue from a bondage, need be no offence to honest nationalists. When Jesus was subtly tested about 'tribute to Caesar' he threw the onus to decide back upon his questioners and no sanction was given.

As for an incompatibility of motives with their adherence as disciples, were the Iscariot and the Boanerges ones different, save in their politics, from others in the fellowship? It seems clear that in measure *all* were confused about what their devotion meant and where they expected it to lead. The question: 'Have I been so long time with you and yet have you not known me?' has a clear Johannine ring. Yet it told a situation present to the last. There in Gethsemane there were swords to hand and the impetuous were ready to use them. All were burdened and perplexed about those warnings concerning 'going up to Jerusalem to what must there befall'. 'You who have continued with me in my temptations' (Luke 22.28) described them all. There were none for whom 'the trials of Jesus' were not their 'trials' also in their varying capacity to know them. All alike were pledged 'a kingdom appointed'. How they awaited it was by their own lights. The wonder is that they stayed – until they could stay no longer, however disparate in their incentives and their visions.

We cannot, therefore, argue against the perception of a Judas devoted for so long *both* to his Master and to his 'zealotry', or against the possibility that he conceived of a way in which the two might be fused into common cause. Trivial objections about there needing no 'kiss' to identify the familiar person of Jesus, albeit after nightfall among low spreading trees, miss the whole point of a loaded symbol.

More exacting is how to understand the puzzling points of the narrative of that Passover Meal in the Upper Room and the strange words passing from Jesus to Judas about 'doing quickly' what he meant to do. Was Jesus somehow aware of his intent? The Passover with its aura of emancipation of an oppressive people was a potent arouser of nationalist passion over against the Roman parallel to Pharaoh, giving recurrent rein to 'zealot' will. It, therefore, ocassioned the more tension among the gathered twelve. What, in that setting, could Jesus mean by 'a new covenant in his blood'? The Lamb imagery would be regnant in their minds, but what could it connote as to impending events he meant both to foreshadow and to commemorate as central to his whole significance and to their destined future?

Did this inter-association of meanings present itself to Judas as final confirmation of the resolute passivity of Jesus in letting his fate come to him – the fate he was necessitating by his refusal of the 'zealot' solution to Israel's 'Passover' from Roman bondage? If so, then Judas might be finally resolved that the 'game' of his discipleship was up.

Or, remotely, might the allusion to 'his blood' by Jesus signify apprehension of the risk of violence, or even some apocalyptic event in which he might pay with his life for the divine intervention?

It cannot be that Jesus had not divined something of Judas' leanings during their long companionship and not known that his allegiance might be dubious if the Messianic issue, so contradictorily present for them all, was not resolved his way. That dubiety about him, turning as it did on how Jesus acted, might – under all the pressures of the hour – conduce to the sequel on the part of Judas which we know too well and to the emotions that welled into that pathos-laden kiss.

It is not suggested here that, in this weighing of his Judas, Jesus ever reckoned with Judas' reactions taking the shape of an effort to force his hand and to precipitate an explosive act of self-defence when, short of meek submission to arrest, there would be no other possibility.[17] But we have to realize, from the Gospels, that during the Last Supper, surmise about Judas on the part of Jesus was darkly present and this Judas-factor could not fail to have been a vivid care in the mind of Jesus in his prayer and travail.

There was always a physical way of escape from Gethsemane, eastward over the Mount of Olives and into security in and beyond Bethany, Jericho and the Jordan. Or there would have been, had Jesus not lingered so long, having bidden Judas 'do quickly' what he had in mind to do. If 'what he had in mind to do' was to take final leave of the 'marriage' he had sought between his 'zealotry' and Jesus, as at length a futile folly against which his whole spirit now rebelled, then why not choose a last despairing throw of the dice and compel his Jesus to a change of will by dint of sheer emergency if he did not. 'A band with swords and staves' would show him how.

The upshot was unequivocal and left Judas self-doomed to the tragedy of his own ambiguous fidelity and the collapse of his last desperate act of salvage from its ruins. Both the fact and the manner of the answer of Jesus were unmistakable. He decried the implication of those 'swords and staves' that he was the sort who either used them or merited their use against him. There is a majesty, especially in John's narrative, of that 'I am he', in answer to 'whom seek ye?' and a protest that he was 'daily with them in the Temple' entirely vulnerable as no *lestes* would ever be, because his role was his as 'Messianic'.

V

The apostolic Church was always going to take a baffling legacy from one named Iscariot, but there was no mood or mind to have him a whipping post for Jewry at large. How could there be when the reach into a thorough 'Gentile' inclusion in its fellowship was an entirely Jewish initiative and in no sense a 'Gentile' clamour to be 'let in'? Judas could only serve any anti-Semitic bias long after that Jewish openness was overtaken, beyond 70 AD and the Fall of Jerusalem, by a heightened will for Jewish exceptionality. This could not well co-exist with the meaning of the Church in that first vision, thus – by default – requiring it to become an increasingly 'Gentile' community.

The burden of the memory of Judas could not fail to be acute. How could he ever lack that identifying phrase 'he that betrayed' with the words having no retrieving feature of the sort examined here. Anti-anti-Semitic critics perceive some gloating in the lurid details of that most famous suicide in all history.[18] Only their animus requires it. The Gospels are terse and factual enough and nobody but Jesus had emerged from Gethsemane unscathed by wrong and misery. Their dereliction had more to do with Jesus and his future than with the Judas-deed that had been party to it. Their supposition in the Upper Room about his puzzling going, as for 'dispensing alms', tallied squarely with his being 'the keeper of the purse', and could have engendered the theory of his 'covetous' spirit of which there is no evidence otherwise. Hence that easy theory about his nexus with the chief priests. How else would they have explained Judas' own remorse so grimly attested by those 'thirty pieces of silver' flung down at holy feet, and suitably invested in a burial ground for those excluded from Jewish burial, since even cemeteries must eternalize seclusion?

We might conclude that not even the 'zealots' among the Jesus-company could have envisaged what Judas meant to happen. Some discernible 'zealot' motive excluded, and given his habitual role as 'trea-surer', the cash-nexus of his conduct was plausible enough. They could not fail to want to understand, so much having ensued from his doing. The bitterness could well mislead their reading and their verdict.

Loved imagery pervades the whole, those 'thirty silver pieces' recalling Joseph 'sold treacherously' by his brothers, the one among the many quite reversed. The deed against Jesus had been in measure a deed against them. Were they not in their calling a paradigm of 'the twelve tribes of Israel'? What then of the empty place in their symbolism? In breaking ranks Judas had jeopardized the future. Matthias would be needed to make good the breach his suicide had made.

There is no trace of that jeopardy of the future in the Fourth Gospel's Gethsemane of Jesus (Chapter 17) with its post-Easter perspective of the Christology the faith would reach.[19] None of them is lost but 'the son of perdition' (17.12) does not silence the triumphant testament of 'They have known . . . ' 'they have kept thy word . . . ' 'I am glorified in them . . . ' 'the glory thou gavest me I have given them . . . '

Judas may have fitted into the pattern, so characteristic of the Passion narratives, of details anticipated by prophet and psalm.[20] For there were several about 'familiar friends' and the 'one who eats bread with me'. Judas readily matched these tragedies which did not have to elucidate the reasons why their 'sweet injuries' happened. 'The kiss of the suicide' would be fastened into Christian memory as the symbol of them all.

Do we have to follow the Semitic mind of the Gospels when they speak of an explicit moment when 'Satan entered into Iscariot'? Was he not always there in the potential for violence, the habit of a 'faith half unfaithful' in its very story? The Semitic habit tended to inter-associate divine will and human in one transaction, excluding all intervening factors and causes without which nothing. It was also liable to fix that immediacy at a discernible point in time where a process became a purpose and a purpose translated into fact. Things do not happen *to* people in that impulsive way unless they are *in* them, long latent and lingering with intent. It is only the sequel that can then seem sudden and dramatic. The presentiment Jesus had concerning Judas at meat with him belongs with what was in the disciple's heart. 'Satan entered into him' is the formula congenial to Semitic thought. It is not untrue, while it registers the elision of all else in the intense moment when pondering becomes doing.

The context of John 17.12 in its reference to Judas as 'the son of loss' hints at the evangelist's perspective within the Church of his writing, when 'apostacies' under persecution were liable to enfeeble it. The noun *apoleia* belongs with the verb *apoleto* 'None have I lost except . . .' Jesus' own retention of his disciples required the Church to do likewise with its own culprits. Yet they had only been 'not lost' following their bitter abandonment of their Master. Only Judas could serve as a warning against irretrievable apostacy. Yet none of those in Church history, apostacizing from the love of the Risen Christ, could ever have had the appeal of the 'zealot' motive in the first place, nor of the unique occasion afforded it in the antecedents of Gethsemane. The 'Satan' in the Judas story was none other than he who had conjured for Jesus in the wilderness a vision of 'all the kingdoms of the world'. Did not Luke observe that Satan 'only left him them for a season'? The reproach of Judas lay in that he occasioned his final reappearance in Gethsemane.

Yet, mysteriously, 'the kiss of the suicide' happened within the story of our redemption. The Church and its theology would always be pre-occupied with the negative role of Iscariot in the positive story of salvation. Perhaps that explains why they so steadily fastened on the simple theme of 'treachery', bedevilled further – if that were possible – by a covetous, deceptive, devious lusting after filthy lucre, as if a genuine 'zealot' cared for petty cash irrelevant in a consuming cause.

Early Christian preaching, according to the first chapters of Acts, did not hesitate to bring into one causation the very salvific purpose of YAHWEH *and* the contributory machinations of religious authority in dubious league with Roman power. Did these evil forces, then, make for where we might 'behold the Lamb of God' and identify his 'bearing of the sin of the world'? If so, again, was the Cross that saves the cross that unwittingly – until too late – Iscariot helped to rear?

The questions have always presented themselves to thoughtful faith, as well as to mischief-making aliens to it. They are the wrong questions to ask – not because they may not spring to mind, but because a right perception rules them out. For they assume that 'the purpose of God' is some arbitrary blueprint which requires human puppets to manipulate. Instead there is something integral in the moral liabilities of the human situation. With these, a divine responsiveness will co-exist – not, thereby, the less divine and 'providential', but redemptively so in its inter-action with those liberties, the inter-action of grace bent to divine ends by divine will.

Christian faith, from its birth and its outset, saw the Cross of Christ as the sign and seal of this engagement of God, of 'God in Christ', with humans in the wrong of an order and at a place where both could be identified for what either was, as there in event and symbol. Those who politically, physically, morally and socially 'occasioned' the Cross of Jesus, epitomize for all time how wrong we humans are, what wrong we do. Judas, Caiaphas, Pilate and the crowd were all necessary to each other to bring the Christ where they did. So doing, they represent us all and, so doing, they 'intend' and 'fashion' the Cross, but they do not 'make' it redemptive. Only Jesus in his pattern of 'bearing' does that. They only willed to stage it: the meaning of the drama was his own.

Judas Iscariot takes his place in that history. Had his version of discipleship prevailed with Jesus the 'Gospel' might have ended in something like the Jewish Revolt. Everything turned on the calling and the meaning of 'Messiah'. Judas had been an ardent volunteer of the reading that would never divinely engage with 'the sin of the world'. That Judas-dimension among the disciples at least ensured that the stakes were not misread by Jesus by the fact of posing them so sharply. Yet, by the same token and for the same reason, Judas could never cease to be in the tradition 'he who wanted it otherwise', his very 'treachery' being for ever salutary for a right 'discerning of the wounds of Jesus', in the faith-vigilance of the Church.

The 20th century poet Edwin Muir did not think so. In his poem 'The Transfiguration' – itself a deeply Christian theme – he wrote of Christ's 'coming again', 'when time is ripe', as somehow an undoing of the Cross. Christ would be 'the uncrucified', 'discrucified, his death undone, his cross dismantled'. Perhaps recalling George Herbert's line about 'teaching all wood to resound Christ's Name' in that he bore it, Muir pictured the cross passing back into a green tree, while Judas too

> . . . his long journey backward
> From darkness into light . . . be a child
> Beside his mother's knee . . . [21]

It is a moving vision. Yet only the actual Cross fitted our sort of world. Only by its having happened – and that irrevocably – could we realistically know of a divine love in final sovereignty over our humanity as only that love can know our story. Any 'second coming' – as in Edwin Muir's confidence – could ever only be because of the suffering dimension of the first. There could be no 'discrucified' about the love of God as, for evermore, that love 'in Christ'.

On that very ground, however, and only so, could not the part of Judas, once so pivotal in its tragedy, be also embraced in the redemption and Muir's vision be approved, in heaven and by ourselves?

There is great tangle here. William Temple in his commentary, notes that 'Judas was fulfilling Scripture', citing John 13.18. Indeed he was, if we accept the import of Psalm 41.9 that way.[22] But the inclusive, not the incidental 'fulfilment of the Scripture' was the whole reach, the entire significance, of the wounds of Jesus. Had Judas' depth of remorse and self-repudiation not seized him so direly, had he allowed himself to survive their desperation, can we doubt that he could have been gathered into the sure embrace of the Cross? The dying brigand, who had never been a disciple, was party, in the extreme, to the cause Judas had 'trusted to redeem Israel'. He lived till where he could identify and grasp where alone the trust

71

belonged and there to cry: 'Lord, remember me . . . in your Kingdom'. If only Judas had lived to breathe the same prayer it could not have been denied.

7

Understanding Gethsemane

I

That the central event of Christian history and theology should have been attended by the desperate suicide of an intimate member of the group of first disciples is a circumstance rarely weighed in its full tragedy, its point obscured by misreading of the vital verb in the narrative concerning Judas. If the logic of the preceding chapter is in focus, and Judas more fond enthusiast than cruel 'betrayer', we have a surer light on the positive significance of Gethsemane in the mind and will of Jesus. The disciple, ardently in the wrong, serves only to underline the Master's truth.

'A garden', writes the Fourth Gospel, 'into which Jesus entered with his disciples' (18.1). How contrastedly they would be departing out of it! Only this Gospel calls it a 'garden'. The writer's care for imagery holds him to the other 'garden' 'in the place where Jesus was crucified', and another where a 'gardener' might be mis-identified.[1] Both 'gardens' might be linked – were readers more alert to the evangelist's mind – with an antecedent crisis-ground in the Book called 'Genesis', also called garden.

Gethsemane was more an orchard, an extensive olive-grove, lying 'over the brook Kedron' but stretching far upward on the slopes of a truly named 'Mount of Olives', a place fit to be lost in. It had intimate memories for the disciples since 'Jesus oftimes resorted thither with his disciples'. Thus Judas, too, knew the place well. It would shortly make him arguably the world's most notorious suicide, in the direst self-homicide so darkly attendant on the age-long drama of a Christian redemption.

If, as we have argued, Judas was presenting Jesus with a supreme opportunity for martial Messianic fulfilment, could it not be further argued that its decisive rejection must have an aura of wilful suicide on the part of Jesus himself? To refrain from incipient insurrection against Rome's oppression in the dire moment of counter-decision could only ensure the fatal consequences, the very fate that Judas' strategy meant, to leave Jesus option-less and so force his hand. In no way optionless, but letting himself be seized for a tragic sequel, must not the popular mind have seen something almost suicidal in Jesus himself? He was certainly deliberately foregoing *in situ* the only life-saving choice.

How should we understand that language about 'giving himself as a ransom' and of 'the Son of Man giving himself up'? What did that phrase with which he so often denoted himself signify in his using and in the mind of the disciples?[2] As for his 'life', John in the Gospel has him saying: 'I lay it down of myself: no man takes it from me'.[3] According to John 8.22, his hearers were prompted to ask: 'Will he kill himself?'

Certainly there was a decisiveness, on his part, about the event in Gethsemane and an alert awareness of its only possible sequel. If the immediate scene left with its observers something enigmatic about the whole person of Jesus and his action, it can only be explored by history and understood by theology within the entire context of his ministry and his relation to God. We have to say that it is he himself who creates the perception by which alone he can be understood, in the oneness of his doing and his being. If, in due reserve of reverence, we are to have the Christ of the Gospel saying, as it were: 'I die in earnest', we must learn what transcends 'self-homicide' by discerning the 'self' that 'lays down its life'.

II

Doing so necessitates a critical trust in and reliance on the consensus of the Gospels, as arising from the mind of the apostolic Church. Such critical dependence on the verdict in their narrative and the reading of the story that it produced is a prior condition of our taking the Cross of Jesus as 'in earnest' both on his part and on ours. For, beyond all legitimate interrogations of New Testament witness, the salient fact is that it arose at all and that it had the assured character which detractors undertake to contest. A right faith will always concede the right of critics to interrogate its credentials, but a Jesus too loyally Jewish to be capable of what his post-Gethsemane disciples ascribed to him, or too Muslim to assume a divinely suffering role in human history, or too elusive to be identified at all – these contra-verdicts will always encounter the sheer fact of a faith that discerned him otherwise and became the orthodoxy of 'God in Christ'.

How remarkable that decision was is measured by the total dereliction in which they were left by his crucifixion as the bitter extinction of all their hopes – an extinction made the more desperate by their own failure to participate in his travail and their 'desertion' of him in his darkest hour. That failure stemmed from their incomprehending love, baffled and distressed by the path he took. That they should so promptly and assuredly have come to read his dying as redemptive is surer testimony to the secret of his mind in the Cross than the conjectures of a remote scholarship, reached in academic aloofness alike from pain and grief.

What 'happened' in history and what 'what happened' meant for its historians are always at likely odds. Arguments about the perspectives of those closest and those long withdrawn will always persist. But that the Gospel concerning Jesus as 'the Lamb in the midst of the throne', 'learning in that he suffered',[4] came about so promptly and spread so far so soon and endured so long merits the conviction that the mind that had it so communally rightly knew the Christ who had it so historically.

This assurance belongs with four other dimensions in our 'understanding of Gethsemane' as 'the earnest of our redemption'. From these it derives and with these it shares itself. They are: the logic of Jesus' ministry, the vocation of the prophets in Messianic terms, the character of God and the necessity in the human predicament. We have to think of all these as a fourfold cord of meanings mutually requiring each other.

III

The logic of Jesus' ministry takes us back to 'the garden'. In its meaning as 'an olive-press', Gethsemane was a haunt of habitual prayer in the fellowship of his disciples. In one burdened night, it would become the supreme sanctuary of their belonging with him because of the meaning of their having been 'long time' with him. Those antecedents entered into their climax all the way from Galilee, their boats and homes the setting of his preaching. That shared past they were bringing with them towards its point of crisis.

For the impression the Gospels leave concerning Jesus' ministry is one of deepening crisis shaped by an encounter with ever more explicit hostility. Radical points at issue emerged between Jesus and the Jewish establishment and even the fact that 'common people heard him gladly' served to sharpen them. They had to do supremely with his perception of their YAHWEH as, at once, Lord of the universe and uniquely their Jewish patron. There was an instinct for 'the outsider', the 'Gentile', in the incidence of his parables and the pattern of his conduct.[5] He discounted in both the instinctive Judaic 'distance' from Samaritans and taught of a 'heavenly Father' with an undiscriminating love for all His human creatures. In His name, he invited his hearers to shun the familiar habit of restrictive greeting and conform to the heaven that 'sent rain upon the just and the unjust'.

He assumed an awed familiarity of human acceptance before YAHWEH whose unfailing percipience of each and all numbered one's hairs and read one's yearnings for forgiveness and grace. This divine inclusiveness in his message drew down the suspicion of those whose formula was 'what the elders had said', while Jesus assumed an authority ready to proceed from ' . . . but I say to you'. It followed that traditional status felt threatened and superseded by this language and closed ranks to sustain the *status quo*. There were issues aplenty around which this tension could gather – the incidence of the Sabbath law, as between rigorist and human realist, the demeanour in worship, the laws of ritual cleansing and dietary 'meats', the role of the Temple and the prestige of Jerusalem.

We have, therefore, to appreciate how the ministry of Jesus was a deepening encounter with official disquiet and incipient rejection. There was on many occasions an implicit 'crucifying' in the enmity his stance and his person aroused – things sinister when 'the Scribes and Pharisees murmured' and ugly storm clouds gathered. In alerting to this situation, we should avoid seeing it in terms of mere censure of the values and attitudes it evoked. For they had their 'righteousness' as something to be 'exceeded' in Jesus' paradoxical ways, and not merely accused. His inclusiveness was not fulfilled in their reproach except as redeeming their intentions. He was 'on trial' in their being 'tried' – in double sense – by him. As it would become in the climax, the *Ecce Homo* of his condemnation told the *Ecce Homines* of their society. The popular verdict proved an arraignment of the populace.

The reader of the Gospels has, therefore, to take the measure of this situation of 'words against his word',[6] and so also of the impact of its experience on Jesus and his disciples. It underlies that otherwise puzzling question in all three synoptic Gospels: 'Whom do they say I am?' and – deeper still to the disciples: 'Whom do you say . . . ?' (Matthew 16.13f, Mark 8.27f and Luke 9.18f).

The locale and timing of the question and its linking with 'the Son of Man' theme are significant. At around mid-course in his ministry, Jesus had withdrawn northward far from the normal scenes of his ministry to the foothills of Hermon. It seems right to understand that it was for a deep assessment of where all was heading and what was to be apprehended from actuality thus far. The interrogation only makes sense as an index to Jesus' pre-occupation with his own vocation and with the identity it must entail. In the later terms of the Incarnation of 'the Word made flesh',[7] it is idle to think of 'omnipotence' asking to be informed, still less of a petulance anxious about reputation. The questions, bearing as they do on 'the Messianic role', can only belong existentially – as we might say – with the gathering evidences thus far, as these were to be discerned in the logic of experience, both his and theirs as disciples truly, if questioningly, 'with him'.

Messianic identity could only be confirmed, or otherwise, inside the issue of its first teaching, preaching dimension – and these in the daily context of the society in which they were pursued. 'Messiah' being so elusive, so loaded a concept, its meaning and its destiny could only be credentialized by inter-action with the constituency of its cherished expectation. That it should be so is entirely consistent with any 'Word made flesh' and with the entire human-ness entailed in Incarnation. Messiahship could only eventuate inside an epitome of the human situation it meant to address. That epitome was historically present in the society to which Jesus ministered in word and deed. It was proven present in the reception it gave him as registered by his mind.

This conviction is confirmed by the parable of the custodians of the Lord's vineyard which comes in the three Gospels and played so crucial a part in the climax of his ministry. It read the 'Son of Man' role as closing the long sequence of prophet messengers sent by the Creator to receive the fruits of the human custody of the good earth, as expressed in Judaic privilege. Clearly their messenger-reception in its aggravated character matched exactly the logic of Jesus' own experience at the hands of the tenants of his time. He, too, knew the cumulative sequence – known also to the Qur'an (2.87) – 'Some of them they said were liars and some they put to death'. Was his destiny, then, of the same order and by the same logic – not as a strange 'death-wish' but as the theme of a classic vocation in the divine Name?

Thus the logic of Jesus' ministry presented the hidden clue to the Messianic meaning by the sheer convergence of the two, and they in the vital context of human society as the arena in its perversity to which both belonged.

IV

Consistent with this is the fact that the task of Hebrew prophethood was the very nursery of the Messianic concept and of the hope it held. Where else could the vision of an ultimate 'solution' to history arise, if not from the energies of those who called for righteousness in history's midst and reproached the wrongs and compromises of the people 'chosen' to be the divine exhibitant of its meaning? 'The vineyard of the Lord of hosts', His 'pleasant plant', was meant to exemplify the human meaning of the Creator's intent, and be His test-case of creaturehood at large. The claim of their story, when it went awry, must surely invoke His responding purpose of will to retrieve it.

The great prophets had themselves emerged from the tradition of diviners and seers, apt for the location of lost asses or the satisfaction of curious counsels with the dead. But Amos first among them had realized how YAHWEH was indeed 'Lord of history', if He could employ heathen Assyria to requite the sins that called for the requital its invading tide would bring. With Hosea, Micah and the first Isaiah, they would be the conscience of the nation, demanding righteousness in the courts of power, but always only with the voice of moral passion. Thus they ensured that the call of true national destiny was never silenced. When exile supervened, first for the northern and then the southern Kingdoms, the Isaiah of the exile and the martyred Jeremiah came to discern the lineaments of the Messianic task, as it would need to be, in the mystery of their own travail. Where else, more aptly, could it be identified? As the vineyard parable told it, there must be a discernible continuity in the sequences of prophethood – a continuity which conveyed its persons into suffering in its vicarious relation to their world.

The secret would seem to be latent in the very coupling into one of 'suffering' and 'servant', as the gathered logic of prophethoods in their long story – a service which passed steadily into travail by its own *raison d'être* as a holy conscience in human affairs, its burden and that burden's cost. Certainly much mystery – and much baffled scholarship – waits on that figure alike in life and imagery. In the person of Jeremiah, it is fair to say that the two were made biography in one, so that the message was incarnate in the messenger, the burden of either explicit in the other. As his 'Confessions' told it,[8] Jeremiah's ministry was lived as well as discharged in his own person.

Here the language of 'the lamb' he was made to be, by the symbol of events, concealed a sorry ambiguity which, when misconstrued, did great disservice to theology. For, in his experience it belonged integrally with his being an anguished victim as YAHWEH's 'messenger'. That alone was the import of its borrowing. Yet sadly it harked back – if reading was so minded – to the old context of animal sacrifice in the Levitical system, where suffering was arbitrarily inflicted on incomprehending animals – a far cry from the reality of the Jeremiah saga. Just as there was nothing less like a lamb that Jesus in Gethsemane, so likewise with Jeremiah at the Temple gate,[9] if the bizarre associations of Leviticus are in view. For then the whole significance captured in the words 'God-in-Christ' – the reality of divine love itself present in and with the Cross – is forfeit in some purely ritual and artificial act. This distortion would be further present, were we to link Calvary with the grim story of Abraham and Isaac in Genesis 22 and imply that YAHWEH also had slain His own Son in going even farther than the patriarch. What a travesty of the meaning of 'God will provide' were Christian faith told as if the Lord was Himself engaged in merely ritual act in the oblation of another.[10] How far are we then from the reality of Gethsemane and of the Cross as authenticating the very character of God (see below) in His authentic, not Abrahamic, terms.

Jeremiah's travail, taking to words, not of preaching to other hearers, but searching his own soul's burden, anticipates Jesus wrestling with 'the cup his Father gave'. He foreshadows the vicarious nature of all prophethood which serves as the sure clue to the calling of the Son. Thanks to their fortitude in holding to their task, there is a moving in it from suffering-because-of to suffering-on-behalf-of. Thus they become 'bearers of wrong' which, thanks to their witness, is not allowed to prevail. Not being 'overcome of evil', truth lives because of them.

This is surely how we have to see the sequence between prophet and Messiah, the latter in the pattern of the former but in the due progression represented by the precedent and necessitated by the evil of the human world.

This is where exposition now has to take the point of the next dimension earlier proposed, namely what the human predicament made urgent and vital. For that is the meaning of the sending of 'the Son' in climax to the long succession of 'messengers' alone. In that meaning we reach the whole reality of Christology as the first Christians came to comprehend it.

V

It is clear in the parable of the husbandmen as a paradigm of human earth-tenancy, via the Judaic as its covenanted 'pilot model', that there comes about a steady downward spiral in the relation between tenants and Lord. It is one which mirrors the experience of wrong-doing. There occur a series of rejections of the bid for the fruits. One makes another more likely, a second the third more ingrained. Refusals confirm and sharpen each other. Such are the habits of human sin. The shape of the ill-will becomes steadily more violent. Recalcitrance, once embarked on, becomes self-renewing in aggravating terms.

This sorry sequence expresses what it first hides and then begins to pursue, namely an ambition to take over the lordship. Absentee landlords were a familiar feature of 1st century Galilee. There was bitter social resentment against them. If tenants could be skilful in playing their cards they might attain to becoming usurpers, simply by disavowing the owner's right, resisting his claims and by conspiracy ousting him altogether. Was not 'possession nine tenths of the law'?

The whole point of the necessity of 'sending the son' is here. For only he, in his person, signified – as no 'messenger' could – his right of ownership. It alone could be his answer to the strategy of usurpation plainly being pursued against him by the rough handling of his emissaries. It was, after all, a strange analogy for Jesus to employ but it held three vital lessons. One is that the 'absence' analogy indicates how real is the human status of 'dominion', and its exercise of responsible tenure – the 'over-to-you' of our human privilege. The second is the gravitation of evil into its own excess. The third is that creation entrusted to creaturely care entails the Lord in genuine liability in the situation which his enterprise comes to contain of human treachery and shame. The mystery of creation for our creature-hood must be corroborated by the reality of redemption. The Lord does not 'weary of mankind'. So 'I will send to them my Son' is His sublime Self-fulfilment, the ultimate evidence of sovereignty.

But, given those antecedents out of prophethoods coming their way, the tenants sense their supreme occasion: 'Come, let us kill him and *the inheritance will be ours.*' Their will to wrong and usurpation reaches the full end of its own logic. Thus the parable reveals the evil tide in the human predicament, our capacity to betray the privilege of being, by deliberately defaulting on its very nature as an entrusted thing. Rejecting the first summons to integrity is like enquiring: 'Hath God said?' suspecting the whole 'good faith' of creation. The second contempt of the 'messenger' is scheming to live 'to the exclusion of God' (a frequent Quranic phrase) or it is akin to the altogether 'secular' view that wants to insist: 'There is only us, we humans.' Any divine relation is either illusory or intrusive.[11]

So it is that the Gospel, by the 'Son-sending' at the heart of it, addresses the wrongness in the human situation in the very fact of bringing it to light, to have it know itself in its own image. The heart of its redeeming action is this 'suffering-because-of' being, by the same token, a 'suffering-on-behalf-of'. The love and the law behind creation take up in Christ-the-Son the vicarious redemption which prophethoods in their travail had foreshown.

While there must always remain for Christian faith a reverent reticence about exploring the self-consciousness of Jesus, there is no doubting that the actual course of his ministry moved in precisely this pattern of malignity. Is it not to this that the 'Lamb' language refers? Jesus as 'the Son of Man' becomes the history of 'God in Christ'.

That very sequence from activity out of Galilee and final faith-verdict about its meaning is the reason for the marked difference between the narrative of the Synoptic Gospels and the language of Jesus in the Fourth. The deep contrast – notably in the setting of Gethsemane and Jesus' words there – is so striking that it needs to be truly registered, a necessity which has not sufficiently happened in the popular mind, though it has pre-occupied New Testament scholarship. It needs, therefore, to be studied here in the context of the evidences of the human vineyard and the 'son-sending' thither.

Plainly we have what musicians might call a different 'key' in the language of Jesus. Nothing, for example, of the discourse in John 6 could have been apposite in the there and then of the hillside 'bread-breaking'. Nor does the Sermon on the Mount resemble the inner discourses of John 14 to 16. Nor does the human pathos of the Synoptic Jesus in Gethsemane tally with the supreme assurance of his prayer in John 17. These are not mutually alien but they are certainly in contrast.

So what is happening here? There always was a need to be alert around simply saying, of any citation from the Gospels: Jesus said . . . ' For 'said' needs a watchful wisdom. Plainly there were no microphones around, no recording means of memory. All was in the retentive minding of listening folk, to be cherished, recited, pondered through a long custody of love till it came finally to be distilled into the text we know, with each evangelist or their precursors exercising some authorial control. Thus Matthew, for example, assembles in one 'Sermon' teachings of Jesus on many occasions, because – with his mountain and gathered following – he seeks to present Jesus as a new 'Moses' on a greater 'Sinai'. A discerning faith has no right to ignore these circumstances in having a sober confidence that is not disserved in trusting their fruition.

The vital point about the Fourth Gospel is that this 'John' is presenting the Jesus of Galilee with the insight of the maturing Christology to which that Jesus-significance gave rise as known to the mind of the Church. This does not 'falsify', but it certainly 'perspectifies' and enlarges. There is a circle of conviction, namely that faith perceived Jesus in Christhood out of the mind it reached concerning him, but did so only in that he had himself evoked the mind that saw him so. He created the faith-credential in which he should be identified.

That it transpired so is the way all historiography works, only that here – thanks to Jesus – it had to be deeply theological, whereas in normal history-telling it need not be so. Thus a Johannine Jesus saying: 'I came to save the world', or 'I and my Father are one' (12.47 and 10.30) is Jesus in his synoptic record speaking in the Christological terms of that historic mission. The issues of these Chapters 5, 10 and 12 in John, in encounter with Jewish authority, enshrine expressly what was always latent in the physical scene and have to be understood in this bifocal way. They would not be intelligible in the first until they had been appreciated in the second, but there is one integrity in that sequence.

There are evidences, notably in Matthew 11.25–31, of this situation but it is the Fourth Gospel which brings it into final focus in the theme of 'having the Father in having the Son', just as the vineyard parable had suggested.[12] Hence the difference already noted in the Gethsemane prayer of John 17, which is a sublime celebration of Incarnation, its mission and fruition – the very same Incarnation that the Synoptic Gospels tell as ground observers.

VI

This crucial integrity within difference of the Gospels as to Jesus known as 'God in Christ' takes us back to the context in which we needed it here, namely the necessity, in the human predicament, that divine action be of this order. We noted the descending spiral of caviling and rebellion about moral duty, the conspiracy of usurpation against the Lord which schemes in human wrong. That point needs to be stressed by noting how law itself, that right to the fruits of good, does not – *qua* law – ensure its own claim. For it is precisely the claim, no less than the dues, which is being defied. Law *qua* law does not redeem. Nor does it repair what is wrong. It only accuses, reprehends and requites it.[13] Doing so, it aims at a certain justice but will never be undoing what was done to the messengers or, better, what that doing manifested. The logic of the parable means the crucifying of 'the Son', as in time and place it proved so.

This dilemma of law in face of human anti-law is given sharp focus in the experience of Paul, where in Romans 7 he identifies the parable in personal terms. The tenants know they are violators. So does Paul but he, in his very will to be right (unlike the tenants) finds a law-flouting nature inside him and prays to be delivered. 'The good I would I do not, the evil that I would not that I do'. Where, then, is answer?

The answer is the Messiah, the advent of 'the Son', and that answer comprehensively understood as 'God in Christ'.[14] It takes us to our final dimension in 'understanding Gethsemane', namely 'the character of God'. For it must be there, and there alone, that our sequence in 'the logic of Jesus' ministry', read via 'the vocation of the prophets', and taking in 'the necessity in the human predicament', can come to solution.

'Answer' is the needed word. For we have posited creation, the world as a human 'vineyard', divinely owned but humanly administered. That human custody – ever under divine solicitude for right administrating – being never withdrawn (thus far), never rescinded, is acutely the place for an answer. Answer it will not, cannot be, if it ignores the human wrong or if it disowns the Creator's stake. Creation, if we heed it, must bring on redemption, just as a drama must bring on its climax. 'God in Christ' will be the Self-consistency of God in creation, the human scene being the fit realm of both. That it happened so is the very heart and nature of the Christian faith.

It is noteworthy that Charles Darwin disallowed creation, substituting something he called 'nature'. It follows that nowhere does *The Origin of Species* refer to 'God in Christ'. The omission signifies a final irresponsibility about the good earth within this universe. Explaining all by 'Mother nature' it had no need to wrestle with the vagaries of human nature. A final nonchalance, a sort of *laissez faire*, could attach to everything. Darwin's 'Nature' could be unbothered about human history. Not so the Lord whom John's 'Prologue' tells as 'the Word letting all, and us, be' and 'the Word made flesh dwelling among us' in order to be *for* us in the only adequate terms.[15]

It might seem pretentious to write of 'the character of God', were a God of no 'character' not a contradiction in terms. The word, however, is so deviously and diversely used. When the poet Shelley noted it in his essay 'On Christianity', he ventured a definition that ran:

> . . . a common term devised to express all of mystery, of majesty or power that the invisible world contains.[16]

What, though, of the visible world where – as we have argued – only the divine relevance can belong? It might be, as Shelley went on, 'the most awesome and most venerable of names', but wherein and how? Would these descriptives belong with the natural order, as this human 'vineyard' suggests, and not also with its tragic register of human 'husbandry'? Consequent upon the messengers, there was that 'suffering-because-of'. It passed for the bravest of them into 'suffering-on-behalf-of'. So intimately, as with Isaiah and Jeremiah, was their task an experience of the travail of their sending by YAHWEH (as they read it) that it drew the outlines of 'the suffering servant', 'a man of sorrows and acquainted with grief', who was – by these tokens – 'bearing transgressions'. The 'character' of their 'Sender' could be manifest in the cost of their sending, by Him into, in truth, a 'sin-bearing' from which He too would not be exempt. For some 'spectator' sending would be a betrayal of the end in mind, namely the retrieval of the wrongness against which it witnessed. Could it, on divine behalf, witness against, without also bearing what such witness meant? 'A faithful Creator' (1 Peter 4.19) must argue a redeeming one.

Was not the faith, which gave the Church its very soul in the truth of its story, then right in seeing this 'character' told in the identity Jesus made – as here argued – between that 'suffering servant' and himself as the Messianic 'Son of Man'? And, further, that he should have done so in the light of his own ministry as itself, in the context from Galilee to Jerusalem, a confirmation of the same paradigm? Or, further again, that such ministry underwent, in deepening measure, the wrongness faith would come to call 'the sin of the world', what the human 'vineyard' is and does?

Then to perceive and trust that sequence, to discern its telling logic, is to arrive, as the New Testament did, to 'God in Christ', and a conclusive theology of His 'character'.

If so, we understand more aptly the Johannine language about all things reciprocal between 'the Father and the Son'. For in them – as John puts it – we have God's own 'exegesis'.[17] That mutuality is the steady theme of both John's Gospel and the Letters of John. 'He who has the Son has the Father also,' in that truly having 'the Father' means that 'sending' by Him of 'the Son'. One who knows the music knows the musician. 'God in Christ' is that sort of mutual unison, or – in archaic language – 'consubstantial' in the proper sense of the inter-defining inter-defined. If the 'sending' term implies initiative that is precisely the impulse to have it so – the dramatist embarking on his drama. If it implies a 'journey' that is to tell how real the granting of the human territory to its creaturely custodians, in the design of creation by an 'over-to-you' 'landlord'. If the initiative and the impulse require the 'father/son' analogy, it is because entry into time and place, i.e. 'incarnation', is always the pre-requisite in belonging with history. Such 'sending' by the same token constitutes a 'coming'. For without departing there is no arriving, no whence without a whither, and the two one in their association.

Hence those discourses in John 14–16 and the theme of the Prologue and the call: 'Believe in God, believe also in me . . . ' (14.1)[18] because 'the word you hear is not mine but the Father's who sent me' (14.24) – thanks to the unison which made it his also as the very nature of his 'sentness'.

All our thinking, then, about 'the character' of God is pretentious unless God has 'characterized' Himself and, if He has done so, our theological task ends in recognition.

VII

Yet recognition is a perpetual duty of exploration, alike to comprehend more truly and commend more fully. The sequence of argument here has been necessary because of the over-all concern with 'dying in earnest', as happening in Jesus' Gethsemane as also Christ's Messiahship. That its eventfulness should have been so promptly followed by the grim suicide of an allegedly traitorous disciple is the strangest commentary of all upon its incidence in the there and then of 1st century Judea. That tragedy we studied in the previous chapter.

It throws its own desperate light on the logic we have traced. The scene is the human 'vineyard' on the good earth, a creation entrusted and under a law of divine expectation, made present and vocal by prophet-summons to its obedience. Messenger-experience makes evident how perverted is the trust, how wrongful the custodians. It intensifies into dimensions of tragic servanthood from which we learn that the divine stake in the sending cannot, will not, be exempt from the suffering it has drawn upon the servants. The divine law-giver, by the very summons of humans into good, becomes the divine bearer of our practice of evil. The reality of creation requires us to believe in the cost-bearing of redemption. The God of the prophets will also be the God of the Son's sending, only so being Self-consistent.

This, we argued, is known to be so by the fact that in his ministry Jesus experienced the Son's measure of what had happened to 'the goodly fellowship' of prophets. He took it as the timely clue to what Messiah should be and how Messiah should suffer. Thus in the responding percep-tion of the Church, his Cross was seen to enshrine 'the very sin of the world', the coalition of moral, political, private and official sins which concerted it being truly an epitome of earth's vineyard tenants.

That acceptance on the part of Jesus to be the Messiah of God tells the full meaning of his Sonship and thus, in turn, the whole truth of divine Fatherhood. What the human predicament necessitated of the divine nature that divine nature sufficed to encompass and did so where – and in the terms that – the faith they evoked could recognize in responsive love and wonder.

This must banish all those suspicions that Gethsemane was somehow the 'suicide' of Jesus. Let us not mis-read those hints of the curious: 'Will he kill himself'? when controversy in the Johannine context has him telling of his reading of suffering vocation. When of his life he says: 'No man takes it from me, I lay in down of myself' (10.15) we have the Christ speaking in and beyond the Jesus who prays: 'Let this cup pass from me' in the same Gethsemane (Mark 14.26). Both are one in the deed and the Christology where they co-existed in the economy of 'the Father and the Son'.

There are other theories of some 'suiciding' Jesus over which we need not linger here.[19] They would never have given rise to the historic faith, just as that faith could have had no origin but for its 'begetting' from 'the only begotten of the Father, full of grace and truth'.

All is a far cry from 'Suicide in Contemporary Islam' to which study must now turn. There could be occasion to bring them together in the concern of Chapter 10 and faith's bond with life.

8

The Suicidal in
Contemporary Islam

I

The fascination of the Samson story and of the Masada zealots and the strange role they have played in the ideology of Zionism and in the conscious prowess of the State of Israel are evident enough in narrative and literature. The 'Agonistes' of Gaza is celebrated by the annalist in the Book of Judges in soberer terms than those of the Song of Deborah but legend salutes him as having 'judged Israel' and been 'avenged on the Philistines'. The sage of Eleazar and his suiciding followers in their last rampart on the borders of the Jewish land served well the Israeli army[1] in heartening its ranks through all the vicissitudes of confrontation, seen as needing to be read in kindred terms and in the toils of survival. The lore of their fore-bears summoned them to worthy emulation. Samson and the Masada zealots lived a 'faith at suicide', the former as a supreme opportunist when occasion offered, the others in the ultimate gesture of defiance their faith demanded.

The 'faith at suicide' of contemporary Islam is of a radically different order. We move, in the one case, from something like 'faith in the act of suicide' (i.e. 'told through it') to 'faith in the use of suicide' in the other. Samson may be a prototype but he only seized what chance, or providence, presented. The suicides of September 11, 2001, contrived their deeds by long malice aforethought. Those who died on Masada by their own hand took no others with them in doing so, as they would have done had combat been joined inside the fortress. The sense of 'dispensation' by which they violated their own selfhoods was of quite contrasted order from that by which the agents of Al-Qa'idah did so. The point of comprehending both, under the one category of suicide obtaining, is only to underscore the great disparity between them.[2] Clearly the theme of 'dispensation' as leading to violation of selfhood in such terms is congenial and readily discernible, at times explicit, in the respective histories. Yet there is something about such inclusive disavowal of selfhood and its mortal irreplaceability which in due course disserves or atrophies the faith that takes to it. There is this certain nemesis for any faith avowal in such terms. The self of both the faith-person and the faith purpose is forfeit in the violence of the deed. For what terminates the individual tarnishes the cause. Such is the inherent paradox in suiciding faith. In dying for his faith that way, the suicide advertises his faith as something with which he is not prepared still to live, in whatever eventuality of circumstance. This differentiates him altogether from others who only risk their lives in hazardous combat from which they may survive. These do not serve notice on the world that there are situations where their beliefs can no longer sustain, interpret or appreciate existence. Nor do they indicate a faith no longer fit or ripe to live by, as the suicide too grimly does. Contrary-wise, he tells a faith that usurps from him the very gift, the irre-placeable treasure, it was faith's *métier* to have him duly cherish and fulfil. If, so doing, he is Muslim, he flouts the entire sovereignty of God, from whom his sacred 'caliphate' was derived, by whose design came the mystery of procreation that gave him birth, in whose hand his time and times belong.

II

That Islam, of all faiths, should be so tragically linked in the public mind with acts of licensed suicide in the contemporary world has surely to be seen as grim anomaly, as faith in utter subversion of itself.[3] How is a believing suicide 'letting God be God', if privately revoking His divine: 'Be and let be' as the very *Fiat* of creation and the theme of the Qurʾan's infor-mative mission as 'a mercy to the worlds'?

It is important to realize how such suiciders are desperate subversers of their religion. Then the immediate task here is to enquire how, from within Islam and Muslim culture, it could have arisen in such highly organized and thoroughly ruthless form.

It was argued earlier in Chapter 5 that the impulse to wilful or pseudo-martyrdom – and thence deviously to suicide – came inevitably in the prior context of religious belligerence. Authentic martyrdom happened when faith, physically threatened, refused to apostacize. Example then might instigate in some a fantasy to covet that high honour and induce its happening. But both types belonged with faiths only verbally relating to their persecuting setting, faiths bent on uncompulsive witness. Killing came when strife was joined in combat – killing given and received, killings exchanged. Only so could there develop a notion that, deaths being thus reciprocal, one's own might be contrived as a 'tactic' in that context, whether as a fitting example, a gaining of advantage or a gesture of defi-ance. Such acts were of a different order from the wilful demise of the deluded, the fantasisers, or the despisers of themselves. What we might call the purposeful or strategic suicides come only in the context of confrontation physically willed and forcibly joined.

Islam in its Meccan defining origins was not of that order. There was 'confrontation', to be sure, but not then in any martial terms. There was only long and steadfast preaching, bravely sustained in face of much contumely, enmity and contradiction. Mecca's merchandise and pilgrimage admitted no denunciation of their pagan nature on Muhammad's part. The vested interests of the Quraish in possession of these sacred assets resisted this upstart Prophet's plea (as they saw it) for their worship as due to Allah alone. Nor did they approve the message of resurrection after death into divine assessment of their human story. Muhammad's being 'a native son' and suspiciously in touch with 'alien' sources for his disruptive theme embittered them against him.

It is idle now to surmise whether those Meccans might have been somehow at length persuadable. Might their grounds for obduracy have been discounted from within? For enormous assets accruing to Mecca as a *Haram* shrine were latent in Muhammad's significance, if never made evident before surrender. The thirteen years of Muhammad's *balagh*, 'word in witness', might have lengthened, either into his mortal passing, as the Qur'an hints,[4] or have 'borne their fruit in due season', like the 'corn of wheat' or 'the bread on the waters', 'found after many days'.[5] For, remaining non-combative, satisfied to witness and wait, everything was with them in respect of sanity, peace beyond feud, and Allah over all things regnant.

With sequentials that would become definitive for Islam, it did not happen so. While Muhammad's tenacity in witness was undimmed, his personal situation became less tenable.[6] He prospected outside the range of his resistant Meccans, notably in the northward direction of Yathrib and up the escarpment to Al-Ta'if on the Arabian plateau. The latter repulsed him harshly but when the former gave word of a protecting haven in its midst, the die for the emigration, the Hijrah, was cast and has decided the shape of Islam ever since – a fact symbolized in its originating of its Calendar around 'the years of the Hijrah'. Islam is 'of the Hijrah' institutionally in every sense, but only in being also essentially 'of those years of Mecca'.[7]

The invitation to Yathrib, soon to be re-named Medina, was precarious enough. It only pledged a will to protect on the part of only some of its population – people who had responded to the 'teaching' they had received. Even so, it was a hint of opportunity on which Muhammad acted. It remains noteworthy that he cast himself and his cause upon people who 'heeded' his *balagh*, the sort of folk he had always wanted to find in Mecca. It was that readiness to heed that prompted the will to migrate. It was heeders above all that he sought. If Mecca denied them to him in satisfactory numbers, Yathrib showed a will to do otherwise.

Thus the Hijrah was a calculated move for and to a heedful reception, though there seems to have been no express directive for it in the Qur'an. Muhammad was not forced, chased or driven out of Mecca. He positively reached for the promise of Yathrib. It meant that his relatively few adherents broke their local or tribal ties in making a religious venture. The Quraish were unwise to let him go. For within their *haram* and its precincts they had far readier control over his mission, than when he was beyond their vigilance some nine score miles away.

Moreover, the Medina-to-be was well placed for mutual hostilities should combat be joined, with trading routes along the Red Sea littoral exposed on the flank to any would-be marauders from its eastern hills.

It might be argued that, for these reasons, conflict became inevitable in the wake of the Hijrah itself. His voice would no longer be heard in the suqs of its first sounding-board. The witness of his devotees had been withdrawn with him, yet not so symbolically as when an earlier migration had sought sanctuary over the sea in Ethiopia some six years before the Hijrah. His exit did not diminish the hostility the Quraishi establishment had for him. Encounter became almost inevitable between an angry shrine and a wanted fugitive.[8] The verbal mission in no way conceded defeat but its vindication moved into another key and assumed another guise.

Islam became a faith in arms, a mission realized in conflict. The history is long rehearsed and is, perhaps necessarily, obscure about the onus of blame – if blame it be – or of responsibility round the initiation of what ensued. By mutual encounters in arms and forays, raids and rallies, Islam became inured to the theme of 'retaliation', developing within and outside the Qur'an a sort of *lex talionis*, no longer as in tribal or family feuds and avengings, but as the religious legitimacy of a right to attack when attacked. As it had been in its prime Meccan form, it would have discerned, out of its own adversity, that it had 'to suffer in a state witnessing exile'.[9]

But, ceasing only to preach its meanings, and being steadily embroiled in winning physical conflict, it grew into the philosophy of necessary power-wielding which ever since has characterized its centuries and internally under-written its schisms.[10] That it proved eminently capable down those same centuries to generate the strains of humility, of quietism and the will to simple godliness, which history knows as Sufism or *Tasawwuf*, is the more significant. Could it be that these were how a Meccan faith might in time have been, had it outlived its adversities and been achieved by its patience, had no Hijrah occurred to change its ethos and martialize its image? But Hijrah from Mecca did not stay Meccan.

The 'might-have-beens' of history are idle speculation in which it is futile to indulge. In point of fact, Islam lacked the pre-Constantinian experience of the first three Christian centuries which retained the imprint ever laid upon their founding story in Jesus himself.[11] The Church was free, if not always able, for his 'imitation' and apt to reach a defining Scripture that sufficiently commended and preserved his 'flesh thus made Word', for its abiding guidance.

By contrast, the 'Constantinian' in Muhammad's Medina – if we may so speak – is permanently enshrined in the text and mind of the Qur'an where it abides authoritatively to condition the Qur'an's other mediation of its Meccan message. Islam has come to enduring confidence in their authentic co-existence in the hallowed pages, the Surahs insistently identify themselves by the two cities of their incidence. The undoubted priority of Mecca remains, nevertheless, tributary to the power aegis of Medina.[12] There is a clear license to resist that, by its own logic, can readily pass into a will to attack as the very duty of alert resistance. The things that belong to peace become the things potential to war. The hand that avails must be an 'upper hand'. The significance of Muhammad's magnanimity in Mecca after victory has its due place in the history.[13] The principle, however, and the instinct, for supremacy was nevermore to be in doubt.

Thus, if the spiritual Meccan message holds the defining image of Islam, the physical Medinan mastering was its fulfilling image. The verbal message merged into the armed mastery. Without what, six centuries later, the famous Muslim historian/sociologist Ibn Khaldun called 'the power of wrathfulness',[14] Islam would not be itself. Only in power terms would it be an honestly or a credibly religious mission. No faith could be genuinely from God, if it did not have God fulfilling God's rule, through it and because of it. It needed to have Allah for it and with it, saying: 'God wills us. He wills us as the due custodians of the final revelation and the perfected religion, the religion He avows as His.'[15]

Would it be fair to set this conviction alongside Paul's famous cry: 'If God be for us, who can be against us?' when writing to the Romans, with the further question: 'Who shall lay any charge?' (8.31). His question was rhetorical. It was not that he was dubious about a possibility but assured about a reality. Arguing from firm conviction of God as 'theirs', their sanction, their hope and, therefore, the ground of their courage, meant a courage which could then take rhetoric further into a fervent protestation about having no viable enemies in the world, none to deny them this bold assurance concerning their Lord. Paul's language comes from his perception of God and Christ, of 'God in Christ'. His context is the often menacing, potentially hostile Roman Empire. He is disqualifying any daunting role or threat on the part of that irreducible power. The Medinan 'question' in Islam would rather be, more fitly, 'Who should be against us seeing that, if they are, our mandate is to bring upon them our régime.' That situation was captured in the tradition, shortly before his death, of Muhammad's summons to neighbouring rulers to bring themselves under Islam.

'The power of wrathfulness' that had brought Mecca round would thus determine the Medinan shape of Islamic history down the long centuries of its one post-Hijrah genius. The Meccan/Medinan dichotomy is nowhere more neatly caught than in the growth of meaning in the term *fitnah* through the Qur'an. What was constant in the situation throughout was that faith and its faithful were under stress, at odds, whether in witness or identity with circumstance around. But initially that stressful-ness was a 'trial' for them in the sense of testing their will to witness, their nerve in innocent fidelity. After the Hijrah, their allegiance became also a matter of risk in actual or possible 'trial' of arms. Then their personal 'trial' or 'test' lay in shrinking from the hazards, out of fear of death or dismay at leaving widows or orphans behind. This reluctance to face danger needed to be reproved in the Qur'an as *fitnah*. The 'testing' earlier of persecution had now become the 'test' of due courage in face, not of ridicule, but of prema- ture death. At a still later stage, when Islam became victorious, *fitnah* was the 'sedition' or malign subterfuge that sought to conspire against success. It was the 'hypocrisy' (*nifaq*) which resented and resisted the success of Islam and took to cunning and guile to undermine it. The way to deal with *fitnah* then was vigilance from strength which first had been perseverance under scorn.

At length we reach in Surah 2.217 the affirmation that '*fitnah* is greater (evil) than slaughter', the context having first listed several areas of action against Islam – 'turning folk away from Allah's *sabil* and refusing to believe in Him and His inviolable shrine and expelling people from it'. It prefaces these with the ruling that 'slaughter' (*qital*) in the sacred month of truce is great wrong, conceding that the cause of faith had only reluctantly broken that tribal Meccan rubric about leaving pilgrimage free of molestation under truce. *Fitnah*, in the first days of Muhammad's Meccan mission, never had occasion to be in any comparison making it 'greater wrong than killing'. *Fitnah* had then been as 'bad a thing as cowardice', or, simply, 'commitment means discipleship', therefore, 'fear not to belong'.

Once the sanction of combat was invoked and the exigencies of war took over, Islam assumed a new version of authority, a different temper of mind. It had always been categorical about its faith credentials and their demand to be affirmed.[16] Each semitic faith is so. Its Prophet was the spokesman of Allah, its Qur'an His speech and language. In Medinan conflict that reli- gious 'ultimate' of mission became an institutional absolute, no longer only 'speaking in His Name', but contesting for His cause.

This engendered a changed perception of His – and its – adversaries. From the outset its message had firmly discriminated 'believers from unbe- lievers', 'gainers from losers', *muslimun* from *kafirun*.[17] Those identities, in their rivalry, became the more loaded and even venomous in the later context of Badr, Uhud, and beyond, as armed engagements and fields of desperate confrontation, into whose sequel matters of spoil, or ransom, or booty supervened. It was not that the pre-Hijrah witness ceased to matter but that it was compromised and overlaid by new pre-occupations of mind, new passions of will. The Hijrah was proving, in more than spatial terms, an emigration from an original self. Like so much else in religious history, it was a watershed, or a Rubicon, within itself.[18]

It is this feature in Islam's primary story which explains how there might develop, after long centuries, the phenomenon of suicidal aggression we currently perceive, the more so in a strong sense of adversarial dimensions from 'the other side'. It would belong with this deeply-rooted tradition of 'vigilance against', of Islam supremely 'self-defendant', as the very form of self-awareness in the world. Thus, the legal concept of *Dar al-Harb*, 'the realm of non-Islam' still to be brought into Islam, the realm outside the single *Ummah* of *Dar al-Islam*, demanded action.

There was enmity aplenty for Muslims in Mecca in pre-Hijrah adversity but the Medinan time gave it a response no longer that of suffering regret and hopeful reversal. The faith became in deep measure an enmity-brooding, enmity breeding thing. There was a new version of 'intolerance', no longer now of idolatry as wrong and folly, but of idolaters as mortal enemies apt for the other 'persuasion' that defeat in battle might accomplish.[19]

When spreading empire rewarded the wide advance of Islam, the *dhimmi* system, designed for tolerated minorities whose scriptured faiths were conditionally allowable, perpetuated something of the same 'enmity' in sharply differentiating within a human co-existence. The status of *Ahl al-Dhimmah*, being mercifully less than persecuting, was also less than dignifying. It retained for the human 'other' much of the same will to inimical differential *Dar al-Islam* cherished in its own identity. It may be argued that such concessions should not be judged by other norms it has taken long centuries to reach. Yet the pattern of an Islam on every count *sui generis* is clear enough. It also contained a deep irony, in that while Islam was only – and by post-Hijrah necessity – religious in being also political in its own power-mastery, other religions must survive in complete forfeiture of any power-dimension. Their being tolerated turned on their being dis-empowered, and that by their own pledged surrender, retaining only their strictly religious freedoms of worship, belief and customary social laws.

In these several ways, Islam grew into a strongly self-sufficient, deeply self-possessed institution both of belief and practice. It was self-referent, but in a quite contrasted way from Jewry via Judaism. Jewry had the ethnic identity of land and people under covenant with YAHWEH. That richly conscious self-understanding needed, if it did not create, the necessity of 'Gentiles', as 'the other', the rest of humankind as the contra-distinction for which, in every sense, they were needed.

Islam was at first liable, and then bent, to the same pattern, but on the quite different ground of *shahadah*, or faith-holding. What the ethnic meant in Jewishness, doctrinal word-in-trust meant for Islam. Broadly they saw the world in terms of their final truth possession, not of their covenant status. To contrast in this way, both being inherently Semitic, is to clarify a subtle similarity. Jewry too read covenant as truth-possession requiring Judaic *shahadah* to the nations. Islam, thanks to its Arab matrix and its Arabness at core, had something ethnic as 'the best of peoples'.[20] In the width of either canvas, the distinction holds. Muslims had the distinctive solidarity, not of a 'people' *per se* but of an *Ummah* of truth, of truth in the custody of its final repository, 'sealing' and so monitoring, all earlier revelation. Those who did not 'come to this light', or could not be accommodated under its tolerance as *dhimmis* could be, were its 'Gentiles', ignorantly or wilfully 'other' than the selves Muslims were proud to be. Was not the term *islam* about 'submission', alike to Allah and His religion? Being, in fact, a 'submission' both to belief and régime made the distinction between the *Dar –* and the non-*Dar –* all the more a crucial apartheid. Conceptually Islam has long lived with this powerful 'we and not we' version of the human world.

III

If the foregoing has fairly discerned Islam in its own instinctive quality, it is possible to understand why it might desperately find within itself, however direly and darkly, the will to the suicidal scenarios in which desperadoes engage as in an alleged 'clash of civilizations'. It was a Western analyst who coined the random, dubious phrase pitting 'West' against 'East'.[21] It was fit for the retort of some within Islam: 'Our formula is Islam and the Rest', and since your arrogance makes the West all, our slogan shall be 'Islam against the West'. Circumstances, or reading of them, might prompt into play the latent anger against that other *Dar*, still unsubdued, indeed blatantly hostile to *Dar al-Islam* seen at odds within itself, and in sorry hostage to that insidious West.

An obvious new factor in the contemporary suicidal in any 'terror' terms is the sheer range and grim potential of contemporary technology. A solitary Telemachus throwing himself into the arena in protest against gladiatorial barbarity, a priest dying soaked in blazing petrol to denounce oppression, or a lonely hunger-striker in prison – these could be greatly influential in terms of demonstration. A would-be suicide armed with bow and arrow would have no suicidal efficacy, however fine his archery. It is the concentrated power-explosive means, its conspiring reach, strapped on private bodies or rammed in vehicles through normal hindrances, that enable the devastating reach of today's suiciding 'martyrs' in their enmity. There was an eloquent irony in two monuments of western technological prestige as the targets of an emulating efficiency, harnessing that supreme symbol of current mobility, the multi-seated jet aircraft.

And not only so. The organization of current criminal 'war on the West' is furnished by all the techniques of communication, the web, the net, the mobile phone and an entire capacity to deploy the means to plot and sustain long-range action across territorial boundaries and in defiance of the countering arts of detection and control. It is served by the same sophistication that it hates and would destroy. The main currency of its high finance is the US dollar. Its suiciding 'pilots' needed only to learn how to high-jack not how to take off, making weapons of murder out of means of flight.

The symbolism of encounter is all too vivid and has its counterpart in the contest between Islamic competition, both social and economic, with the West in the wake of the 'space' created by the collapse of the Soviet Union, which also removed from western reckoning the long familiar adversarial theme of 'the cold War'. If, thereafter, American thinking had a psychic need for an object of hate, so also a differently alerted regional Islam gained a heightened sense of enmity to the USA.[22] The excessive accent in US foreign policy on economic self-interest and market aggression has only served to sharpen the answering sense of resistant anger. It follows that the economic aspects of Islamic violence tangle on every front with the world finances it exploits and poisons.[23]

Realists might insist that these economic factors are paramount in the confrontation and that the religious element merely fanaticizes and obscures their functioning. That verdict and its cynicism would be deceptive. The organizing 'fronts' or 'cells' of concerted violence use Quranic terms like *Al-Ansar*, those 'aiders' of Muhammad in Yathrib,[24] or they clothe their purpose as arrayed in the classic quality of *Jihad* and Hijrah as 'venturers of faith', the *mujahidun* and *muhajirun* of today. Qur'ans were likely to be found in their vehicles and its study the main pre-occupation of their training camps.

'Terrorist' is, of course, a variable word and much injustice has been done by invoking it without discriminating between situations where it is identified. Suicide as a policy or strategy gives a radical shift to the order – or disorder – of conflict, the more so when, for obvious ideological reasons, it is likely to be unilateral. For where life is prized, it is not a tactic which will be reciprocated. Muslims, devising or promoting it, have to disavow or distort the reading of their own Scripture. It is important to realize that it has no warrant in the Qur'an. That sacred Book is familiar enough with the fact and fruit of a faith at war – of war which accepts its normal hazards of death and wounds as part of war's incidence on a faith's devotees. Even so, as studied under the concept of *fitnah*, it harangued its people about not shirking these out of fear or family bonds. The rules it promulgates about booty and/or ransoms, when 'war lays down its burdens, suggest a measure of human feeling but only to mitigate what war exacts.[25]

Nevertheless it flouts what we may call 'the mind of the Qurʾan' to extend the art of war to the indiscriminate hurt or death of the 'civilian', though this very term, with its modern ring, has no Quranic equivalent. The issue over *shirk* was all engrossing. 'Neutrals' found themselves in a hard role in the years that followed the Hijrah, as Jewish communities knew to their heavy cost.[26] War had to be relentless until 'sedition', that ultimate *fitnah*, ceased (2.193). 'Civilians' in today's world, especially when they are fellow-Muslims, are a far cry from the fervid, local *mise-en-scène* of Islam's founding conflict and the stark immediacy of its religious issue.

If that scene-set in no way matches what current suiciders at war do in thronged streets, towering buildings, crowded trains or popular resorts, there may be a latent clue in how the fervour of fight ignores 'civilians' now because it passes into a pathological condition. The zeal of religion, of which the Qurʾan leaves us in no doubt, can certainly lead to impulses its saner mind would disown. Aum Shinrikyo (he with nerve gas in a Tokyo subway, 1995) explained: 'We regarded the world outside as evil and destroying the evil as salvation.' Something of that utter negativity may move the Muslim zealot, the more so as he believes that Allah wills it. The very vulnerability of present-day civilization can make that passion the more fascinating in being the more efficient. A pathological condition thrives on the sense of victims anonymous and easy.

The persuasion that is ready to conclude: 'There are no more civilians' finds logic also in any long tradition, as in Islam, of desirable martyrdom. Why should an all-possessing passion think of 'others anonymous', immune from its own range of reckoning, or enjoying a sanction on life exempt from the version of a zealot's world? Meccan caravans might have given themselves a sort of 'civilian status' by buying off marauding Bedouin with a share in the profits, just as protection rackets are often found going well with violence. But such calculations find no place where absolute passions religious belong.[27] While there has been strong reluctance in shaihkly circles to allow deliberate suicide as legitimate martyrdom, there seems no doubt that a long and deep culture of martyrdom somehow can encompass it.[28]

Is the enigma present in the words of Surah 6.162: 'Say: My prayer, my rite of sacrifice, my living and my dying, all belong to God, the Lord of the worlds'? The second term *nusuki* has come to mean 'my asceticism' in some usages, but tells essentially 'my utmost devotion'. The term also covers the rites of pilgrimage which fulfil the pilgrim cry: 'Here I am at Your call.' On almost every count, this reading would have suicide quite ruled out by the final words: 'My dying' – a timing Allah has within His own will. Yet even this a suicidal zealotry might override by coinciding divine and private wills.

IV

One might well be dubious, if not wholly sceptical, if one studied the issue without the adjective 'contemporary' with which this chapter began. Thus far the factor of provocation has been muted, while we studied the abstract perceptions out of which it would be answered. While martyrology looms large and with it much that might seem altogether suicidal, what we are examining is recent in its vehemence and range.

And thus what is recent in the emergence of the suicidal strategy is precisely the perception that the odds of conflict have been dramatically changed by the 'compound interest' advance of western technology. Its power-wielding can no longer be matched – or even faced – in familiar terms of frontal war. An Iraq may successfully invade a weaker neighbour but can rapidly be evicted by the super-power. A Muslim diehardness may entrench itself on the far highlands of Afghanistan and still be dislodged from them in the frontal terms of combat. Palestinian militants are no match for a local nuclear power, furnished with all latest techniques by its staunch western patron. Such boast no tanks, can deploy no helicopter-gunships, nor patrol their Gaza with naval armoury. Islam, by and large, finds itself physically inferior to the other 'hemisphere' its passions are liable to perceive as *Dar al-Harbiyyin*, 'the realm of the to-be-warred against'.

If that realm's techniques are to be employed against it, this can only be by their almost private adaptation to strategies of surprise and cunning, whose detection will be costly and circuitous and whose efficiency works by creating apprehension and anger.[29] 'Terror' then finds its own compound interest, but the price is liable to be suiciding self-immolating, for which Muslim martyrology readily supplies both rationale and incentive. The bomb-and-nail-loaded body-belt becomes the 'answer' to 'superior' foes. The self-forfeiture is justified by the self-satisfaction, though the victim does not survive to see the toll he takes. It was even so with Samson. 'No time for lamentation now.'

It is crucial to realize that there is much Islam in the treasury of its Qur'an to set against this mind-set and its logic – the mortal trust of self-hood of which the body is the token; the worth of forbearance and *sabr* in what should be 'a mercy to the worlds'; the virtue of 'submission', not usurpation, of the will of God. There is that, however, in Islam by which Muslims can argue to supersede or disqualify these other counsels, when perceptions of the non-Muslim world sway the choices made. If that other world is such that it can only be countered in suicidal terms, there will be 'Muslims' rising to the answer, seeing that other world as grossly deserving the enmity with which it is so desperately rewarded.

But much more than these dimensions of encounter in military terms are the large adversarial emotions roused by western penetration into other cultures and society. These see them as invasive, arrogant and hate-provoking. Hostility to the United States is fuelled by bitter resentment over its lapse from earlier ideals of international community and a responsible posture with wealth and privilege. American films, media, news-presenting, sexual imagery, are seen as flouting or thwarting the self-image of Islam in its culture and mores. There is a sense of something inwardly self-betrayed and insidiously promoting a self-betrayal, wherever it reaches and does not belong. This infiltration of the undesired is the more provocative of envy and resentment because its inroads seem irresistible. The perceived aggression breeds an answering counter-aggression likely to reach for emotions and passions fit to sustain it. It could also seem to such emotion that the West needs the tuition of Islam in its own grievous *Jahiliyyah* and that the lesson, on every count, must be violent in its incidence.[30]

Stark contrast sometimes best captures the truth of situations. Just months after September 11, 2001, a book was published in the utterly different sphere of minority Muslim scholarship in India, in which an eminent scholar-leader, Wahiduddin Khan, took his theme: 'Islam, a Religion of Peace', citing a tradition about how Muhammad answered a simple enquirer who sought from him 'one simple truth by which to live'. The Prophet answered: 'Avoid being angry at all times'. Wahiduddin continued:

> Never being angry is the essence of Islam. All disputes should be resolved by dialogue. Violence has no place in Islam, Islam means peace.

Jihad meant precisely this self-struggle against anger and violence. He cited *Al-Salamu 'alaikum*, the familiar peace greeting between Muslims, as if it were not normally a restrictive greeting.

The book to which Wahiduddin contributed had the title: *You Are, Therefore I Am: A Declaration of Dependence.*[31] How grimly, how readily, that 'You are, therefore I am' fits the violent suicider, ignoring any 'canon 'gainst self-slaughter' in defiance of what he sees as non-Islam. 'I am what I am because you are what you are.'

Such sharp divergence about 'essential Islam' takes us to the heart of the global crisis. Since there is something inter-human and mutual in its making, there must be something inter-human and mutual in its repairing. In that way Islam may be seen as at risk within itself (?) but with no exoneration of the West.

V

Clear as the divide is between an Islam according to 'Usamah ben Laden and an Islam according to Wahiduddin Khan, there is a deep irony in any 'risk' language about what contrasts them. The Indian mentor has the assurance of divine patience, the Arabian the suicide's sure Paradise. The confidence either way has to do with Allah as everything must in Islam. What is at issue is theological and no hopes or fears concerning 'global crisis' can ignore this.

'Allah wills and Allah wills us thus' we noted earlier in this chapter as the ruling principle of suiciding servants of that will and of their conviction as to it. It is a theology whose writ runs beyond the mortal scene where the believer's presence is so readily abridged. The Lord they so radically serve below will amply serve them above. The two realms inter-penetrate. The devout Muslim's private world is steadily alerted by the Qur'an to an ethics of eschatology, to an eschatology of ethics. Daily deeds are 'forwarded' to celestial account. 'Books are opened'. 'Last Judgement' supervenes. There are 'scales' weighing 'light' and 'heavy', telling the trivial from the worthy, the defaulter from the fulfiller.[32]

The martyr by his dying short-circuits these grim assizes or, rather, wins eternal verdict into bliss by the inclusive worth of how and why he died. 'The book in the right hand' belongs by immediate right to him, to him whose hand was selflessly against himself for Allah's urgent cause. The assurance proves immensely fortifying against the odds of certain and untimely death. For, on two counts, 'untimeliness' is cancelled – mortality is fitly complete and death could not be more fitly timed.

Minds in the West, schooled to abhor this 'presumptuous sin' since such it seems to them to be, need to appreciate how deeply the ethos of Islam inter-meshes the two realms of 'here and hereafter', whether in the daily business of living or in the ultimate business of dying. It is impossible for the outsider to guess what other psychic factors – pathological, mental, or maniacal and personal – corroborate or exploit the religious vocation to self-homicide. There is no doubting its textual warrant in the Qur'an or its working in the phenomenon we study. It was noted earlier in comparing varieties of *fitnah* how any shrinking from death in dutiful *Jihad* was reprehensible. Nor should the faithful dissuade themselves from risk by thought of kindred and kinships grimly suffering the loss of them. Expectation of life is always a societal, no less than a personal, assumption. Though an ultimate act of self-isolation, self-homicide is never only privately such. It must be a large, but not an inconceivable, step to discern something like that Quranic *fitnah* in the prose and cons of religious suicide.[33] Zealots of suicidal order might well override their human hesitations by appeal to those verses about disallowing all prudent, fearing, exempting counsels.

Yet, given any will to think Quranically at the impulsive point of last resolve, there could be three deeply Islamic criteria to lay an utter veto on it. These belong with the meaning of *Allahu akbar*, its total warning against *Shirk* and, thirdly, a quarrel with Muhammad's *Sirah*, or prophet-career, in its primary shape. Brooding on these three may serve to set the religious strategy of suicide in proper light and firm disavowal.

VI

That there is something utterly absolute in this form of self-homicide cannot be in doubt. Deliberately to forfeit intelligent youth hardly over the threshold of maturity – as is normally the case – is to absolutize one's will in the most drastic way, a wager with no 'hedging of its bets', a foregoing of all that life's future holds, the most ultimate of irreversible decisions. All such absolutes, by their very nature, deny any absolutes beyond them. What then – the Muslim's question – of that 'God is greater' truth? Has it, somehow, been abrogated as a referent proper to have cancelled the other? Has divine sovereignty been usurped, the divine will taken into private human hands? Ought not reference to Allah be 'greater' than one's personal policy to die?

Certainly the two have somehow been identified. Such, indeed, will be the answer, and the pride, of the self-foregoing actor in Allah's Name. How, then, is 'God greater' than one's own presumption?[34] Has the freedom of the divine will been taken over by the private self? It could only not be so, if one were assured that the criterion of the human will coincided with the criterion belonging only to Allah. How should one know? Or better – how could one presume concerning a sovereignty ever transcendent?

The point may perhaps be served by that clause in the prayer Jesus gave his disciples to use, namely ' . . . as it is in heaven' qualifying 'Thy will be done on earth . . . ' The Qur'an would certainly posit the same linkage. The doing of 'God's will on earth' is to be conformed to the divine mind. How do we know that we know this? Must not all else refer back to the divine character, so that everything in politics or ethics becomes a referent for theology? Deeds, in Islam and everywhere, ought to be 'characterized by the character of God' and on this score should there not always be a reticence?[35] It is always vital to 'leave room for the judgement of God'. Suicide, by definition, will not do so.[36]

In this way it has 'not let God be God' – to use the clause most definitive of Islam. On three occasions the Qur'an makes this point about the rule of theology in ethics when it observes of pagans that 'they did esteem

Allah as He should be esteemed'. Their actions proved that they had no right 'measures' of Allah.[37] Their idolatry enshrined their misreading.

Shirk in the Qur'an is the negation alike of divine unity and divine sovereignty. It diversifies the former in the worship of a medley of tribal, local, notional deities to whom it allocates – by trust, or plea, or reverence – the sole prerogative of the latter. By its *ilahat mut'addidah* it flouts *Allahu akbar*. Allah is now only peer among the many.[38] Only social confusion and spiritual futility follow.

Could it be then that the suicider in zealot Islam, in disallowing *Allahu akbar* also becomes guilty of *Shirk*? Away, surely, with the thought! – unless somehow, in the light of the argument, 'the cause' has become his 'idol', his ultimate allegiance, his, literally, final worship. 'Letting God alone be God' might have given pause to a 'self-omnipotent' posture with himself. Or was there a 'tyranny' to which he brought allegiance, seeing how all-commanding its claim was allowed to be?

When, in the light of 19th and early 20th centuries, Arabism was girding itself for liberation from the Ottomanism of the Caliphate, one of its thinkers, 'Abd al-Rahman al-Kawakibi (1854–1902), coined the formula for agitation against it from the concept of *Shirk*. He argued that political tyranny was a form of idolatry because it violated the very sovereignty of Allah. His book *Taba' 'al-Istibdad*, 'The Nature of Tyranny', was very influential, seeing that this incipient Arabism was minded for revolt against the most venerable of Islamic institutions, the Caliphate as the legacy of Muhammad himself.[39] It brooded its case from the premise of 'the nation', compromising the theory of a unitary Islam as a single *Ummah*, or 'household', in which 'nationalism' had no place. Many contemporary suiciders now hold that conviction. Al-Kawakibi in his time and place grounded his Arabism in the charge that 'idolatry' belonged in the tyranny that Arabism suffered. Thus even an 'Islam' could be idolatrous, in not honouring the theological norm he held to be alone consonant with a true worship. The argument, of course, could well be turned against his own 'conspiracy', which Ottomans saw it to be. Either way, issues political become matters theological. It is clear how far the familiar Islamic passion against *Shirk* can be double-edged. We may not simplistically assume that we are doing Allah's will. 'Idolatry', therefore, is always more than anathema concerning it can comprehend or remedy.

VII

Reflections of this order, for all their urgency, may avail little to stay the hand of ardent suicide in the stress and turmoil of its long and anguished brooding in the soul. Perhaps more effectual in immediate dissuasion might be the third to which the other two have led, namely what was primary in the *Sirah* of Muhammad himself. It involves our reading of that Hijrah, the nature of its watershed between the twin cities of Mecca and Medina. There is no doubt, from the naming of its Surahs, that the Qur'an finds the two identities central to either, since of their contrast there can be no doubt. Islam has one origin but a second version.

At their first inauguration and for long centuries, unity of origin and version was not in question: in a global modern scenario it has emphatically become so. It was a unity which enshrined its two dimensions firmly in its Qur'an, while yet designating its Surahs to their proper city. Thus the house of Islam renews its awareness of both in the flow of its *Tajwid* from the first to the last. The Christian Church, by contrast, has no scriptural lections of its Constantinian version, post-315 CE.

It has been and can well be argued that the fusion of message and power that ensued at and after the Hijrah was entirely valid then, Muhammad being harshly faced by an establishment that might never, otherwise, become persuadable by his essential message. For as we have seen, it challenged their vested interest in pagan shrine custody, pilgrimage and trade. The emigration on which he embarked out of that impasse proved eminently successful. Yet it radically altered the guise of that for which it was meant. The irony of that fact persists to this day and this 21st century. It is only a minority that thinks that Islam has *now* to forego its Medinan shape. It is, however, no minority but an inclusive unanimous perception that Islam is abreast of every flux and toll of time. Its finality as a 'mercy to the worlds', is sure.

'Worlds', manifestly, alter in the role, the task, they present to every religious structure. Islam's 'world' is no longer in a context remote from the main-stream world, nor one sanctioned in tribal rivalries by patron deities whose aegis sustains our quarrels. We inhabit a global scene where tensions are bred of economic imbalance, racial injustice, political rivalry and the vagaries of a single super-power. We are not, therefore, in a world that Islam can aspire to coerce into unilateral religious adherence after the manner of a far-off Medinan deployment of the physical means which then availed. The legitimacy, then, of its recourse to a militant fulfilment of its call to faith cannot persist into the global setting where its first *balagh* must now belong. The onus of being and staying final must demand its acceptance of a vocation more arduous than that of Badr and Uhud, the encounters by which its zeal once prevailed across the Hijaz. The vocation abides but the discharge of it has to adjust from there to here, from then to now.

This in no way means that religion somehow relinquishes the sphere of power – a notion Muslims would instinctively find a treachery. It does mean that participation there is on its mettle, no longer in terms of the force that rules and requires to be monopolist. It belongs in terms of how the primary *balagh* guides, motivates and inspires the religious conscience.

Where Islam is culturally and historically dominant, it means that it admits a full and genuine participation of minorities, religious or secular, in this activity. Where it is participant in nationhoods of more balanced population, it will do so in its Meccan shape of 'witness' and 'the word'. It will, in either case, renew that Meccan priority but no longer with the ancient persecution, seeing that the world at large is ready for a tolerant Islam of that order. Where Muslims are in a diaspora in which there is no realistic prospect of political power – or one only at the price of being subversive in a most dastardly way[40] – this vocation will be the more fulfilling for its very challenge to patience, gentleness and peace.

There are voices across Islam now perceiving and commending this version of a contemporary self-image as its current destiny. Nor are they merely visionary. Their formula is buoyed up against heavy odds by three factors. The first is that they recover the first edition of Islam, the one for which Hijrah was devised, the one towards which, at Mecca, every mosque is focused, the place-mind to which the pilgrimage repairs and the defining essence of Muhammad's own *Sirah*. On every count there can be no denying or revising the absolute priority of the Meccan, nor of sustaining here and now the Medinan amendment of it, once susceptible of legitimacy only in its there and then.

Secondly, there is nothing new about it thus far into Islam's 15th Hijri century. Back in its 13th, for example, Indian Islam thought itself deprived and languishing because the British Raj and Queen Victoria called the political tune. Muslims were not ruling themselves. But need this spell some kind of doom? Along came Ahmad Khan, founder of Aligarh, noting that the mosques were open, *Salat* practiced, pilgrimage made, *Zakat* paid and the Ramadan fast observed. 'What lacks,' he asked, 'of Islam?' It was irrelevant to protest: 'But we do not govern!', or it would be if Islam had not been truly minted in Mecca or that only Medina now ensured its definition as it had once assured its survival.

Thirdly, the hard fact is that around one fourth of all Muslims globally are now in that British India situation, in diaspora across the world, lacking the corridors of power except insofar as they will frequent them in bringing the insights and moral wisdom of their *balagh*, as its voice inside a shared citizenship. One quarter of the whole is a significant segment of contemporary Islam. The quality of its counsels, the depth of its introspection, can yield dividends both for itself and for the stimulus of Muslims where they dominate in traditional heartlands.

Physical diaspora now means also a generational ferment inside the Islamic mind. Dispersion apart, current 'worlds' inter-penetrate. Old categories of 'East' and 'West' become partly obsolete.

Given the high significance of this diaspora, it would be idle to think these three factors finding fruition in the immediate future or that suicidings in the aggressive mode would be deterred by them. The way must be long and hard. It is arguable that the Al-Qaʿidah-style belligerence itself arises precisely from confused apprehension about diaspora, seen as 'menace'. Ferocity, as often in religion, is born of defiance.

Even so, the principle of 'change via consensus' is present in Sunni Islam, given the 'right *Ijtihad*, or enterprise' to initiate it. As for its conditionality by reference to the Qurʾan, the rubric about 'non-repugnancy' admits of lively exegesis.[41]

Rather than deploring and denouncing the Islam it perceives as implacably 'terrorist', the West would be more wisely relating – beyond fulminations – by contributing all it carefully can to the emergence of the Islam the world needs Islam to be, an Islam in the rightness of its own mind. That task is already in part academically in hand. Only in the world scene at large is it well discharged.

Suiciding 'terrorists', as we are apt to figure them, might give the careful observer pause about what will be bland as a dismissive. Self-obliteration – for such it is save for some imagined continuity within a 'cause' – should not be virtually ignored in the manner of, reportedly, an American officer during the late 2004 battle for Fallujah. As insurgents' died where they stood, or where they appeared as snipers above some parapet, Lt. Colonel Rainey, a bluff veteran, cried:

> I think they are committed fighters out there who will want to die in Fallujah.
> We are in the process of allowing them to self-actualize.[42]

'Self-actualize'! the irony of the verb is malicious, but what of the flippancy? Scorn and abhorrence have surely to find some will to commiseration in the presence of so dire a mad bravery, so pitiable a brave madness? These mangled corpses have been the literal embodiment of bombs, their selfhoods diminished into collateral damage.

It follows here that these fearful acts of self-homicide need to be set in the larger context of suiciders in general, without whom the study would be incomplete. The Ernest Hemingways, the Virginia Woolfs of a life-weary world are a necessary counter to our main pre-occupation, if only because their measure of what we may think to be 'unfaith' serves to interrogate the very excess of 'believing' via the uniting fact of a desperate ending. All the foregoing will then suggest some measure of the 'bond in continuing to live'.

These themes are the business of succeeding chapters.

9

Suicides and Shares

I

When in 1865 Charles Dickens was serializing his last completed novel, *Our Mutual Friend*, he confided to a colleague:

> It is a combination of drollery and romance which require a degree of pains and a perfect throwing away of points that might be amplified . . . [1]

It was verdict which might well apply to human biography itself and the tale of every private self in the chances and changes of a mortal existence through allotted years. It also captured – though Dickens did not directly link them – two loaded features of his complex novel, namely wretched suicides and the vagaries of stocks and shares. Take the latter from the realm of cash and trade and let it tell the lottery of human fates and we have an immediate context of the former. Dickens frequently dwelt satirically on the irony of the cash nexus in the human scene.[2]

> As is well known to the wise in their generation, traffic in shares is the one thing to have to do in this world . . . Have shares . . . in capital letters and be great. Where does he come from? Shares. Where is he going to? Shares. What are his tastes? Shares. Has he any principles? Shares . . . [3]

Such are the Veneerings and the Lammles of Dickens' imagination in the novel. No names attach to the sundry corpses fished from the dark Thames in the grim opening of the tangled story. Their value belongs only to the odd coins that may be filched from their bodies and the fees that cheaply reward their salvage from the waters. Scavengers in sinister boats prowl along the muddy banks to drag the week's suicided wretches from the stream and gloat or gibe about their body-finds.

> What world does a dead man belong to? 'Tother world. What world does money belong to? This world. How can money be a corpse's? Can a corpse own it, want it, spend it, claim it, miss it? Don't try to go confounding the rights and wrongs of things in that way.

Could any one of these hapless human flotsam on the river be 'the mutual friend' of Dickens' ambiguous title?[4] For 'rights and wrongs' in the bundle of life had been bitterly confounding them.

Hence the point of 'shares and suicides' of this desolate order in any study of 'Faith at Suicide'. This chapter is no less relevant than the rest. For 'lack of faith' – if such it be – among these forlorn ones only queries and quenches the faith-bravado of the fanatic kind. It also squarely inter-rogates the confidence of the heroic measures of the Samsons or the Masadans of this world. Perhaps also it under-writes the darker meanings of Gethsemane. If we are concerned with 'wrongs and rights' of self-homi-cide we may not well ignore the 'wrongs and rights' in society and history of all, otherwise, would-not-be suicides.

For the literature of existence has of them so many. Nor will Robert Browning deflect us with his poetic rescue of a 'morgue in Paris' due to be demolished, by hearty celebration of the three who newly were its tenants, three 'who most abhorred their life . . . so ended it'. Each had made their exit by drowning – we assume – in the Seine.

> Poor men, God made, and all for that.
> The reverence struck me: O'er each head
> Religiously was hung its hat,
> Each coat dripped by its owner's bed,
> Sacred from touch . . .

Two, the poet conjectured, were failed insurrectionists. He counselled them: 'Be quiet and unclench your fist.' The third, 'poor fellow that is blue', Browning guessed, had come adrift through women and lust, whence 'ill luck gets . . . '

> the copper couch and one clear nice
> Cold squirt of water o'er your bust . . .

His homily concludes: 'It's wiser being good than bad,' but ends with 'a wide compass round' to final hope.[5]

The strange and cruel vicissitudes of mortal time that take the poets to such mortuaries have kindled the imagination to still more dramatic read-ings of the earth itself as summoning the life-weary into its waiting bosom. Matthew Arnold, for example, mourned the Greek Empedocles who threw himself into the flaming cauldron of Mount Etna, a philosopher answering the fascination of its elemental fire. His leap into the crater was his gesture of self-assertion and a bid to be one with earth as the realm of air, water and fire, those four elements which corresponded to the frame and the moods of humankind. The will within his mind had brought him to a terminal despair, 'dried its self-sufficing fount of joy', 'lost in the fantastic maze'. His mentor, Callistes, musing further down the slope of Etna, affords Empedocles no solace. What if . . .

> . . . we might gladly share the fruitful stir
> Down in our mother earth's miraculous womb! . . .
> But mind – but thought –
> If these have been the master part of us –
> Where will they find their parent element?
> What will receive them, who will call them home?[6]

Such self-analysis prompts him to find analogy from the flaming earth for the fire of his own emotion of thought. 'To the elements it came from everything will return, our bodies to earth, our blood to water, heat to fire, breath to air . . .

> They were well born, they will be well entomb'd.[7]

Far from that Greek world, less articulate minds, musing on their ill-share in life, might well sense the occasion's equivalence of the crater edge – the dizzy heights of the Suspension Bridge, or the white cliffs of Beachy Head. Or there is always the dark mystery of the strongly flowing river, as in the poem of C. H. Sorley, writing before his death in France, aged only twenty years. The poem broods on the image of a man standing in thick darkness on the bank of a swift flowing river.

> The mass of blackness moving down
> Filled full of dreams the eye . . .
> He had an envy for its black Inscrutability
> He felt impatiently the lack of that great law whereby
> The river never travels back but still goes gliding by . . .
> We are two living things
> And the weaker one is I.

The silent thrust of the river contrasts with the seeming futilities, the bitter inexplicables of his private and his public world.

> He had a yearning for the strength that comes of unity,
> To be a part of that great strength which moves and cannot die.[8]

The man in the poem throws himself into the stream which received him silently . . .

> And there was left no shred, no wrack
> To show the reason why,
> Only the river running black, beneath the blacker sky.

Such 'weakness and strength' equations between frail mortality and mother earth need find no Etnas to climb or be halted by the infrequency of volcanoes in eruption. The thought of being 'rocked around with stones and rocks and trees' suggests an exit strategy on many counts of circumstance and anxiety as – in literal terms – a 'native' death-wish.

II

Literature in many nations is full of them, the Virginia Woolfs, the Cesare Paveses, the Sylvia Plaths of this world. Among the most celebrated of the 19th century was 'Papa Hemingway' blowing out his brains with a shotgun his wife Mary strove to keep out of his reach. For the menace of the use of it had long hung around his life-style and his mind-set. Dogged in his later years by ill-health, alcoholism, weary of electrodes in hospitals, and writing out of a long tradition of violence, had he any further 'onus to live'? In *Death in the Afternoon*, he had written:

> All stories if continued far enough end in death . . . he is no true story-teller who would keep that from you. There is no lonelier man in death, except the suicide, than that man who has lived many good years with a good wife and then outlived her.[9]

There was a saving grace in that proviso and many a suicide has known and disregarded such thought of the 'out-liver'.

All his life, Hemingway had lived with savagery – in wars he deliberately sought out, in Cuban strife, in African game-hunting, in Spanish bull-fights and endless escapades with death. Of these he had made his name and when notoriety both rewarded and embittered him, he suffered quarrels with the media trading on his fame. The young and intensely ambitious would-be man of letters became the nation's celebrity, the icon of its muscular tradition. Sometimes the malignity he depicted stemmed from the forces of nature, as in *The Old Man and the Sea*; otherwise, more frequently from the wrath or recklessness of men. The courage which so long described him in desperate confrontations with hazard and gore did not suffice him at the last.

There was even a brashness, an austere bravado, about his literary style – terse, clipped and raw in calculated disregard for finer reaches of eloquence except when landscapes warmed him to some emulation of their majesty. The tautness of his prose matched the metal in his soul. His narrative concentration was on physical experience as the paramount idea and there was a degree of cynicism about his glamourization of violence and a certain register of war-weariness. His heroes are often puzzled over sexual identity, given his ruling fascination with being masculine. Affectation he deplored and, with it, a rugged avoidance of adjectives in his writing discipline. There was little of the pathos of John Donne's words as Hemingway borrowed them in *For Whom the Bell Tolls*.[10] He could tell of traumatic experience with a detachment that renounced pity and abstract rumination as if sensing vacuity everywhere, only redeemed by active dexterity, 'snatching a lesson from life', and demonstrating 'doing something well'.

Had he always been somehow 'suicidal'? The theme preoccupied him in several stories. In *To Have and to Have Not* he mused on the sundry ways in which people could contrive to die by

> ... those well constructed instruments that end insomnia, terminate remorse, cure cancer, avoid bankruptcy, and blast an exit from intolerable positions by the pressure of a finger . . . so easily carried, so sure of effect, so well designed to end the American dream when it becomes a nightmare . . . [11]

One critic saw the story as:

> an extraordinary re-creation of the chaos, brutality and fear of a society on the edge of an abyss.[12]

The 'consolations' in Hemingway, if we have any, are not those of religion but of sensation. Not being made for thinking, the immediacies of the senses and an itemizing their incidence meant for him a wholly visual relation to the world. 'Now, as it is, is all you have.' The fact of Hemingway's enormous popularity is a strange index to the society he made enamoured of its mirroring.

For all his yarns and risks, Hemingway (1899–1961) arrived to three score years. A writer of a very different suiciding, the Piedmontese, Cesare Pavese reached hardly two score (1908–1950). Not his the brittle violence of the Hemingway saga. A solitary who never married and knew of despairing suicides among his native Piedmontese farmers, he sought meaning for a time in Communism and remained a committed anti-Fascist. His Dickensian 'shares' were those of political unrest and private alienation. His searchings brought him under the spell of Herman Melville, whose *Moby Dick* he translated into Italian. In the year of his death he published *La Luna e I Faho* ('The Moon is on Fire'), his earlier *Lavorare Stanca* (1936) ('Work is Wearisome') alike sensing the irrecoverable lostness of childhood, quite unrelieved by the American robustness of Walt Whitman whom he also savoured. From other sources (Mexican) he developed a strange feel for ritual sacrifice and its origins, as presented in *The Golden Bough* of James Frazer.

It was a dark amalgam of emotions that led him to contrive his own exit from a brooding fatalism, always expressed in the first person by his characters. His personal diary was published in English as *The Burning Brand*, where he had written: 'No one ever lacks a good reason for suicide'; 'the only joy in the world is to begin'; 'when living has become a habit one might as well be dead'.[13] Walt Whitman would have approved on the last in 'I Sing of Myself' but only by having 'living' perennially a challenge to the self that must fulfill it.

No writer in Italy was more pained and puzzled by Cesare Paveses' grim death than his near contemporary, Primo Levi (1919–1987), famed survivor of the Shoah and through turbulent Fascist years a revered figure in Italian Jewry. Their paths had sometimes crossed.[14] The tragic demise of the foremost among Italian literati troubled Levy deeply, contending as he was with the trauma of the post-Holocaust mind and burdened with the legacy of the Fascist years. The grim depletion of the Italian Jewish community through stricken years, he emerged to symbolize in resilience and despair alike. There was a heavy dubiety, to his mind, about what long ago had been called 'the consolation of Israel' in the ironic form of post-1948 – the 'Zion' of an independent Israel.[15]

Most arduous of all in his mental world was a latent sense of 'guilt' lest he had owed his exemption from the fate of those millions of his fellow Jews to his having been a 'useful' industrial chemist, apt to be spared for no human reason but a scientific function, so that his very prowess accused him. Such at least were the forebodings that supervened when his own family sky darkened with the crippling illness of his aged mother. His attaining to be so far and so well the icon of his Jewish community and, for many Italians also, in the far reach of his name, weighed also on his soul. He wrote of how he tired of being always the exemplary object of some general yearning that found its solace in the repute they justly accorded him. That very repute turned, in part, on a perceived role, for ever taxing his own resources in a sort of vicarious irony. All the years from his youth into his sixties, he who had 'lived with Auschwitz' would be dissuading other survivors from taking their own lives.

The writing on which his literary fame rests was his means of 'personal stabilization' against bouts of despair, as his pen affirmed for readers that what 'tests us' spells the measure of who we are. The wit and humour of his muse had its intriguing play in his 'chemical' study of nature's 'elements' – carbon, sulphur, mercury and the rest – as analogues of human moods, minds and stories.[16] Through all the positive, courageous qualities of his character he was struggling against a deep mistrust of all human experience, Jewish and 'Gentile' alike, as somehow a blighted, ill-fated mystery. His last complete novel, *The Drowned and the Saved*, was written, as he said, *de profundis*, as having lost all *lebenslust* in an *atavismus*.[17]

Thoughts or fears of suicide run through all his writing.

It was, finally, as if the weight of anguished years and the evident malaise of all the human world, left impulsive termination life's last and now only option. There was a grim sign at its climax. Primo Levi threw himself down the stair-well of 72 Corso Re Umberto in Turin, his life-long home, emulating how his own father's father had leaped to death from a second story window. The stair-well had always fascinated him as habitually he surveyed it in his comings and goings, with its 'giddy sensation of a spiral void'.

It was a dark close to a life lived worthily, for ever to dispute the logic of its end. The officiating Rabbi at his funeral waived the ruling against allowing Jewish suicides the seven days of ritual mourning, holding him a survivor who had been murdered by the Nazis. They recalled his camp No. 174517. Many outsiders felt somehow betrayed by his shape of death, its apparent mindlessness of his family's aftermath. Others concluded with his bereaved wife that 'all it took was a moment's inattention'. That dire 'moment of inattention' had sealed what another called 'one howl of freedom in sixty-seven years'.[18] There is no relating the eloquence of that moment with the abrupt exit of the suicide bomber. 'Casualty' is the only common factor, but of what dire substance are casualties contrived? 'Made victim at their own hand' is said of both, with no likeness in the 'dyer's hand'.[19]

If Ernest Hemingway's death 'at his own hand' captured the life-adventure of his chosen saga of violence, risk, war and their fame, and Pavese with Primo Levi were tragedies of time and scene and their literary telling, the pens behind the deaths of Virginia Woolf and Sylvia Plath wrote a different music to accompany their passing. The one, aged 59, walked weighted with stones into the River Ouse, the other, aged 31, laid her head in a gas oven, leaving two tiny children.

III

Highly personal as were the subtleties of these two, the noted essayist and novelist, the young ambitious poet, were 174517's of a different imprisonment and release from those of the two Italians. Two World Wars had massive place in Virginia Woolf's story but both these female writers were private, not political, martyrs in their suicide, Plath with less cumulative reason than the older woman. They serve us here to learn further how the 'undoings' of selfhood in suicidings answer the 'undoings' by which birth and life are held to have made disauthentic the very selfhood they came to tell. They are a verdict on a painful inconsequentiality, the final commentary on a self-awareness that became unwanted.

How does living come inwardly to desire its own cessation? With Virginia Woolf, privately inside the years of war and their public tragedy, answer seems to belong with memory and childhood, the tyranny of things societal and the questing liberty of the pen. She brought the three together in the pursuit of writing, as striving after great sympathies by the effort to learn conflicting truths. For writing was

> . . . the token of some real thing behind blind appearances (and made) it real by putting it into words.[20]

It was this overwhelming sense that 'there is a significance in life' she 'wanted to make real by putting into words' that inspired alike her fiction, her diaries and her essays in criticism. The great onus, however, on that writing was the duty to reach back into memory and unravel the influence of her parents, their marriage, her childhood in its traumas – and all these inside the conventions of the Edwardian society into which her maturity emerged.

In her growing years inside the double families of both her parents' previous marriages, she was darkly abused by her two step-brothers, whose cruelty permanently wounded her psyche and intensified her interrogation of the world. 'What awful lives children live . . .' we read in *The Years*: the comment follows: 'Yes! And they can't tell anybody.'[21]

Physical abuse apart, there was the perpetual image of the ever busy, philanthropic mother, Julia (Duckworth) Stephen, her image all-engrossing yet somehow also love-withholding in the intimate endearments that are truly individual. There was the literary prowess of her formidable father who, with his irascible temper and exacting ways, symbolized the hurtful social conventions she must sharply challenge and authorially amend.

These 'formations' of her childhood years and later adolescence were further harmed by illnesses, nervous and other, besetting her family and disrupting its closest ties. There were suicides in their tradition and thoughts of them burdened the mental climate in which she struggled for her vocation as a writer. She became an intermittent prey to depressions that deepened from time to time into near prostrations of spirit that made her the more apprehensive in the ardent welcome she must give to times of vigour, clarity and literary achievement.

Her very creativity was an inward battle of wills between a mind and pen affirming 'there is significance in life',[22] and the fear of its proving otherwise. Feodor Dostoevsky was chief among her literary inspirations, with his exploration of things submerged in social mores, like unplumbed under-water valleys in the sea-bed. Society is immersed in things inarticulate that people do not, or cannot, say, like silent white 'gaps on the page' in *Jacob's Room*, making nonsense of E. M. Forster's dictum: 'only connect'.

> The streets of London have their maps . . . our passions are unchartered chasms in the continuity of our ways . . . Civilization built on an astonishing gift for delusion.[23]

Hence the 'stream of consciousness' technique of narrative which found such vivid expression in Woolf's *Mrs Dalloway*, and which would become her major authorial influence, using writing itself in the very tracing – as well as the telling – of human emotions. Are identities illusions in the very flow of their possession? How do we both tolerate and escape the conventions by which society is ruled? What capacity, outside letters and the art of them, have we to do so? Yet despair, however enervating, must be resisted.

For all Virginia Woolf's extensive literary output, both critical and fictional, was imbued with a religious sense of 'something there', the very pain of finding, and defining, it the sure form of its veritable presence. The question could be asked only because the answer must be Yes!

> Why is there not a discovery in life, something one can lay hands on and say: 'This is it?' I have a great and astonishing sense of something there.[24]

The better the fiction, the truer the facts. Yet such 'positive capability' had to wrestle all the time against what could only assail its hopefulness. Two of such factors for her were the wretched futility of war and the disesteem of women. Woolf felt she was a defeated pacifist and a necessary but reluctant feminist. She may have shrunk from wearing either label but life's enmities had to be disowned. The reversion to war on such a scale in 1939 was a powerful factor in her final exit. In 1914 she wrote:

> Certainly it was a shock to see the faces of our rulers in the light of the shell-fire. So ugly they in the light of the shell-fire. So ugly they looked, German, English, French – so stupid.[25]

The maelstrom of conflict made her feel a loneliness as one inside an inscrutable society. If the art of fiction was portraying, by authorial mind and deliberation, what belonged with what, in plot and character, how was the world ever doing so in the horrors of the trenches or the malice of the bombs?

It was when invited to lecture on 'Women and Fiction' that she came to write *A Room of One's Own*. She was not an activist but could bring satire, verve and caricature to a cause whose rationale she deeply shared. Women, she averred,

> . . . had the role of looking glasses possessing the magic and delicious power of reflecting the figure of man at twice its natural size.[26]

Caricature can often be a potent weapon to drive home meaning precisely by deft distortion. The truth was that she ' . . . found the gendered behaviour expected (of women) by society incompatible with her sense of herself as a writer'[27] as a daughter and a sister and a woman she might have added. Her mother, she felt had conceded – indeed coveted – a role 'as angel in the house' (and community) in having 'never a mind or wish of her own'. Revering yet exorcizing the image of Julia Stephen, her mother, was no small part of Virginia Woolf's psychic tribulation. Never let any one guess you have a mind of your own was a spur of all her writing.

Could there, conjecturally, be some affinity between misogyny and imperialism? Woolf believed strongly in the interplay of attitudes social with patterns political.

> The public and private worlds are inseparably connected, the tyrannies and servilities of the one are the tyrannies and servilities of the other . . . [28]

If social masks hide private sorrows, and institutions shape personal griefs, it is the duty of the writer to sift and tell their mutuality in angry protest.

Her prolific authorship brought a kind of 'verbal thrift', and economy of language and image, that require attentive readers. In our *Moments of Being*,[29] 'we are the words, we are the music, we are the thing itself', urgent to comprehend how realism and reality are 'there' in any dependable text unless, as she sometimes conjectured, 'we are strangers within ourselves'. Caring in private perplexity the burden of the public scene, surrendering hopeful belief in the remedying of society and faith in human bettering, dreading the onset of another unbearable depression renewing those she had already suffered and resolving not to linger on the verge of her sixties into a withering old age, Virginia Woolf chose to drown with herself all the insoluble ambiguities of the world she could so vividly scrutinize and decipher in her array of characters. There was no failure of verbal ingenuity or mental insight, only their forfeiture of will to stay longer in the loom they wove.

For all her residual sense of an almost religious passion for that 'something there', she also wrote powerfully of its radical absence, pleading 'do not credit me with a creed'. For 'the fumes of that incense obscured the human heart', she wrote in *Between the Acts*.[30] How far, meanwhile, were people really strangers to each other, mutually isolated by the habits of society and the chaos of opinions? In a kind of autobiography unpublished at her death, she wrote:

> There is a silence in life, a perpetual deposit of experience for which action provides no proper outlet and our words no fit expression.[31]

Earlier, writing on 'Modern Fiction', she wrote of

> . . . the sense that there is no answer, that – if honestly examined – life presents question after question which must be left to sound on and on after the story is over in hopeless interrogation that fills us with a deep, and finally it may be, with a resentful despair.[32]

It was this sense of being 'a Hamlet' for which there was no 'Shakespeare', that found her wading, stones in pocket into the friendly Ouse flowing between English meadows.

It is instructive to set this self-immolation alongside that of the air-borne bombers of September 2001. They had too crudely read the human riddle, too savagely concluded the business of their lives. It would have been well if they had let 'question after question . . . sound on and on' before presuming on a deadly travesty of their own Qur'an's plea to 'people with a reflective heart' (Surah 50.37). Their sense of destiny, wholly directed on to an external 'enemy', had not stayed to know an interior 'involvement with mankind', in the reach of that mortality for 'whom the bell tolled'. Despair about history led Leonard and Virginia Woolf to agree on dual suicide had Hitler invaded their southern England. Defiant prevention was the Churchillian resolve her death hid from her, as an authentic courage. By contrast, were the attacking suicides on the World Trade Center and the Pentagon, for all their grim courage, only a more fated version of despair? Given that Islamic confidence we noted in the Introduction of Muslims made such in very wombing by Muslim parenthood, in what lost boyhood or rearing had it been gathered into this form? In the will to be Islamic this way they were 'undoing' both Islam and the 'birth' it gave them. Was true identity precluded from their calculus in the very passion of their conviction with it? The ardent, living, dying introspection of Virginia Woolf, writing to decipher and report the human condition, had no counterpart in the vehemence of their lives and of their deaths.

IV

'Why did Virginia Woolf commit suicide?' We find Sylvia Plath asking in her voluminous diary.[33] The year is 1950 and she a talented self of nineteen years, adding 'I am in the position of a blind girl playing with a slider-rule of values.' The suicide theme was often in her thoughts until finally, aged thirty-one, she made her mortal exit in desperate contrast to the drama of an Empedocles on Etna – no flaming cauldron on a peak of nature but the prosaic refuge of a cooking stove.

Only a little more than half the length of Virginia Woolf's struggle with her literary life, that of Sylvia Plath is of a very different order. It does not belong less fitly in this highly selective study, as providing a foil to the main concern with the suicides of Muslim zealotry so determinedly deadly to themselves. Theirs was a consuming death-claim on the meaning of their life: hers a cumulative anxiety to find the authentic point of living.

Was that anxiety deepened by the lively sense of gifts and assets she undoubtedly possessed, confirmed and encouraged as they were by scholarships to the prestigious Smith College in Massachusetts and on to Cambridge, England and exciting marriage to a fellow poet of rising repute? There were mysterious debits to be sure, there to haunt her psyche, but she could be rightly conscious of a certain poetic genius, though it is well to sober the extravagance that could write of her: 'Plath altered the map of English poetry.'[34] Her literary power of phrase, her boldness of metaphor and her command of imaginative prose are all amply attested in her *Journals* of the years 1950–62, aged 18 to 30, filling a large volume of more than 700 pages all exhaustively garnered from cherished archives at Smith College.[35]

Yet it is their very bulk which gives the student pause. Why should intro-spection need such perpetual scrutiny and self-assessment want such incessant record? There is a residual scepticism perpetually undermining an eager awareness of talent and a thrusting ambition. If she sat still and left off 'doing', the world would for ever beat 'like a slack drum' (p. 210). Dreams of a future and attainment there had to be. For without them what romance? Yet what if they only conveyed to us 'peverty' (sic) – an impov-erished pen and self in one? For whom were the steps she heard coming up the stairs? She was depressed if they were not coming for her.

She wrote of disliking her girlhood. Not being a man would mean that she would have to make captive her energies to the interests of 'her mate'. She would work doggedly and only 'expect the minimum' (p. 405). Inward exhortations to be stoic ally with vows of dedicated effort throughout her *Journals*, noting 'black, lethal weeks' (p. 292). There was a steady preoc-cupation with a public image of mandatory success and apprehension when it was not realized, through the years of college study and, later, a faculty role.

She felt there was much to blame in her Polish origin and her American nurture and then the re-location of her story into England. Had her sternly imagined father deserted her in his dying when she was only eight? What of the tender ties she cherished with a perhaps over-caring mother? Even self-heartening marriage, to the poet Ted Hughes, when it came, somehow only made latent fears to lurk the more because it was so re-assuring. 'Ted . . . our possible impregnable togetherness' (p. 295) reached feelingly into the dual 'our', but why that 'possibly' reverting as to a suspect singular again? The utmost security might harbour the utmost self-undoing. When so it proved in his marital betrayal by his resort to Aisia Wevill, driven home as it was by grim transit from the homestead in Devon to a London flat and loneliness with two tiny children, it proved the final chapter.

How might she have found escape from the dark imprisonment of self-non-acceptance at the core of such vivid self-awareness? Was it – to anticipate the theme to which we must return – that she never found 'the transcendent that could transcend?' Sexual love might hold promise of it and prove all too prey to what disenchanted lovers. What of pregnancy and motherhood and the charm of utterly dependent infancy. She shrank from these as what only fuelled her apprehension. She feared for the kindled awareness of her own womb and its darkly fated progeny. Motherhood held aspects which made her want to crawl back into the womb of her own birthing as something never more undone.

The emotions and fulfilments others found heartening in their gift of sacramental wonder, their procreative promise, found no such purchase on her scepticisms, for all her yearning to be rid of these.

They found somber expression in her poetry. It is at times as if human consciousness intrudes into a negative universe with birth, its inaugural, a nightmarish irrelevance. Mothers feel regret for not aborting in what would seem the proper self-despising of womanhood *per se*. It is in 'Three Women', a disease they carry until death. Was it of recent pregnancy she wrote:

> I am terrified by this dark thing, that sleeps in me;
> All day I feel its soft, feathery turnings, its malignity.[36]

Where a veritable meaning might have brought its solace – from love, from tasks, from ties and chores, and more than solace, meaning, she found only an oppressiveness that sickened on itself, as mirrored in the verses in *The Colossus* and *Ariel*.[37] Resembling Primo Levi's haunting stair-well, the Charles River at Cambridge, Mass. seemed a river of despair.

Of course, around the private maze of yearnings, 'there were other faces

> . . . the faces of nations . . .
> Governments, parliaments, societies,
> The faceless faces of important men.'[38]

Against these, she would be 'an Earth-Mother in the deepest sense',[39] yet never seeming to invest herself in any significant venture in the common good, some counter enterprise against the farce of things. The atomic holocaust over Hiroshima, the execution of the Rosenberg 'spies' – these troubled her, but only ever asking: 'Is there no way out of the mind?'

How should an honest sense of pathos read this story of a life's hostage to a comfortless ego, so endowed with capacity to tell itself but never to achieve itself, except in final exit and periodic debates with suicide? Why was a life-acceptance so far a fugitive thing and, with it, some eager bearing of the kinship and the social role, as both its healing and its wisdom? Do we invoke neurosis, pathology, brain-chemistry as sources of this solipsist shape of life, yet so eloquently protesting and pursuing aspiration?

Might perhaps the answer lie in the absence of any sacramental measure of selfhood that might bring liberating dedication in terms of 'a service that is perfect freedom'. For only in grasping the 'self for' within the 'self in' this mortal scene do we find that which 'justifies' existence in its quality as 'serving beyond itself' as the 'meaning for itself'. There is healing self-transcendence only in what worthily transcends. If it takes more than I am or have to be me, by the same token there is that 'more' which it takes enlisting me. There is a 'wound of absence' which we carry as the pointing witness to 'the healing presence'.

There is a point in Sylvia Plath's crowded *Journal* when, aged 18, feeling both choiceless and powerless, she wrote:

> I turn wearily to the totalitarian dictatorship where I am absolved of all personal responsibility on the altar of the Cause, with a capital 'C'.[40]

How uncannily close to the Muslim suicide bomber that entire dispossession of the personal self in absolution, via the all-warranting 'cause', of all
individual identity and liability! Yet the 'cause' as all-decisive had no right
to usurp the individual conscience, being itself malign, violent and
demonic. Any all-commanding cause has to be itself worthy of that claimed
surrender by being itself fit to transcend.

Sylvia Plath never attained to give herself to the all-fulfilling, all-enlisting
transcendent which would have given her back to herself by the positive
surrender where she let it belong, both forfeit and fulfilled. This theme of
'shares and suicides', etching its conclusion, though – in Plath's range of
human tribulation – quite at random, is the more telling for deriving from
a still youthful sufferer in the early ruin of a romantic marriage.[41] Its span
is so haunted, its documentation so gifted, its language so taught and full.
'I shall doggedly wait and expect the minimum,' she wrote in 1958.[42] How
bewildering are all conjectures as to meanings. What, though, of 'Reality
making me' by credentials that persuade the mind only in being a summons
to the will? The false ones engross us in the ruin of our selves. Better than
such deadly suicide, or the weary sort that never find, in those fulfilled by
worthily dispossession, we learn ourselves authentically our own. Only
what is truly transcendent gives us to ourselves by requiring ourselves
fulfillingly. How and where and whether are the part that rests with us.

V

That 'part resting with us' must seem only a bland or cruel conclusion, if
we are fully honest with the 'shares and suicides' of this chapter. What
'share' fell to them, whether in the heavy vicissitudes of circumstance,
inheritance, temperament and personality, or these in the incidence of
wayfaring consciousness, could have made possible that reach of deliberate
response? The battle with the letter 'I' may be unwinnable on its own
ground, and there is no other. If the theology that told itself in churchyards
by the edifice around which it lay, assigned to a separate corner those who
had 'perished of themselves', did it not thereby confess its own defeat?
Must not authentic faith concede its own enigmas and take upon itself the
more 'the mystery of things'?[43]

How it may be so was the point of this present and the previous chapters as a study of 'Faith'. For those the one perceived as 'martyrs' would
never be in that secluded area of 'the barnacle dead'.[44] Faith-spawned
dying clings on the living for a memory admired. What earlier chapters,
especially 3, 4, 5, and 8, have meant by 'faith at suicide' must reckon well
with 'faith-less suicide' as the likes of Empedocles, Hemingway, Pavese,
Levi, Woolf and Plath have here conveyed its logic and its sorrow – such
is the task of their inclusion.

Doubtless the realism it has for them, and has them fully tell their souls, must set itself to the ministries by mind and deed of a caring society, compassioned by its casualties. But, that assured, was it right to see those exemplars 'faithless', as 'mirrors' only reflecting human tragedy and not 'windows' through which to read a measure of faith? Believers must beware of adopting 'unbelieving ones' too roundly. Yet is there not a measure of faith in the very search for it and perhaps more genuine for the very failure of the research? Empedocles on the lip of his volcano must always be enigma and Hemingway with his ready gun the epitome of his chosen style of life. But the final despairs of our other 'martyrs in themselves', random as the choice has been, told in the ending of their lives the urgent will to have its meaning even in its forfeiture. We must read the courage of their narrative and the eloquence of its telling, the frankness of its probing, the conviction they had of its unreached significance. Such were not 'at ease in Zion', cushioned by its certitudes. Their anguish sets the standard of sincerity by which all faith-tellers must be judged.

It would, therefore, be patronizing to ask: 'Could faith have rescued them?' For the effort of confidence all faith requires was itself precluded by the want in them of what these pre-supposed, whether by reason of whatever diagnosis of their selfhoods could be reached or as belonging with 'the mystery of things'. Love and hope alike must be willing to leave the issue thus.

What, in the toll and task of human selfhood, abides from all the fore-going is finding and loving what must over-master us – we remaining masters of the decision, in the twin requisites of faith as freedom and of freedom in faith fulfilment. 'To serve is to reign'. The captive to faith's meaning is freed and fulfilled in the destiny it shapes. Sane discipleship needs no rash 'undoing of birth'. For birth proves the deliberate occasion to which the entail of the years conveys it as its proper theatre. Such is no drama of over-weening pride in self-homicide, subdued to a divine demand that had no concern with whether a human conscience should co-operate. That conscience was only fit to be compelled. *Servare non regnare.*

If only on moral, not to say doctrinal, grounds, it would seem that there must be something ever reciprocal between the divine and the human order of relation, a mutuality by which either is alone defined and understood. There is a 'towards-us' in that which is 'beyond-us', neither being so without the other.[45] This means a sovereignty that contrives a creation where our human wills are relevant and truly ours, while – being such – they are meant for ennobling partnership with the sovereignty we learn freely to obey and love.

For Christian theology this means its heritage of Semitic faith under-stood to have reached its inner logic as 'God-in-Christ', God with humankind, who reigns and who serves, either in the other. In the more partial context of verbal communication, Paul in a letter had the sequence exactly: 'Not ourselves' – in any self-preening capacity – 'but Christ as Lord' – in our self-dispossession – 'and ourselves' – restored to due role but only as 'your servants for Jesus sake' – taking duly rightful place in God's economy.[46] It remains to ponder finally the liberating authority of this 'bonding with life'.

10

Faith and the Bond
with Life

I

Absent thee from felicity awhile.
And in this hash world draw thy breath in pain
To tell my story.[1]

The tragedy of Hamlet, Prince of Denmark, ends in a grim conspiracy of swords and poison. In its throes three 'principals' lie dead or dying beside the stricken Hamlet. Horatio, innocent and ignorant of how and why, the ever loyal friend, resolves to die by suicide among them. How may he survive when all his world is perishing before him? But this dire finale, with all its dark antecedents, its unraveling sequence, requires that Horatio must live. The 'felicity' from which he must 'absent himself' is the satisfying bliss of quitting a world so desolating in its anguish and futility, the blighted scene these dyings leave him, a world where he can no longer stay.

That noble impulse, Shakespeare knows, can only mean a desertion of the situation. The more loaded the past, the more liable the future. To have lived through the one entrusts Horatio with living for the other, 'things standing thus unknown', and 'a wounded name' to rescue.[2] An onus to live belongs by right to the tragedy of death, in the due entail of one mortality.

The suiciding Muslims we studied in Chapter 8 do not see themselves as 'absent from felicity' except in the gore and horror of their demise. Rather they think to find themselves in the 'felicity' of the Qur'an's paradise and the 'felicity' of what they could inflict on *Dar al-Harb*. The parallel with Shakespeare's drama is remote, yet not so far that logic may not borrow it, if we could bring such forbearing-to-die *inside* the prior will to suicide. Hamlet's dying before Horatio, needed his living beyond it by the very nature of its incidence, since 'a wounded name' belongs only to a victim not to the perpetrator. For a travesty is all that the event bequeaths.

120

Whereas, with Hamlet, tragedy had contrived a death which yearned for an interpreter, these self-homicides in Islam should acknowledge that what had deserved dying for, deserved living for the more. If they thought to make a legacy that others must undertake, they had better stayed themselves to be its servants. Their deaths had been a premature departure from their own Islam, both as a 'cause' in the world and as a discipline of life and person.

These conspirators in self-assassination brought their malign salute to the 21st century when it was hardly a year old. The deed might be resembled to the action of a scythe swinging its havoc among the standing grass of an alien Manhattan rearing so arrogantly tall, as icon of a culture and a commerce meriting a vicious censure. Given the ideology with which it muscled its swing, it darkly symbolized the crisis in contemporary Islam with which Chapter 8 concluded. As a poet had it elsewhere: 'The cutting edge drank thirstily and deep.' Would the men of arms be likewise vowing: 'Tomorrow, by the living God, we'll try the game again'?[3]

In the resolving of that crisis and due reading of its passion, there is so much in Islam to which they might have appealed for their own correction, if ever to be their own Horatio. Such culpable self-homicide on Muslim part entirely contravenes the onus of life-service explicit in the Qur'an's doctrine of our human *khilafah*, our inclusive self-charge told in its doctrine of creation. For our creaturely presence here, being divinely willed, is also divinely summoned to the stature that revelation ordains and its guidance educates.

Birth, as we have argued, inaugurates this status, while the religion of Islam purports to be its ever vigilant mentor towards its proper end, both goal and terminus. In the opening of the womb we were

> Thrust from the mother warmth
> In the nakedness of birth . . .

only – beyond the debts of infancy – to take up the venture of mortality.[4] This onus to live, initially so haplessly physical, becomes steadily personal and spiritual, to engage with all its meanings as the prize of existence in a here and now and thus.

This high Islamic vision of our selfhood rules out all option of a self-contrived demise. Whatever the impulses otherwise may be, they cancel the womb's fidelity and make of life a sort of belated abortion. Thus the suicide for any Muslim cause makes himself a renegade from it and forfeits all relevance to its future. Only those who survive to reckon with the aftermath can save its lost intent. Suiciders deny a living service to the ends for which they rashly throw themselves away. Life demands our patient 'absence from whatever felicity' we think to find outside it or beyond it, since death – in any event – leaves an incompleteness to others. It finishes things unfinished.

Thus the grief in war in memorial terms over the fallen soldier or the drowned sailor in the wastes of war cries to the living to take up what these seconded onwards. What is tragic from the past bequeaths the necessity of devotedness about its future. Mortality must find a sequence, when individual life-tenures are in forfeit, for the purposes they served. When those purposes have been malign, vindictive and ruthless, their appeal to their future only perpetuates their enmity. It grimly incites their repetition. Not only do Muslims suiciders desert a future they have not willed to see or serve, they commend it to a further, longer cycle of malignity and fear.

Doing so, they show no kinship with those yearning disesteems of life explored in Chapter 9. Their 'shares' were only in the grim dividends of fanaticism prompting immolation of their own selfhood and excluding all heeding relevance to the 'still sad music of humanity'. They are of a different order also from those dubious dyings studied in Chapter 5 on the margins of authentic martyrdom, when it was only ecstasy or madness that left integrity in doubt.

By every human as well as every Quranic light, Islam has urgent reason to disavow its renegades of that September mind in 2001. Not only did they abandon a future they might have lived for, they bedevilled it the more. They embittered what they antagonized and proved themselves 'untimely born'.[5]

II

This sane, yet darkly negative conclusion only makes more evident the point of Paul's one ambition about 'abiding in the flesh' and in the terms for doing so. He had a mind to stay undaunted, un-withdrawn, in the purpose to which his spirit called. He would not curtail a vocation further time might yet more earnestly fulfil, despite the distresses through which it had already passed. Remaining time was greeting not farewell. For him as for the aged Simeon, any plea about 'departing' would be 'according to Thy word'.[6] That *Nunc Dimittis* in Luke's narrative of birth argues a steady anathema for suicide, as something the more morally bankrupt in ever being religiously contrived. True personhood can never finally consent to its own undoing.

In our sort of world, 'the bond with life' faith has must argue the constant presence of a redemptive factor countering the moral sequence of selfhood in waste, amid the mortal vesture of decay which is our temporal scene. It must mean a morally caring society, or rather elements inside it which undertake the ever present plea for active compassion. It will be a caring in exact antithesis to the Nietzschean world of power-pursuit in its necessarily disdainful regard for human frailty. Society will need a suffering soul, in the suffering that is its willing identity with what any realism has it comprehend from the common story of who and how we are.

If it is not Christian, it will need to find another metaphysic which both educates and enables it, via the knowledge that 'reality' also – the ultimate mystery that underlies the very nature of the burden – is on its side. For, without such knowledge or conviction, it will be involved in a contradiction, an operation no heroism unbuoyed by such assurance will long sustain. Whether or not we hold that moral values are rooted for their content in the being of God,[7] their practical translation in the fabric of the world needs more than merely human resources.

We can defer that 'whether' awhile and think of human ministries before and around those 'death-beds' where these tragedies 'expire' on ashes of their own kindling. When Philip Larkin brooded in his poem, 'Dockery and Son' on ' . . . age, and then the only end of age . . . ' he forgot that, even in being 'the only end', it could have many shapes whether, 'of honour and dishonour', attending its merely physical finality.[8] Dissolutions of self-hood in place and time by suicides, fanatical or desperate, accuse the societies, the cultures, that breed them. The most private of deeds is the most public of reproaches. That was the case for bringing those of Chapters 8 and 9 together in the larger context here in view. When 'the bond with life' is violently cancelled, their liable societies are the more scrutinized for their preventive or redemptive competence.

The Quranic and intellectual disavowal of suicide in Islam was earlier noted. Random suicides are notably far fewer in Muslim culture than elsewhere, or in the West and Japan, but there is something uncommonly virulent round the Islamic will to self-homicide in the alleged claims of loyal faith. The only final corrective has to be a contemporary disavowal of martial versions of *Jihad* and its reading now as the personal, communal commendation of Muslim faith by word and life alone, in constructive co-pursuit of shared citizenship outside Islam. That the way there is taxed with difficult re-self-imaging by Muslims is obvious enough – and strenuous. In contrast with this virile task, the suicider's way must seem a coward's option. Certainly the one version of Islam must disown the other and only so prove itself a worship of the ever 'compassionate Lord!'[9]

How such worship might educate and enable its proving so might be captured by bringing together two narratives broadly linked with the neighbourhood of time, and partially of place, where the ferocious Isma'ili sect founded by Hasan al-Sabbah, had its long tradition. In their own idiom they bore strange resemblance to the current Al-Qa'idah grouping. They swore binding allegiance to their leader, exercised a rigorous control over their discipline and pursued their politico-religious ends by calculated assassination of enemies, singled out individually for maximum advantage to the cause. In their day and age, only stealth and steel, not suicide, were necessary to their purpose.[10] Hence they were termed *Hashishiyyin*, or

'Assassins', in reference to their alleged habit of taking cannabis (*hashish*) to induce ecstasy or indoctrination, to fulfill their goal of 'judgement' on false rulers alleged to be 'killing' the true Imam by vile 'usurpation'. The parallels are uncanny between their régime (*c.* 1090–1256) with this 21st century.

The celebrated Sufi poet Jalal al-Din Rumi, born in Balkh (Afghanistan) in *c.* 1207, was at risk from them before their demise at the hands of advancing Mongols, from whose depredations he and his family were fleeing westward. He was a youth of twenty when his fugitive family finally arrived in Konya (Turkey) where they settled. He died there in 1273. The Assassins specialized in hill-fortresses from which they made their forays of death. They held many in Syria. Whatever the route of Al-Rumi's migration, he could hardly fail to learn of their repute. His inspirations were wholly elsewhere but it signifies, for our purpose, to coincide these two tales of demise or of migration at the hands of an advancing threat from beyond Islam.[11]

Nothing could more totally throw into contrast the violence of the Assassins as 'Islam' than the Sufi devotion of Jalal al-Din with his fervour in discipleship to the ardent love of God. To be capable of the poetry of religion in such terms as his is the surest answer to the other, and the most insistent evocation of the better wisdom of Islam. His was religion in its deepest cognizance of the human predicament, always on condition of an active investment in the tuition and the redemption of society. Though there are forms of Sufi piety tempted to withdraw into a private indulgence of the ecstatic, Jalal al-Din saw his poetic muse and the meaning it distilled as the active response his living made to the ills of human society. Its mind and music have for long centuries since brought an Islamic ministry across his own frontiers of place and time.

This random but inclusive contrast between the 'Islam' of the poet-sage of Konya and the 'Islam' of the Assassins of Qazvin educates us in the 'bond with life' by which faith holds on to living and prizes the changing occasions of mortality. From the suiciding fanatic it learns the vocation to be no less totally committed to vital self-expenditure, but in its own different cognizance of what requires it to be sacrificial.

For that requirement takes our once-for-all selfhood into an investment, not with death, but with an 'absence from felicity' taught by its reading of the world. It is a reading which perceives 'the shadow of death' in its social incidence hovering over so many. In so far as society is inherently competitive and, therefore, 'nasty, brutish and short', there must be those who reverse the competition into the counter-factor of compassion. If society is a theatre of the vulnerable and the wounded, it is a stage fit for the wound-menders and the healers. These, to be such, will not read their life-span as a private luxury or their mortality their own to gratify or violate, but rather 'send to know for whom the bell tolls' and, having learned, will act.[12] They will register the significance of the drug-users, the burden of the exploited and the poor, the wretched wastefulness of war and the chronic ills of man-made bigotry. In so doing, they will need sustaining warrant and sure imagery.

It is the supreme business of religion to identity that warrant and portray that imagery. Only so may it direct its discipleships and enable their vision. A religious faith has, therefore, to inter-relate the divine and the human in such terms that the one moves in and with the other, somehow ordaining, on the one hand, and on the other fulfilling, the same mind. Then what transcends in sovereignty translates in what obeys. What is willed 'in heaven' is 'done on earth', but only as 'the will in heaven' freely recruits and informs the earth-dwellers. There is, at once, law and love, but only law as loved within and only love as minded from beyond to be reciprocal. Shylock's old question – outside his own 'merchant' context – 'Upon what compulsion must I?'[13] rings through all ethics. There has to be motive to constrain as well as reason to obey, the objective 'ought' and mutually the subjective 'Yea, I will.'

Law is often signaled as the central concern of Islam and love the vital accent of Christianity. Such generalizations are dangerous. Whatever may be the case of the two belief-systems, the two elements have to be under-stood as counter-parting in their incidence. There is, indeed, a difference in the ethos of two faiths, but there need be none in the 'law of love' in the relation between God and humankind. *Regnare* and *servare* are not antitheses. 'Whose service is perfect freedom'. We humans 'reign' in that we serve, and by our 'service' God reigns too – reigns the more.

But is that *regnare, servare* formula somehow reversible, so that God also 'serves' in duly reigning? The question is boldly Christian and many would at once rule it out of court. Yet is it not implicit in every notion of creation as recruiting into creaturehood? Human *khilafah/'* dominion' can hardly be 'for God's sake' and not 'in God's interest', and the 'interest' in our hands 'served' in our response.

That dimension deepens if we will follow the Biblical perception of deeper involvements still, with at least 'the things of God' expended and expendable for 'things of ours' – needs, hopes, directives and – may we add – beliefs? Divine 'otherness' does not preclude 'togetherness' in human history. Were it thought to do so, 'otherness' itself would be meaningless. All is somehow relational and this must be true both for faiths religious and for ethics social. Or, in more direct language, can we ever find to say: 'We love because He first loved us'?[14]

Grateful souls, kindling to awareness of the natural order, could cry: 'Yes'. But, that order being also sometimes ambiguous, is there any fuller, richer order of divine *servare* we can recognize and comprehend? If so, we will have, supremely, the warrant and the imagery we were looking for. If we could bring together this divine *servare* with ours as its ground and spur, we would reach a theology by which we could truly find our 'bond with life'. There is a Biblical analogy which eloquently does so in its 'the Lord is my shepherd' and setting His emulation as the image of its caring for the world.[15] That 'pastoral' version of its world has to immerse it in harsh reality but also to curb the instincts of religious authority and draw them to a gentler quality than belongs with fatwas, bulls, edicts and anathema decrees. For while there is no lack of authority in the shepherd role, it consists in the worth of its relation to its charges. Inasmuch as tempering the zeal of dogmatism in contemporary religion is a vital factor in the life of Islam, the shepherding imagery and the prize of self-restraint are the more evidently urgent.

Moreover, a caring quality, infusing 'official' authority, can interact with the faithful, and hold for all and sundry in community, whatever the formal relation between 'clerical' and 'lay'.[16] The 'bond with life' then becomes – by the same token – 'a bond with society' where its ministries must avail as faith reads and understands what availing demands, whether of imagination in compassion or resourcefulness in will. Or, as Charles Wesley had his people sing:

> Ready for all Thy perfect will.
> My acts of faith and love repeat,
> Till death Thine endless mercies seal
> And make the sacrifice complete.[17]

For him 'the bond with life' is lifelong, since 'leave of absence' is not in his hands.

If such is duly the set of the religious mind, it differs sharply from the frequent present demand for 'human rights' while addressing them more surely. While it is an easy truism to say that 'rights' are always required to be mutual to 'duties', the 'ministry' word we are exploring comprises both more truly. While the word originates in Christian tradition of 'the Word and sacraments', it has passed into the parlance of politics, with 'ministries of foreign affairs, of trade' and the like. The word takes 'obligation' into 'fulfilment', 'task' into 'satisfaction', and 'capacity' into 'humility'.[18] It hallows what otherwise might be perfunctory and dignifies the common-place. Thus it has the potential to make of self-expenditure the fabric of self-expression, so that selfhood is most deeply self-possessed in being self-spent. It is thus the clue to self-realization by dint of its surest definition and as such the surest antidote to private futility and public tragedy. 'Ministry' in all its range is the ultimate religious word, the measure of the length of life.

To be realist and honest, it has to find and be itself in behaving and belonging and, in some sense therefore, in believing. It recruits both person and citizen and so worshipper. If it is faith in action, it can hardly be action without faith. The person plainly is the ground of all else, in the immediate 'ministries' of mutual order in childhood, family, home community and means of livelihood and, in so far as these can reach to them, the wider realms of common good. Since 'no man is "insular" but party to the continent', continents must be the measure of where 'common good' must reach.

It could never adequately do so without the role of the citizen, schooling (or voting or inciting) the state into 'ministry perceptions' of its role both 'insular and continental'. For there are many privations, injustices, afflictions and enmities that can only be answered by the concert of politics and the will of governments. The 'undoing' of all these wrongs and evils demands the vigilance, the conscience and the will of the political order and that on two counts. The one count is the guilt of the economic order in their incidence and their perpetuation, the active 'penance' required of it as part of its correction. The other is the positive will to the moral discipline of the market and the conscience of the structures. Both have to evoke the pressure of the citizen as, for ill or good, participating in them all. Such 'ministry' is the only sanity. We have neither without conviction.

III

What, we argued, recruits alike both self and society calls for the worshipper. Belonging with the world means believing its significance. But how do we 'signify what signifies', minister to what belongs, identify the summons we must answer? It was no accident that when Friedrich Nietzsche intended the power cult of self-realization deploring the enfeebling evil of Christian compassion, he also abolished the futility of theism. Sanctuaries of worship had no place in his universe of the uninhibited ego, whereas the old psalmist had sung: 'I looked for You in the sanctuary . . .' (63.3) by which he meant the Temple, but the Temple only as the sign and seal of the whole earth as 'hallowed and for hallowing' in being the human realm, with Jewry as the index to its destiny.

That Nietzschean repudiation of a Christian ethics of inter-human compassion was also – and by the same token – a dismissal of a Christian theology of the divine/human nexus realized in Christ. Its very negativity was eloquent of how the two belong together. The Christian thesis is that, if we would have a caring world, we must have a caring quality in God, a quality deep enough to suffice our human case and satisfy divine sovereignty within it.

However other faiths or belief-systems perceive the worship that teaches and enables their compassion, this concerning 'God in Christ' is the Christian one. Christology – as the term has it – means this relatedness between the divine *en soi* and the divine *pour nous* in their inter-action, the musician and the music, the dramatist and the drama – or in New

Testament language – 'the Father in the Son'. The 'caring' about us which we identify in Jesus as the Christ makes his birth, ministry and passion God's own biography whereby 'who has the Son has the Father also'. What is for ever pastoral in God concerning humans is the mandate and the energy for a caring society, as the life-task of such a faith. Both are caught in that analogy of 'the good shepherd'. The psalmist who first glimpsed what the Christ would make good and actual in history (Psalm 23) was content to know it so 'all the days of his life' as one who would 'always be in the house of the Lord'.[19] and will behave accordingly.

It is almost as if, in the idiom of the psalm, the 'sheep' learns from the shepherd's role, to be ready for the practice of what he has experienced. But such readiness hinges entirely on the divine originality of 'shepherd-hood' which his world has decisively received. What can ever be humanly compassionate turns on what has been divinely so. By contrast, Edgar Allan Poe's biographer wrote that 'Poe remained convinced that the world lacked a protective deity'.[20] A figure of life and literature starkly exemplifying the bitter 'shares' studied in Chapter 9, the early reason why was the churlish atheism of his own foster-father from whom he had the 'Allan' name. The glad nexus of Psalm 23 between loved experience and loving practice was there in tragic reverse, but only to prove that the nexus is real. We learn as Browning knew, that – in what has to do with compassion – the human may be clue to the divine, but only in that the divine for ever was and is the impulse in the human sort.[21]

But where was the divine convincingly so? The natural order which, in many moods and symbols, might qualify to that end remains in part contradictory. Maybe the will to accept them nevertheless needs the persuasion of the great alternative credential – that of 'the Christ in God' via the living, dying history of 'the God in Christ', 'the Word made flesh' and 'flesh in the obedience of the Cross'.

But what if, identifying that history so, it were only an assertion of the faith that yearned for the satisfaction it told? Such yearning might be the very strategy by which the meaning chose to make its way – its necessary way into a welcoming heart. For it is no part of the content of such faith that its credentials should be self-imposing, or that they be exempt from the risks that must belong with whatever betakes itself to history and to language. For these would be intrinsic in any relevance to the human situation, only to be evaded or escaped by recourse to an eternal silence – a silence quite incompatible with any significance in our creation.

Thus, as the Fourth Gospel realized, confidence in the Incarnation belongs with conviction concerning creation as the divine 'intending' of the world. 'Let there be . . . ' and 'Let there be the Christ' belong together. That the New Testament presentation of this Christ in Jesus has always been eminently scrutinized by an incredulous dubiety has been inseparable from its content as an invitation to faith – to a faith anticipating such a situation as the quality of the welcome it awaited. The cynic may say that 'only faith makes it so', but what if 'faith doing so' was precisely how truth's own nature would have it be? Truth's credentials could have such sympathy with the pre-requisite of their reception, such partnership with the honesty of the heart. If, then, 'the good shepherd giveth His life', the lives of human 'shepherds' may be in His life-long employ.

II

These Unbelieving Believers

I

Might 'fideocide' be a permitted neologism seeing that the 'faith' in 'faith at suicide' will likely mean what motivates action rather than what doctrine tells.[1] The ambiguity has always been present in the English word. In our context here we mean the active that acts because of the belief that prompts it. The first has so far been our concern, with its origins in zeal or hate, its logics of anger and its defiance of traditional veto. But the second is made the victim of itself in the interpreting image of the first. We have to say that suiciding Muslims are the narrative of a suiciding Islam. There is no doubt that they are traitors to great counter-positives of their own Qur'an. In this shape of their faith, the faith itself is in dire forfeit. In their dying this way there is a measure of dying around the faith to which their deed brings deathly tribute.

There is thus a desperate 'unbelieving' at the core of a most violent assertion of belief. Any re-kindling of hope has to know and tell it so. There is not only the perverting of a public image: there is also misprision of its deepest private conviction.

It is often alleged in daily life that suicide is a highly selfish exit strategy, even callous of the grievous burdening of others who survive – assuming that its own vehemence allows of these dissuasives. Somehow the faith-suicidings of Islam turn all to splendid pride. The 'others' can dwell in the glow of vicarious martyrdoms and wear the accolades of high esteem among their peers, the benison of other worthy proxies.[2] Suicide thus in high social and religious esteem only the more puzzles and dismays a watching world. Death as the most intimately private experience becomes a perplexing public symbolism of unreason and the faith-image is the more bewildering.

Questioning spectators – not to say the sufferers at its hand – are the more dissuaded from any wisdom from Islam. Yet to exemplify 'religion according to Allah's mind and will' has long been axiomatic in Muslim self-regard. Truly 'religion with God is Islam/*islam*' as noted earlier. 'Imageing', then, both as the faith presents and/or as the world perceives it, is a primary Islamic vocation with which it has no mandate to be careless. Thus the outrage which suiciders do to it is no ally of its mission. A faith like Islam which has the world in its sights can hardly ignore a world's misgivings. In truth they are many. No faith deserves to persuade the world by first reaping its scorn. If in 'image' terms alone, 'fideocides' is an honest name for 'suicides' of zealot, lethal, cunning shape in contemporary Islam, faith is thus self-disowned.

But, it may be countered, is not that verdict the outsider's bias, as one who has not reckoned with the crucial Muslim duty of *Jihad*, a 'contention for the faith' that had no option to reflect on how it might be 'seen', esteemed or disesteemed, by a humanity it was only to bring within its empire of coupled faith and power? The 'image' would be rightly understood when its authority had been duly established. The current age, as that writ and rubric read it, might well necessitate and justify the tactic of ruthless surprise, given the physically inferiorized means which the suicides could alone deploy. Much in a Medinan Islam as housed in the one Qur'an could be so read. Islam, moreover, and the conduct of its people, should not be subject to constraints from outside its own sufficiency as both an ethic and a faith-system. The world's distaste for its 'image' could be the very proof of its validity and of that world's moral vagrancy.[3]

Such irreconcilables can only glare and fume at each other, unless, as looked for here, we try to lift them out of mere insistent contradiction and set them in a context where positives, not controversies, can genuinely converse. This must take us out of 'image' – arrogant either way in pride or horror – and take us to the potential of either to comprehend the other.[4] It requires we take seriously what old lawyers called the 'gravamen' either has against the other. This can only happen if we share the human ground of any seriousness at all.

II

The Qur'an has never lent any credence to futility or the absurd. It has its intelligent readers understand that the world was not created and does not exist as a divine folly or a human plaything (Surahs 21.16 and 44.38). Selves are not 'in vain'. They have a re-assuring warrant to be (always an anxious burden for the would-be suicide) which is evident in the mandating intelligibility of 'the heavens and the earth' to human mind and will and soul. The physical order has a dependable – if rarely prone to the irregular – quality which ever necessitates the answering cognizance of our human wits.[5] It then affords the wherewithal to attain the livelihoods that achieve society and culture in a continuity of generations, these too being the supreme occasion, in their procreation, of our competence.

There is nothing 'eastern' or 'western', Muslim or non-Muslim, about this common situation. It makes entrepreneurs of us all in a setting that spells both necessity and freedom. John Milton's Raphael explained it well to his first human pupil.

> Our voluntary service he requires,
> Not our necessitated, such with him
> Finds no acceptance, nor can find, for how
> Can hearts not free, be tri'd whether they serve
> Willing or not . . . freely we serve
> Because we freely love . . . [6]

The poet here has made 'religious' what is also the fact of science. We yield to factuality as mindfully we find it and doing so yields to us a liberty whereby 'we live and move and have our being'. Such is the common territory of the *mise-en-scène* which all religions purport to monitor and explore. Islam is no exception. On the contrary, its very name/term, in being both, captures it with a telling simplicity. There *is* that which 'lets us be' and its being what it is is our being's ground and habitation. Such is the meaning of the doctrine of creation and of the creaturely condition as the hallmark of all humankind. It is worthy to make Islam and non-Islam a pointless distinction, being so plain a theme of unison, while it banishes those intimations of the futile and the absurd which have of late afflicted western minds.[7]

Accepting to be on such re-assuring grounds as the physical sciences furnish to our enterprise of living – the psychic ones being less competent – we move with liberty via necessity to create our creation in turn. Islam's Qur'an is no stranger and surely no resister to this role. For it tells its natural world as a realm of *ayat*, of 'signs', phenomena as clues that make for sciences, via detection, observation and enlistment into usage, but cry also for recognition as the material of gratitude. Things that mean, so as to be harnessed by engineers must also be read by priests and poets as tokens to the spirit. The emphasis on praise and gratitude (*shukr*) in the Qur'an is the vital form of its shaming of the other thing, *kufr*, the absence of all thanks which is the gist of 'atheism'. The God we ignore is thus the more 'denied' than the God we doubt.

Here is another unison which we might all find on Quranic ground, making the sciences no stranger to the arts, knowledge in the one no absentee from mystery in the other and divine worship the due theme of both. It could serve to counter the vulgarity and the obtuse frivolity that Muslims often register in western life-styles and lavish self-indulgence – ills which they know and fear are insidiously subversive of their own societies. The issue is no realm for charge and counter-charge but only for a surer cognizance of the truth of things. The world needs to be loved indeed, but only with a certain kind of love which is first reverent, even reticent, that it may be duly possessive in a right self-possession.

Here, too, we come upon that vexed question of our quarrels, namely the secular. There are some moods of Islam we all need to dispute which want to argue that the secular does not exist, seeing that all things are under 'Allah' as an 'omnipotence' that requires all things to be and stay 'subdued' to inscrutable will. But this is to disown and exclude the human *khilafah*/'dominion' we have just explored in 'signs' and 'gratitude'. These by their very nature lie inside our option. All things are indeed 'under Allah', but by divine will itself all 'sub-vested' in human trust and care, whence must necessarily arise the 'secular' diversion from the 'sacred' shape of that divine entrustment of them to our hands. Surah 2.30 and sundry other passages are emphatic about the 'delegacy', this vice-ruler-ship, as the human privilege 'to be and never not to be'.[8]

Thus the whole point of the secular turns on the open question of the human will. It is manifest in history how critical that situation has been. The tragedies of history are inexplicable without its desolating factor, just as its benedictions have belonged with human sanity and love. Our faiths thus need a concept of divine omnipotence which accommodates this human crisis while never forsaking compassionate sovereignty for it. Would compassion – as distinct from sheer power – have any place at all, if there were no human autonomy, the autonomy whereby the 'secular' abides as both our option and our testing. The sacred only happens by our submission. For it is patently no crisis-free necessity. It has to be willed by due responding to the 'signs' and the awe they must evoke. Were 'hallowing' innate no *fitnah* would be present.[9]

III

It is just this crisis quality of what religion has at stake which carries the course of thought to a feature of Islam that most disturbs the western mind and underlies in some sense the current vehemence of its suicides, who see no fideocide in their homicides but only a necessary obedience in faithful duty.

That feature ensues, by Muslim lights, from all we have reviewed of this human *imperium* under Allah, this privilege 'to be and never not to be'. This dignity, being so precious, so well endowed with means in 'signs', so fraught with history as destiny, is also so critically precarious, so prone to what earlier we called 'vagrancy', deliberate distortion of itself. Unhappy evidences of such turpitudes in the non-Muslim worlds are readily identi-fied to certify the aberrant human and so necessitate a Muslim rigorism.

All is thus pointedly at risk in our creaturehood and, therein also, in the whole created order. It follows that humankind needs authoritative religion, ready to be also authoritarian. The two descriptives spell indubitable Scripture and an empowered faith. A sacrosanct Qur'an and the Islamic State must – and should – equip Islam to discipline humanity on 'the straight path . . . not of those who go astray', as the *Fatihah* (Surah 1) tells it. The dependent question around these two urgent necessities is: Can Islam ever be otherwise? Before we answer with a hopeful Yes! and the reasons present, it will be well to heed the contrary case in some summary of this the most urgent quarrel with Islam from such current assessors.

We may well draw it from a recent assailant of its dark 'image', who totally neglects its deep positives.[10] Islam, he argues, is prone to 'terrorism' because it engages superlatively in the liability of all religions to absolutize themselves. Beliefs are wanton self-delusion, darkly suggestive of mental disease. They assume the form of mortal threat to what should ask of them some modesty, self-doubt and openness of mind. They foster what must be dubbed 'warranted insanities' ousting the rationality which alone can sanitize the world.[11] There is Harris argues, a rooted 'fundamentalism', irrespective of any other sort, in the Islamic view of the Qur'an as 'the literal, inerrant words of the one true God'.[12] This, he avers, rules all other mind-sets out of court. Quranic truth is a magisterial and forbidding monopoly to which we should accord no heed.

Furthermore, for our dismay and fear, this impregnable bastion of credal credulity contrives to be also authoritarian in the political exclusivity, as ideally had, of the organs of governance and the means of power. Its *Din* must have its *Dawlah*. Only Muslim power is proper to Muslim faith. The entire world is the proper range of its *Dar*, *Dar al-Islam*. The authority of the faith duly intends and wields the authority of rule, just as the authority of rule sanctions and sustains the practice of the faith. How then, in the face of this phalanx of ends-with-means, can we think realistically that Islam could ever be otherwise, ever Islamically re-new its Islamic self?[13] Can any historical religion ever undo itself?

All turns on what that 'self' definitively was and is. It will also ask: Who is to say? In rescue from this somber gravamen it will be well to let the political wait until the doctrinal is explored, while delaying pre-emptive strikes required lest 'they' first attain some nuclear capacity.[14]

What justifiying apologia can Muslims offer their critics about that 'infallible' Qur'an of theirs via a celestial 'dictation' to a wholly passive messenger? They can elucidate how it does violence to the Qur'an itself, its perception of Muhammad's role and its incessant plea for intelligent reading.[15] It has anyway in itself a 'sign' quality, requiring – like those of nature too – a perceptive cognizance. Its verses are called by the same *ayat* word. It is not only Sufis and mystics who have rightly seen what must be 'inseen' as more than bare language. The idea of two sides of a tapestry may be elusively suspect, but Surah 3.7 warns against failing to recognize things categorical from things figurative.[16] Rigorists can create no exclusion zones of their own.

The theme of celestial *tanzil*, a word-mediation from heaven to earth, from God to Hijazi time, is – we must concede – a test of faith. Christian 'truth through personality' via 'the Word made flesh' differs profoundly but still appeals to cognizing faith. The eternal/temporal will always be a mysterious transaction but to exclude it altogether is to impoverish the meaning of time itself. Words and language, in any event, are the counters of existence and the Qur'an is clearly pivoted on the role of 'the pen', in human knowledge everywhere. Moreover, there is nothing more at co-operate risk with its 'other' than the author, the speaker, the word-spellers. All are utterly subject, however sacred, to the heeding, the risk, their intended party brings to them.[17]

The Qur'an itself is alive to this situation. It makes re-iterated appeal for *tadabbur*, reflection that de-words into cognizance what is en-worded in text. The Qur'an is in no parley with the vacant mind. It has its hundred times repeated *la'alla*, its incessant 'perhaps', waiting on attendant readership. Its margins may have been the safe havens of the myopic: they were never meant for retreat from liability of mind. The summons was to the same partnership of text and mind that had to be brought to external nature, and with the same result of unison. In its first local time and place the Qur'an's stress on its being 'Arabic' ('We have sent it down an Arabic Qur'an so that you may give your minds' 12.2 *et al.*) was no literalism for literal sake but a concern to be intelligible – a purpose which left no veto on translation but implied the duty for it anywhere else.

Thus there may be a textual 'fundamentalism' in theory: there is no call for it in fact and readership. Nor could its role for Muhammad as its recipient admit of 'cyphering' his mind and spirit, his context and his capacity, least of all in view of its 'sending on his heart' (2.97, 46.194) – seat of all human affections. This would not, need not, make him 'author' of the Qur'an, a role Islam has always ruled out. It must make him 'party' to it, if ever recipience were to be possible. Readers as in trust with the text is all one with that inclusive *khilafah*, or 'soul-possession' which the Qur'an's doctrine of creation made central to the human condition.

This still leaves the apologia, much lightened, with the outstanding issue of finally, inerrant authority for the believer. Have not all religions, via the Scriptures, known the compelling quest for 'certitude'. The status they want them to have is the status they give to them. Once this is realized, it becomes clear that they are still, nevertheless, given into a readership. In no case can they, the Scriptures, rise up and say to erring mortals: 'You read us wrong'. They should not be victims, but they may be vulnerable, seeing that they can only 'mean' as readers 'read'. This hazard of their very being is what requires the protection of their status. There is much more to historic Islam than the Qur'an contains or legislates. The role of its reverent trustees has to be there in the principle of 'non-repugnancy' (rather than literal conformity) to the text. This has proved important in heeding it beyond its silences. The length to which that principle has been applied in modern times is witness to a flexibility and an inter-play of sacred text and reading mind as the corollary of the Qur'an's finality – a finality only obtaining that way.

This may seem a somewhat defensive apologetic but such was what we set ourselves in the will to comprehend. Faiths are more likely to become self-aware if they are handled with respect, their instincts appreciated rather than despised. This means no cheap exoneration from duties of scholarship as well as attitude. It does mean these do not ride rough-shod over complexities and fears or miss the flux and chance in what they diagnose and the bias of dialogue itself.

That bias, of course, is eminently reversible so that the critic of Islam's perceived 'incorrigibility' must know how to reckon with Muslim register of 'abomination' there, elsewhere, beyond Islam and its truth-ensuring *Dar.* The western cult of 'the absurd', the loss of self, the doubt about significance, the frivolities of self-indulgence that display these, we noted earlier. The grim supposal that 'anything goes' seems heinous and 'atheist' to a people inured to hold that 'God is great', and instructed to 'enjoin the good and forbid the evil'. Probity, as well as religion, seem quite forfeit when faith is assumed to be 'a private matter' and is socially assigned to that elusive realm, whereas it should be the public championing of 'public truth'. What of societies in well-being, if beliefs are wholly in the private realm and at the personal option?

Since the Asian tidal-wave catastrophe, there have been passionate sermons in mosques in Cairo, in Riyadh, in Damascus and Qatar, explaining its incidence as Allah's vengeance on the iniquities of western tourism, with its flaunted luxury and 'riotous living'. Did the tsunami not strike precisely on these beaches, the dens of these sinful folk? It was a grim but simple verdict – a sovereignty in requital and the evil that deserved it making one equation. Yet, via sun and moon, that same sovereignty contrived the sandy beaches, washed by the gentle tides that drew the fated bathers. And what of the unequal justice of the vengeance without reference to age or guilt?

The Qur'an itself has a verdict against such wild readings of the divine mind when it comments on how 'idolaters', those 'worshippers of the pseudo', did not 'measure God a true measure' (Surahs 6.91, 22.74 and 39.67). Their criteria of God were all awry, distorted by their own prejudice and errant logic. A right theology cannot be a law unto itself.

It is this mindfulness of mystery at the heart of a right theology that comes into effect in Muslim regard for the 'Names' of Allah, *Al Asma' al-husna* which the Qur'an knows He 'possesses' and bids us use, while long tradition ties us to cautious if not crippling reservations. For the very availability, the feasible currency, of these 'Names' ties them, via language, into human realms, not merely of verbal usage, but of description and narrative. Thus to think of God as somehow participating in human-ness offends against the sacred principle of His incomparability, His transcending 'otherness', whereby 'none is like unto Him'.

Yet, if language denoting Him is not permissible to us concerning Him, how then do we address our worship? Adoration in lack of a theology is aborted in the mind and withered in the soul. 'Names' there must be, at least to 'mean' *for* worshippers, if not to mean *about* the Worshipped. Christian faith satisfies this situation and removes its paradox by not needing to posit any divine reluctance for human descriptives, as already taking them into 'the Word made flesh'. Needing more than the reluctance, the prohibition, Islam leaves the paradox unresolved in doctrine, while waived in worship. Muslims use the *Asma'* – as their formula runs – 'without asking how' and 'without similarity' to their human meaning.

This need not be theological sleight of hand. It preserves a crucial point, with which alert Christians must agree, namely that devout 'use' of the divine Names 'defines' while it always forbears to do so. There must always be that which goes beyond the words, that which the terms cannot ever exhaust. This will be a reservation characterizing Christian and Muslim theologies alike and making them kin. The crucial Christian view must be that what certainly 'goes beyond' all 'wording' does not contradict what belongs in it. Transcend it will but not disown its 'known-ness'. For otherwise all vocabulary in theology is 'language games' and contrived delusion, as rank unbelief has often alleged. Whether Islam would have the same concern about a 'pragmatic' but still 'agnostic' theology is for today's Muslims to say and clarify. Meanwhile, reservations about theological language are, and are not, well taken. And they could be a window of relation to the world that scouts it altogether.

Reservations about the divine Names have brought no restraint to the zealot Muslims' assurance of his access to the divine will. It remains provocative or incomprehensible to the western mind how some Muslims could see suicide bombing as a legitimate shape of Islamic defence and affirmation, with its grievous tally of human horror and its forfeiture of Muslim limb and life. For the critic earlier cited, this feature becomes the referent-symbol, however unjustly, of entire Islam, for he adds:

> Religious moderates are, in large part, responsible for the religious conflicts in our world, because their beliefs provide the context in which scriptural literalism and religious violence can never be adequately opposed.[18]

This verdict, more from exasperation than calm discernment, takes us to the second aspect of Islam's self-image. The doctrinal merges into the political, while neither ever forgets the other. We can leave the doctrinal, assured that whatever the vagaries, the pride or prejudice of its institutional history, Islam thanks to the Qur'an has the defining elements of human meaning under God – a cosmos of created purpose, a viable privilege of human fulfilment in sub-sovereign vocation and faith in a divine solicitude, via 'guidance' and discipline, for its true realization, with all as our dignity in mortal span, our bond in trust with life.[19]

IV

That conclusion is the measure of what, in contemporary part by Muslims, must be truly called fideocide. For its violent terms contravene and sully all the sure positives with which a right Islam consorts. Yet *in extremis* it may be seen as only the rampant, angry form of the traditional belief that Islam has the right and duty to be coercive, if the form and time are rightly judged. The contemporary suiciders have no doubt of this, while many other Muslims altogether disavow them. There are those again who cannot tell or will not say, the tests of 'rightness' being themselves at issue.

Coercion and religion – how should they relate? Faith and the means of power – how negotiate relationship? Chapter 8 explored the hard measures of Islam's immersion in the answer. Late in the Medinan time of the story, Surah 2.256 laid down the principle of there being 'no compulsion in religion', but the Arabic, *la ikraha*, had ambiguity within itself.[20] 'There ought not to be coercion' (absolutely) or: 'there is not . . . ' (a statement of fact as expression of intent?). Either way, the shape of what *ikraha* denoted stayed an open question.

We studied how open it lay in the sequence from pre- to post-Hijrah; whether Hijrah was ever divinely decreed; in the strange evolution of that *fitnah* term from undergoing persecution to countering sedition and, through all these, the passage of Muhammad's own career from verbal tenacity to sharp belligerence. As argued in Chapter 8, there was no doubt of the ensuing Islamic verdict on the power/faith alliance. Religion had to accommodate coercion. Religion would carefully monitor its incidence. Religion had no liberty to renounce it. There is no need to take the case-making further. Islam's years, with its Calendar, are 'years of the Hijrah'.

It is plain that asking whether its violent suicides are 'fideocides' is the faith/coercion question in its sharpest and most tragic form. On one score they could be their faith's superb exemplars, its supremely loyal heroes. On another they must be known its traitors, undoing their Islam's Meccan birth and crossing all the limits of its Medinan shape. They compel us to ask what place the thirteen years of Mecca have in the ten of Medina, whether that Hijrah – if once valid then – remains so now, whether the charge of 'fideocide' is cowardly calumny against the proving of Islamic genius, the utmost *bona fides* of devotion.

Observers may see only criminal lunacy perversely sanctioned by perverse belief-authority, people 'in whose heart there is a sickness' – to borrow from another context the Qur'an's own diagnosis of its populace.[21] Pride and horror, warrant and anathema, are extreme in either case. Perhaps, finally – and with the themes of Chapter 8 in train – 'these unbelieving believers' may be pondered, with the contemporary West as well, by way of one simple question. Can religion genuinely be 'neutral'?

Clearly not, in respect of what it holds. For commitment is of its essence. It does not advertise options, it summons to discipleship. It wants no abstract condescension. It seeks and recruits conviction – the conviction by which it lives and breathes and goes, having its world for its reach. Hence, for traditional Islam, the urge and thrust to ensure that the power in politics is in its hands and at its call. For to suppose that statehood and governance could be left to their untaught, untamed devices, would be utter dereliction of religious duty and spiritual task.

Yet a certain ideal of 'faith-neutrality' spreads and seeks to suit across the world. Religious conviction retreats into the private sphere as a personal choice, a choice all should be free to make or from which to desist. Belief ought not to suppose itself warranted as public truth. It cannot be somehow as mathematics is, since its evidences are always *sub judice* and for ever disagreed, the criteria themselves being elusive or discordant. Nor can it be as skills of technology become. On the contrary, these, with their sciences, do not discriminate in their application, between this or that faith, this and that 'believer'. Hospitals, airlines, computers, and all the media will 'do their thing' irrespective of the faiths of patients, passengers, users and consumers. 'The rain', too 'falls alike on the just and on the unjust', even if we still hold to our 'restrictive greetings', believing like with believing like.[22] The universe, it would seem, has no favourite faith, the elements no 'chosen people'.

This wide 'neutrality' goes far these days to 'neutralize' among many people the urgent claims of religious faith. Indeed, the very thrust of fanaticism or bigotry in some faith quarters arises from the fear, the alarm, which this situation kindles. Faith has to will to relativize its identity into a coexistence, and should learn, it seems, to breathe a tolerance and practice a courtesy on every side. But can it leave the ideology and the control of the body-politic to this amorphous, miscellaneous faith-variegated citizenry, each bringing whatever qualities of person, mind and soul, their ethic and their heritage can attain? All is thus a far cry from Muhammad's Medina, from Ottoman Caliphate or Moghul rule, from Charlemagne and 'holy Rome', from Richard Hooker and *Ecclesiastical Polity*, from the ideals of Edmund Burke or William Gladstone, with his confidence that there was 'no atheism in this House of Commons'.

This seemingly irreversible aspect of modernity is 'a hard place' for traditional Islam, even if – in terms of vulnerability – it takes the mind back to Mecca. But then, there was a solution. There could be the Hijrah, the power option freely sensed, freely taken. There is no such Hijrah now, unless it be that of a diaspora which takes it where a renewed Medina is *ipso facto* forfeit.[23]

Acceptance to be 'neutral' is highest as a hurdle of destiny for Islam, higher than any other belief-system. The reasons have been plain throughout, since no other large religion has the 'founding' equivalent to Muhammad. Whether the stakes can be faced is the nature of its contemporary crisis, how the burden of its collective mind.

We keep in mind the pragmatic things noted earlier, about wide Muslim dispersion, the inter-penetration of cultures and the pressures of sheer diversity, mental and social. These have their place in the prospect of the answer the crisis seeks. But the ultimate reality is that this would-have-you-neutral world itself has urgent place for your non-neutrality. The analysis was one-sided. The truth is that this daunting, even uncongenial, situation leaves room for – and has finer claim on – your faith's resilience. Precisely in being no longer privileged with power, it is more pointedly present in its ultimate witness and its more sifted relevance, namely that human privilege inside divine intent.

The invitation of 'neutrality' is thus a call to be more emphatic in the criticism faith must bring to the public arena and, with it, the moral force it can deploy for society and state, its custody of its own stake in the wisdom or salvation it can bring. Far from being ousted by lack of power from relevance, relevance will be more thoroughly within faith's care and conscience. In being, otherwise, neutralized, honest faith will be the more religiously at work. Is it not this shape of things which will decide who 'the unbelieving believers' are?

Notes

Introduction   Body-Tenancy/Soul-Tenure

1   Whatever the discernible psychic or circumstantial factors in the depressive or other conditions in which suicides occur, there is always, somehow, a kind of 'challenge' to the universe of life for being the way it is, a reproach for what existence has done to its 'victims' to bring them to fatal disavowal of being alive. It is not always realized – from the outside – that this 'life-repudiation' hides a hidden paradox. Only some belief, vague or assertive, that 'it ought not to be this way' implies somewhere a 'liability' that is accountable. Yet, if no such 'accountability' exists there is no *problem* of evil and suffering. The pain and grief, even the anger, will be real enough but only some divine 'given' constitutes them a problem. Thus 'atheism' as 'denial of God' only makes sense by assuming the central note of 'theism', namely a 'responsive' to the charge despair wants to make. A non-entity is not indictable nor can the 'non-existent' be accused of 'absence'.

2   'At' is of the order both of 'life at sixty' and 'men at work'. What the suiciding self as 'at' both terminates mortal selfhood and distorts the 'faith' that prompted it.

3   The years that have ensued since 'date of birth' might be thought to have made any 'undoing' of birth impossible, the natal die being cast (as metallic imagery might say). Yet, for present meaning what enfolded a continuum is certainly 'undone' in being arbitrarily cut off. See further, Chapter 10.

4   The Arabic *Ihdina al-Sirat al-mustaqim* is (lit.) 'Guide us the straight path.' It can hardly be 'into' if Islam places us on it: it must be 'on it', though much hangs – beyond the grammar – on the vexed issue of human amenability, making the prayer in one sense urgent, in another hardly so, thanks to what the 'path' bestows. The prayer has to be closely linked with the negative that follows – . . . 'not of those who . . . ' in contract to 'the graced'.

5   Not, however, in W. B. Yeats: *Selected Poems*, Chosen by Seamus Heaney, London, 2000.

6   See, for example, the eye-witness account in E. W. Lane: *The Manners and Customs of the Modern Egyptians*, London, 1908 ed., Chapter xxvii, pp. 509f.

7   Much more than the rhyme is at stake. The sexual act in human procreation is the elemental part of our *khilafah*, the 'sub-mastery' with which we are endowed, always under Allah's sovereignty so willing it to be.

141

8   William Shakespeare: *King Lear.* Act 2, Scene 4, line 157.

9   William Shakespeare, *Hamlet*, Act 1, Sc. 1, line 1. Even the challenge is awry. Two sentries enter simultaneously. One greets the other: 'Who's there?' – as if he were on the watch. The other cries: 'Nay, answer me . . . ' as if he were not due to be relieved. A sort of reciprocal challenge as to who and what is 'man' reverberates throughout the play. 'Answer me!' is the plea of Hamlet's soul – and all in the gloom on the battlements of Elsinore.

10   Herman Melville: *Moby Dick*, 1950 ed., New York, p. 1. Ishmael here being the private self through whom the action moves and registers. The central hero is Captain Ahab. He, too, is graphically heard first by the tap of his wooden-leg on the deck above, sinister enough to point the legend around him we have earlier learned.

11   In the case of *Great Expectations*, Dickens' ardent readers demanded a happier ending than the one he had contrived. As he prospered on their plaudits, he agreed to 'improve' it, while making sure it stayed ambiguous.

12   *Moby Dick, op. cit.*, p. 517.

13   It was the New England poet, Robert Frost, who wrote in 'The Lesson for Today', *Complete Poems*, New York, 1940, pp. 475–6.
    'We are all doomed to broken off careers,
    I take my incompleteness with the rest.'

14   This theme of the human writ of action inside an ordered cosmos is more fully traced in its Biblical and Quranic sources in *A Certain Sympathy of Scriptures*, Brighton & Portland, 2004.

15   Ludwig Wittgenstein: *Notebooks, 1914–1925*, Albert Camus: *The Myth of Sisyphus and Other Essays*, Eng. trans. Justin O'Brien, New York, 1955, p. 1.

16   There is much prejudice and confusion around what is ideal and what is actual in Muslim attitudes to sexuality. The former may be found in Chapter 4 of Muhammad Abdel-Haleem's *Understanding the Qur'an: Themes and Styles*, London, 1999, but see also: Leila Ahmad: *Women and Gender, Historical Roots of a Modern Debate*, Yale, 1992. One has to maximize the Qur'an's witness to inter-sexual equality as co-believers and long standing cultural attitudes in Muslim society that discount or defy it, taking due note of the lively feminist campaign, e.g. in Egypt, India and the diaspora.

17   The paradox is drawn in *Murder in the Cathedral* where even martyrdom may prove to be self-serving – and the more so by virtue of 'the cause being served'.

18   This is not to argue that 'believing makes it so', but to take due note of how a faith about Jesus rapidly arose from within society with him, thanks to that society spreading so widely because of him, and doing so out of the deep trauma of despair into which his being crucified had brought them. Too much academic 'recovery of the historical Jesus' omits the hard significance of the affirmed Christ. Antecedents are learned from their consequences.

19   Borrowing the familiar words of Thomas Cranmer's 1552 Anglican Litany.

20   Transposing here the status of a religious message to the setting of conscien-tious citizenship in the modern nation-state, in total contrast to what Meccan pagan hegemony had for a nascent Islam in its pre-Hijrah shape. Given Islam's 'finality' in, for and to, all conditions of time and place, the purely 'preached' thing could have that order of citizen relevance now, that actualities in Quraishi Mecca would never admit. Islam's 'being just a religion' then was a

circumstance of privation and suffering only (hence the Hijrah). It is not so now and the original vocation becomes the more viable and, therefore, the more loyally Islamic. In the world as we now know it, Islam has no reason to be physically aggressive, as if its very viability as a faith were otherwise at stake. It can loyally fulfil itself by thus 'revising' itself and – so doing – return to its defining self in its ever decisive form.

21 Noting Luke 2.20, the verb *apoluo* and the nouns *doulos* and *despotes*, Plummer observes: 'The words show that the figure is that of the manumission of a slave . . . his release from a long task.' *Commentary*, New York, 1914, p. 68.

I 'Canon Fixed 'Gainst Self-Slaughter'

1 *Hamlet*, Act 1, Sc. 2, lines 131–2. *Cymbeline*, Act 3, Sc. 4, lines 76–7. If we may read it in allusions in the graveyard scene in Act 5, Shakespeare seems to have been fascinated by the legal debates around a notable suicide in Canterbury in 1554 which lasted almost a decade. His 'Cleopatria' has another view: 'Let us do it after high Roman fashion/And make death proud to take us.' *Antony & Cleopatra*, Act 1, Scene 2, lines 131–2.

2 Born in 1908, Pavese committed suicide in 1950. His diaries of the years 1935 to 1950 were published in English translation by A. E. Murch in 1961 under the title *The Burning Brand*, New York. See pp. 71–8. 'The only joy in the world is to begin.' 'When living has become a habit one might as well be dead.' 'Before being born we were all dead.' It was not from such impulses that the 'suicidal believers' we are studying took their ways. More apt about them would be Pavese's warning: 'There is an art in so arranging things that the sin we commit becomes virtuous to our own conscience' (p. 78).

3 The story has often been told. It was June 2, 1840. 'The labour was a difficult one, and nearly cost Jemima her life. The child itself appeared to be dead, and was thrown aside into a basket by the surgeon trying to save the mother, until the midwife exclaimed: "Stop a minute: he's sure alive enough."' Robert Gittings: *Young Thomas Hardy*, 1978, p. 25. Or there was Tennyson's still-born firstborn son in 1851, 'the dear little nameless one' that lived but never breathed, for whom he wrote a grief-laden poem. 'The remembrance overcomes me.' Such grief only tells the preciousness of life.

4 Dylan Thomas: *Collected Poems, 1932–52*, London, 'Fern Hill', p. 150.

5 See Surahs 21.16 and 44.38. Part of not 'taking the Name of God in vain' is in not taking this world as 'in vain', trivializing ourselves in supposing some underlying frivolity concerning us. 'A serious house on serious earth it is,' as the 20th century poet said, standing in more than a churchyard.

6 'Strategy' may seem irreverent here, but it is only graphic about how Surah 2.30 and Genesis 1 and 20 see the divine 'delegacy' of the earth into human care and custody. 'Associates', therefore is also no more bold than apt, seeing that creation belongs in creaturehood and creaturely enlisting meant the ministries of prophethood for its due surveillance. On both counts then Allah is having 'people' as His 'policy'.

7 The k f r root verb denotes all 'disowning' of God's reality, whether in the ultimate shape of 'atheism' or in what withholds the worship, gratitude, or witness

that properly belong to Allah. Thus *Kafir* is the term of deep reproach, the inveterate renegade from true faith.

8 Echoing the hope of Thomas Hardy to be remembered as ever an observant 'percipient' in the natural world. *Collected Poems*, London, 1932, 'Afterwards', p. 521. Contrast 'The Impercipient at a Cathedral Evensong', pp. 59–60.

9 *The English Poems of George Herbert*, ed. C. A. Patrides, London, 1974, pp. 106–7.

10 'Imperialism' is the Qur'an's own term in Surah 11.61, for human 'fashioning' for 'husbandry' of the earth. Every native soil is thus 'colonial' ground – not by political intrusion but by agricultural occupancy. Daily in the 'worker', supremely in the 'messenger', Allah recruits His agencies. As 'Lord of the vine-yard' (Biblically) He has us all for 'vine-dressers'. The theme is more fully explored in *A Certain Sympathy of Scriptures: Biblical & Quranic*, Brighton & Portland, 2004.

11 *The Dialogues of Plato*, Benjamin Jowett's translation, Phaedo, 63, New York ed. 1937, Vol. 1, pp. 446–7. Socrates added: ' . . . as he is now summoning me.'

12 *Ibid.*, Vol. 2, Book IX, Para 863, p. 618. Omitted are some 'qualifiers' of the reproach of the suicide which come more fitly in Chapter 2 here. They help explain why Socrates was less than downright in his adverse judgement.

13 The last line of Charles Wesley's hymn in invocation of the Holy Spirit as 'pure celestial fire' on 'the mean altar' of the serving heart – adapting the analogy of Hebrew rite where the 'fire should never go out'.

14 The measure of his tenacity is in his very despair.

15 See, more fully, Sidney Goldstein: *Suicide in Rabbinic Literature*, New Jersey, 1989.

16 William Shakespeare: *2 Henry IV*, Act 3, Sc. 2, lines 232–3, cf. *Richard II*, Act 1, Sc. 3, line 174, ' . . . the duty that you owe to God.'

17 Even so, the same Fathers could pronounce the suicide of Samson *Kiddush Ha Shem*, 'the sanctifying of the Name'.

18 The word *yatawaffakum*, lit. 'to call to account', is the euphemism for 'to cause to die', as in the much debated passage in 3.55: 'O Jesus, I am causing you to die . . . ' Being created into creaturehood is being destined to die – and both by the same divine decree. Mortality and responsibility are one and the same coin. Thus creaturely 'disruption' of this bond is heinous sin, unless – somehow – the intervention of the suicidal deed is the form divine decree takes. That, however, would override both inter-bonded realities – Allah's will 'for' us as 'in being' and 'over' us 'in dying'.

19 Is the meaning (closely linked to 'proud' and the 'proudful') the utmost of pretension? 'Taking one's own life' would surely be such – and a sin of a sort 'to get dominion over' the self, and that in the most radical way, ending it alto-gether. If the psalmist is referring to sins that do become repetitive and habitual, preparatory broodings on suicide can certainly be of that order.

20 John Bunyan: *The Pilgrim's Progress*, London, a 1965 ed., pp. 100–1, First Part.

21 The tradition of *Salam* and *Shalom* as only properly addressed to the recipi-ents worthy faith-wise to be accorded them, terms due to be recalled if inadvertently addressed improperly. In Hebraic terms this use of *Shalom* is

akin verbally to dietary laws socially. Muslims too, by some Quranic precepts and assumptions, are 'a people apart'. Is the long Christian tradition of burying 'self-homicides' in 'unconsecrated ground' a dark *post mortem* violation of unrestricted greeting?

22 Cited in Ralph Russell: *An Anthology of Urdu Literature*, London, 1999, p. 147. The point is important, seeing that much 'wrong done' in personal life, while not for exoneration, is none the less 'mixed' with public factors. As Engels reportedly told Karl Marx, man only exercises his 'freedom' in the milieu that society provides for him. The Qur'an, however, in its eschatology, is insistent that final judgement happens in severely individual terms (cf. 6.164, 17.15, 39.7 and 53.38). Guilts are not absolved in the personal by the fact that they are shared in the collective. Yet there are many times and places where 'the individual' hardly exists.

23 *Ibid.*, p. 148.

24 Feodor Dostoevsky: *Notes from the Underground*, London, trans. C. Garnett, 1920, p. 115.

25 *Letter to the Philippians*, 1.23–4, the most intimate and gentle of all his writings.

26 Ludwig Wittgenstein: *Notebooks 1914–25*.

2   The Veto Rescinded

1   Albert Camus: *The Myth of Sisyphus*, Paris, 1942, Eng trans. The opening sentence.

2   This is not to say that there have not been Samsons and Masadas *sui generis* in any and every culture. Nor is to ignore that massive incidence of what may be called 'implicit suicides' in many martyrologies. The distinction, however, is radical between all such and the explicit adaption of suicide as an instrument of religious expression in a politics of 'terror'.

3   The quotations that follow are drawn from Donne's *Selected Prose*, Oxford, 1967, chosen by E. Simpson and edited by Helen Gardner and Thomas Healy, pp. 26–40. There are strange allusions in *Biathanatos* to the death of Jesus which we defer to Chaper 7.

4   *Ibid.*, p. 31.

5   And which he had also treated in his *Pseudo-Martyr* (1610) arguing that Catholic dissidents who were seen as 'martyrs' were virtual suicides.

6   *Ibid.*, pp. 31f. Arguing from the assumption that Papal 'dispensations' can over-ride laws that would otherwise obtain, he notes how the Schools of Paris disputed whether that wilful Thomas Becket could even be 'saved', whereas the Roman Church 'canonized' him.

7   W. B. Yeats: *Selected Poems*, chosen by Seamus Heaney, London, 2000, pp. 130–1.

8   *Loc. cit.*, note 3.

9   Robert Browning: *Poetical Works*, Oxford, 1940, pp. 518–19.

10 Sophocles: *Oedipus Tyrannus*, 1071–2.

11 John Donne turned from his Catholic origins around the age of thirty, after a clandestine marriage and involvement in foreign travels. David Reid in *The Metaphysical Poets*, London, 2000, p. 47 comments: 'Donne is not . . . shuf-

fling into apostasy from a Catholicism that would cost him too much, as looking for a sane and central religious tradition, which he might persuade himself was the true tradition of his family.' His poetry is replete with the stresses of doubt in the fabric of belief.

12   Surah 2.106. Cf. also 13.39. Debate has been long about the incidence and limits of *naskh*. Its being available to God, however, gives no license to believers to think it within the power of their personal 'caliphate' as Muslims.

13   The problems of readership and reading are discussed, with reference to both the Qur'an and the Bible in my: *A Certain Sympathy of Scriptures: Biblical & Quranic*, Brighton & Portland, 2004, pp. 64–78. See also here, pp. 135–7.

14   Echoing the words of Hebrews 9.27. On the loneliness of death see also Chapter 9 below.

15   The sequence can be pointedly traced in the slow change within the Qur'an of the concept of *fitnah*. Being in sum what 'tests' and so 'tempts', it denotes as it moves through the story, first 'persecution endured', to 'risk of death feared', to 'sedition plotted against'. See Chapter 8, note 33.

16   The Greek word (from *meiro*) has the root meaning of to 'decide' or 'divide', as a 'witness' does about things in dispute. Hence the gesture of raising a hand on speaking 'on oath' (cf. Genesis 14.22). YAHWEH Himself in the Bible stoops to so doing (Exodus 6.8, Deuteronomy 32.40, and three times in Ezekiel). This would make the 'pledge' on Masada the more significant. Hence the further meaning of one who 'seals' witness by dying for it or dying in its name.

17   Unless it occurs in a perverted wish for martyrdom where, being pseudo, it has no credible 'witness', thus contradicted by lack of will to live for it still.

3 'Eyeless in Gaza'

1   In that they make the 'understanding' and the 'departing' one transaction and one story, their inclusive verdict on themselves 'construing' life itself as death, with violence the clue to either.

2   In the Book of Judges patron deities belong with tribal bonds as the prescribers of the proper territories. Cf. Jephthah's question to the tribe of Ammon in 11.24: 'Wilt not thou possess what Chemosh thy god gives thee to possess?' just as YAHWEH had bestowed 'Israel' on 'Israel'. In the days of Samson the strife came from the 'sea peoples' marauding or infiltrating into areas deemed as 'Hebrew land' across the Shephalah. While being 'monolatrous' confirms this mind-set, being 'monotheistic' does not resolve it if the Lord of that inclusive worship is not seen as embracing all peoples. 'Chosen covenant' has to accommodate one creation in a single creaturehood.

3   Samson initially thinks they only mean to 'distress him more'.

> 'Have they not sword-players, and ev'ry sort
> Of gymnic artists, wrestlers, riders, runners,
> Jugglers and dancers, antics, mummers, mimics,
> But they most pick me out, with shackles tir'd,
> And over-labour'd at their public mill,
> To make them sport with blind activity?
>
>   (*Samson Agonistes*, lines 1323–8)

4 *Ibid.*, line 1659: 'The vulgar only 'scaped who stood without.' Milton makes his own gloss on the Biblical narrative.

5 'Sacrifice' has become a vastly diminished word but even at its most ample it was always darkly ambiguous, as the two previous chapters have noted.

6 *Samson Agonistes*, lines 1712–13. The tradition Milton follows in the closing commentary of the Chorus and Manoah is the convention of Greek tragedy with 'all passion spent', i.e. purged. It does violence to the ultimate moralism of the Hebraic mind. Meanwhile it suffices that 'Gaza mourns' as Gaza mourns still. 'True experience' Milton calls it, but 'true' was ever an elusive adjective.

7 *Ibid.*, line 564 and lines 594–8.

8 To distinguish it from the 'synthetic'. It rejected gentle gradualism and stressed the plea – and policy – of utmost urgency, a Zionism needing no supine excuses modifying its absoluteness. See Chapter 5 following and David Vital: *A People Apart: The Jews in Europe, 1789–1939*, Oxford, 1999, p. 613.

9 Hosea 13.9. Hosea's mind relates the Northern Kingdom's current – or impending – invasion and captivity to his reading of her 'apostasy' in the cult of the *baalim* for whom her shrines and liturgies were meant, when it was YAHWEH alone from whom her 'corn and wine and oil' were 'found'. They had ceased to be 'His people' by their betrayal of the terms by which in truth 'He was their God.' See 1.9.

10 Cited in Arthur Goldberg: *The Zionist Idea: A Historical Analysis and Reader*, pp. 561f. The fervour and finesse of this presentation are striking evidence of his power of vision, passion of mind and vivid turn of phrase. He affirmed his admiration for all things British except the danger in the 'bias' of their Arabists. His Zionism might even recruit British partnership.

11 Cited without reference in Anton La Guardia: *Holy Land, Unholy War: Israelis and Palestinians*, London, 2001, p. 152.

12 Cited in Eric Silver: *Begin: A Biography*, London, 1984, p. 12. Translated from the Russian of Jabotinsky: *On the Iron Wall*, by which phrase he meant this necessary harshness in Zion's.

13 *Ibid.*, La Guardia, p. 89. Note 11.

14 David Ben-Gurion's turn of phrase for Eretz Israel. While Palestinians might be a physical presence, they had no divine right for their presence in moral or spiritual fact.

15 *Samson Agonistes*, lines 503–7.

16 For the partition idea, first formalized by the Peel Report provided the logic – and in measure – the mapping which would eventuate in 1947 in the UNO vote of that November. While, in Zionist ideology (and certainly in Jabotinsky's) the land was indivisible, a pragmatism, like that of Ben-Gurion, saw that accepting a part could, wisely played, open the future to the whole. Meanwhile it was not to be despised. When in due course the new State accepted its partitioned lease to life, it did not accept the map that went with it. That was explicitly reserved for future opportunism to enlarge as events and ingenuity might contrive. This studied ambiguity about the definitive 'size' of Israel has always bedevilled the case for its 'right to exist'. To which 'Israel' did that conceded 'right' belong? Palestinian tragedy, not to say inter-

national confusion, by Israeli politic contrivance, have darkly turned on that wilful situation.

17   That only Palestine would 'do' was clear enough from the hostility Herzl knew when, initially, he thought that somewhere in Uganda (which the British might bestow) would 'do'. Strong reaction within the ranks quickly dissuaded him from that folly. That enmities territorial were latent and implicit is not to discount the compatibility between Palestinians and long-standing Jewish pietist presence (as in Safad) or, indeed, *vis-à-vis* initial entry of agricultural 'zionists' who presented no political threat and whom traditions of hospitality could even welcome.

18   If play on the word 'arms' is allowable. Those of Samson – for all their muscular strength – would have a yet longer reach. His had the sort of ruthless prowess which in all realms of diplomacy and planning, advocacy and energy, Jabotinsky and his quality attained. David Vital, Zionism's historian, saw him as

> . . . a man of remarkable rhetorical talent (who) with great rapidity made a name for himself as the *Wünderkind* of the Zionist movement.

Samson could have approved of the epithet. *Loc. cit*, Note 8, p. 612. The heavy tangle of Jewish self-awareness and its expression in the Zionist cause, I tried to study in: *Semitism, The Whence and Whither*, Brighton & Portland, 2005.

4   The Masada Mind

1   He was funded by interested parties. The London *Observer* newspaper gave prominence to his reports in sequence. He attracted a wide diversity of volunteers, ready to brave the torrid heat and adverse elements, to share the honours of what resembled a military expedition pursued with great *éclat* and precise organization.

2   Published, London, 1966, trans. From Hebrew by Moshe Pearlman, reprinted eight times in the ensuing decade, with 96 full colour photographs and numerous maps and plans. Exploring together the palaces of Herod and the austerities of the Zealots added a significant irony. On Yigael Yadin see: Neal Silberman: *Yadin: A Prophet from among you: The Life of a Soldier, Scholar and Mythmaker*, 1993.

3   For example, he refused to attend a 'State funeral' staged in the régime of Menahem Begin for Jewish relics of – allegedly – Bar Kokhbah's men found in the Judean desert, when the coffin was draped in the Israeli flag and carried by four Army generals. This was in contrast to the State funeral in 1968 with military honours accorded to bones from Masada. It may have been that 'secular' embarrassments over such 'myth-generating' acts prevailed with him. When, at length, the pledging ceremonies on Masada were abandoned the Army pleaded economic reasons. Perhaps Abba Eban caught the meaning of the use of the epic of Masada, when he called it: 'a pragmatic mood of post-Zionist open-mindedness'. *Heritage: Civilisation and the Jews*, London, 1984, p. 311. In any event it was hardly an apt parallel for the Israeli Armored Corps to invoke, pledging: 'Masada shall not fall again', when – in terms of contemporary conflict – no Israeli fight for survival would ever find itself on a distant cliff top in Masada terms.

4   Seeing that history is never 'bare fact' but only what happened is perceived to
    mean and what reckoning must be made of it. Both these are the preserve of
    the historians. They obviate 'bias' and 'untruth', not by impossibly having no
    verdict but integrity with the logic by which they reach it.

5   *The Works of Josephus*, trans. William Whiston (1736), New York, 1987, The
    Wars of the Jews, Book 7, Chap. 8, 6, p. 765, paras 323–5.

6   *Ibid.*, pp. 765–6, paras. 330–1, 334–6.

7   'Conjecturing at the purpose of God much sooner' – a posture read here in
    terms of re-assessment of the dogma which had led the Zealots there, namely
    that 'the sole rule of YAHWEH' made any acceptance of Rome anathema. For
    such thoughts of pragmatic realism or self-scepticism, they had no room and
    to such surmisings gave no quarter. However, the words *might* be read as a
    finally despairing forfeiture of the very core of Zealot conviction to which the
    scenario had brought them. See below.

8   *Loc. cit.*, note 5, p. 766, paras. 340 and 331–4.

9   *Ibid.*, p. 768, para. 386.

10 See Jacob Neusner: *Judaism and Its Social Metaphors, Israel in the History of
    Jewish Thought*, Cambridge, 1989, 'Israel's past . . . by definition, belonged to
    Israel alone. It followed, therefore, that by discerning the regularities in Israel's
    history, implicitly understood as unique to Israel, sages recorded the view that
    Israel, like God, was not subject to analogy or comparison' (p. 165) (Israel in
    this passage is each time in quotation marks). Must this exclude analogies
    drawn, e.g. by Amos, between Israel and other nations?

11 'Quandary' seems the approximate word here. We cannot say 'enigma' since,
    for Eleazar, God's will as adverse to their hopes is clear enough. Nor is it
    'perplexity' about God, for the same reason. The point is that God is somehow
    no longer as trusted to be, so that their reaction as 'ending themselves' is conso-
    nant with their situation so read. 'Disproven' by God in their self-reliance,
    their self-warrant ends, in the strangest form of loyal faith.

12 Yigael Yadin refers to the strong southern winds on Masada in *Masada:
    Herod's Fortress and the Zealots' Last Stand*, London, 1966, p. 29 and to their
    sudden change of direction, pp. 33–4.

13 Josephus, 'The Wars of the Jews', *loc. cit.*, p. 768, Book 7, Chap. 8, paras
    371–2.

14 Repeatedly, in Josephus' rendering, Eleazar had insisted that the only prospect
    their cast of Jewry had under Rome was 'slavery'. See, for example, *ibid.*, Book
    7, Chap. 8, para 372, p. 768: 'As to the multitude of those who are now under
    the Romans, who would not pity their condition, and who would not make
    haste to die, before he would suffer the same miseries with them?' Should
    Masada not re-enact itself everywhere?

15 It is notable how this concept recurs in Jewish thinking as a corollary of the
    uniqueness of Jewish identity as somehow suffering a self-infringement one
    should not willingly survive. Thus, for example, the historian of Zionism
    writes of 'radical forms (of solutions or plans) the greater part of the Jewish
    population regarded as self-abnegatory, if not downright treasonable'. David
    Vital: *A People Apart: The Jews in Europe, 1789–1939*, Oxford, 1999, p. 877.
    For something to be 'self-abnegatory' is more than being 'unfair', or 'inac-
    ceptable' or 'hostile'. That 'something' is lethal to identity *per se*.

16 The precept in Pirke Aboth 1.1; 'Make a fence around the Torah' was designed, it would seem to make the law the more inviolate and yet provide a 'space' where a sort of 'gray area' might absorb unwitting infraction while keeping the meticulous in place.

17 The reference is to the inroads of Pompey. See: R. H. Charles: *Apocrypha and Pseudepigraha of the Old Testament*, Oxford, 1913, Vol. 2, pp. 88–9, citing the Psalms of Solomon, 2.7 and 17.

18 For sundry examples of the cult of Suicide in the Judaic tradition, see: Martin Hengel: *The Zealots*, trans. David Smith, Edinburgh, 1989, pp. 262–71.

19 *Ibid.*, p. 378.

20 'Undone' in the double sense of, somehow its consequences repaired, or not done at all. The intention is to recall Edwin Muir's poem on the theme of, somehow, Christ's Cross being also as if 'unenacted'

>   And Judas take his long journey backward
>   Beside his mother's knee, and the betrayal
>   Be quite undone, and never more be done.

'The Transfiguration', Edwin Muir: *Collected Poems*, London, 1963, p. 200. On the significance of 'suicide' (Judas) in the meaning of Jesus' Gethsemane, see Chapter 7.

21 So thought Hosea (3.4) Cf. 2 Chronicles 15.3 citing a seer named Azariah in the reign of Asa; lack of the Temple priesthood and the Davidic throne being the dual calamity – the calamitous nature of which Josephus was minded to question. Even zealotry was at odds over the Temple system, or its holders, as also over the nature of duly Judaic monarchy.

22 See Louis H. Feldman: *Studies in Josephus' Re-written Bible*, Leiden, 1998. 'Re-written' refers to how Josephus drew his Biblical characters for Roman appreciation in *The Antiquities*. Had not Gedaliah (Jeremiah 40.7) been 'a client governor'? There were problems over Ruth, for Rome also had laws against inter-racial marriage. Phineas (Numbers 25.11) might seem a torrid 'zealot', but his 'zeal' was redeemed because it was against sexual evils. Other parallels to 'zealots' like Joab and Jeroboam were justly to be reproved.

23 See ed. Louis H. Feldman & Gohel Hata: *Josephus, the Bible and History*, Detroit, 1989, Raymond R. Newell: 'The Forms and Value of Josephus Suicide Accounts'. Pp. 278–94. But see also: B. A. Shargel: 'The Evolution of the Masada Myth', in *Judaism*, Vol. 28, 1979, pp. 357–71.

24 *Ibid.*, p. 289. Newell argues that the heroism of the Sicarii would not denigrate them in Roman eyes which had anathema only for revolt. Eleazar's 'speech' broadly fitted his character and the situation.

25 The tangled theme of contemporary Israel 'conjecturing the purpose of God much sooner' arises from the violent repressiveness entailed in failing to reckon *ab initio* with the human presence of another people and their identical plea of the necessity of land and power to their 'nationalism'. It is studied in: *Semitism: The Whence and Whither*, Brighton & Portland, 2005.

5 Suicidal Christian Martyrology

1 A pagan intellectual could easily allow a divinisation of the Emperor in a way that Semitic theism could not. Moreover, as intellectual he could appreciate

how the practice was a political device to ensure imperial cohesion, just as images on coins and statues in public places signified the authority that ruled over all. At least in our times and mores we could 'see through' this devising and not find it incompatible with a religious doctrine of divine unity. The Early Church had no such option of pondering such 'sociological' notions of the 'utility' of religious beliefs.

2 *Epist. Ad Rom.*, 4.1.53.

3 See G. W. Bowersock: *Martyrdom and Rome*, Cambridge, 1995 for discussion of how *martur* as a term passed from meaning only 'witness' to meaning 'martyr' also.

4 As H. M. Gwatkin remarks: 'It is clear that Ignatius is the very last man to be taken as a sample of Christian opinion in his own time.' *Early Church History to AD 313*, London, 1909, Vol. 1, p. 134. We return to Clement below. Gwatkin's verdict, however, seems over-sanguine. As Bowersock (*loc.cit.* note 3) observes: 'The suicidal aspect of martyrdom remained at the forefront' (p. 64) and: 'Without the glorification of suicide in the Roman tradition . . . the hordes of voluntary martyrs would never have existed' (pp. 72–3).

5 In the Semitic sense of 'loving less', as in Jesus' verdict about 'serving two masters' (Matthew 6.24) or Romans 9.13 about 'hating Esau'. The injunction about 'loving enemies' is not overridden nor the precept of 1 John 2.9.

6 A point heavily stressed by Bowersock, *Martyrdom and Rome, op. cit.*, note 3, in line with his emphasis on the role of Roman factors, social and political, in the long pre-Constantinian world.

7 In Book 4 of his *Scorpace*.

8 As was so frequently the case. The degree of 'dramatization' that served imperial ends so well, could also entice Christians into welcoming the fact of it in their own sense of 'publicity for Christ', an investing of life itself in a feat of 'faith-attraction'. How far it availed is hard to know, whether fascinating, convincing or repellent?

9 Plato's *Phaedo*, Para. 61 in *Dialogues of Plato*, trans. Benjamin Jowett, Vol. 1, New York, 1937, pp. 445f.

10 The passage in Plato reflects the Greek instinct to acknowledge puzzlement and to refrain from sure assertion.

11 See his Chapter on 'the Civic Role of Martyrs', *op. cit.*, pp. 41–57.

12 The word is *tithemi* in 10.18, *exagein* in the other.

13 Bowersock: *Martyrdom and Rome, op. cit*, p. 74, where he adds that this 'Roman feature' would 'conspicuously survive in Islam'. In his insistence that the Jewish temper had an abhorrence of suicide equal to that of the Greek, does he minimize or exclude the Semitic nature of the Maccabees and of Masada, despite a Hebrew horror of suicidal death? In the citation, p. 74 'was redeemed from' would seem more in line with his thought, and Clement's, than 'was deprived of' which suggests the regrettable rather than the desirable. 'God-fearing fanaticism' is not a contradiction in terms – given its version of 'fear'. At a tangent, see also: Anton Van Hooft: *From Autothanasia to Suicide: Self-killing in Classical Antiquity*, London, 1990. On the Jewish tradition of martyrdom see: Martin Hengel: *The Zealots: Investigations into the Jewish Freedom Movement from Herod until 70 AD* trans. David Smith, Edinburgh, 1989, pp. 256–65.

14   T. S. Eliot: *Murder in the Cathedral,* London, 1968 ed., p. 41f.

15   As noted by Christopher Hichens: *Unacknowledged Legislation, Writers in the Public Sphere,* New York, 2000, 'The Wilde Side', p. 4.

6   The Kiss and the Suicide of Iscariot

1   Matthew 27.5 Cf. Acts 1.18. One salient example of Jewish embitterment of scholarship around New Testament study and Judas in particular was Hyam Maccoby in his *Judas Iscariot and the Myth of Jewish Evil,* London, 1992. He regarded the New Testament presentation of Judas as 'almost entirely fictional' (p. 2). The 'myth', however, was useful he alleged because it helped to keep Jewry also in the pillory. He discounts the reading of Judas followed here but only by ignoring the 'publican' dimension among Jesus' disciples. Hyam Maccoby (1924–2004) left a range of sometimes polemical works – *The Mythmaker, Paul and the Invention of Christianity* (1986), *Paul and Hellenism* (1991), *Jesus the Pharisee* (2003) and in 2004 *Anti-Semitism and Modernity.* See below re Judas.

2   How comprehension, replacing both damnation and exoneration, might obtain was ventured, perhaps too far, in Edwin Muir's poem, to be noted later.

3   The theory as to 'messianic secret' goes back to the early days of form criticism and is linked with the name of W. Wrede, writing in 1939. He held that the idea of Jesus directing that nothing be published about his 'being Messiah' is a sort of 'fiction' on the part of the apostles later, to explain why Jesus was only found to be Messiah (by them) afterwards. He had not been proclaimed such during his ministry because of a 'secrecy'. This was to offset the charge that his being so was the theme of their subsequent faith and *not* of his history. It is far more credible to understand why Jesus was reticent over this theme, since obtruding it risked such deep and crippling distortion, given the dangerous ambiguity of the term and the passions that waited on it. The conviction here is that it was the very nature of his Messiahship that its quality could only be known *de facto* by its achieving – and that achieving greeted by the faith that recognized both its fact-ness and its character.

4   It is the very nature of faith that these matters cannot be decisively resolved. We live with the questions. There can be confidence that the apostolic experience to which the faith testified was the most reliably qualified to tell what it was and – only so – give rise to the New Testament as its documentation.

5   It could hardly be that a dimension so extensive, alike in parable and action as was the Matthew/Zaccheus index in the ministry, could have been a later invention. Occasions made it evident enough how offensive to officialdom and pious bystanders were these initiatives of Jesus. How ill at ease the 'zealot' element among the disciples must have been as guests of Matthew's celebratory banquet, introducing his Jesus to all that ilk.

6   Was it some 'Galilean accent' that had *ben* into *boan*?

7   Among the points raised by Hyam Maccoby (note 1) against the reading of Judas followed here is that the very size of this force precludes it, were Judas merely acting out of bitter disappointment in Jesus. Maccoby is interested in his own case-making of Judas *in toto* as a creation of anti-Jewish villainy, a

152

malice he is used to incriminate. See below, where the point recurs concerning the plot.

8 Can Matthew 11.12 contradict Matthew 11.28–30? The word *biazetai* is here passive and means 'to be forcibly treated', as what is liable to violent reaction. To translate ' . . . has been coming violently and keen enthusiasts want to share it' can only be by opting for extreme paradox, perhaps the sharp paradox of Matthew 10.34 ' . . . not peace but a sword'. For the view that *biazetai* does, albeit incongruously, mean that the Kingdom acts violently, see: G. E. Ladd: *Jesus and the Kingdom*, London, 1964, pp. 155–8.

9 For, in psalm and prophet, 'gates' were ever the symbol of 'power', as leading where power lay. 'The rock', surely, is the confession of Messiahship but on human lips so that it meant no abstract reality but a living, active availing conviction. It was also an allusion to the local terrain at Baneas and the foothills of Hermon, whither they had withdrawn far north of Galilee.

10 A word loved by the Elizabethans in the 16th century, meaning 'well suited to fulfil', or 'well-accoutred for a task'.

11 The Gospel is precise about the point at which Judas reached his fatal *volte-face*. On its handling of his memory, see below.

12 Or rather a form so inconceivable that it would never cross the 'zealot' mind or present itself to any Messianic purpose. For, in his reading of what being Messiah meant, Jesus was alone, but for his fellowship of heart with the experience of the prophets, especially those 'Servant Songs' in Isaiah.

13 The word is apt in its strict sense of 'setting a price or value on'.

14 Unless it is a Davidic psalm, there is a puzzling ring to its warning to heathen powers to 'kiss the Son' lest 'his anger' break out upon them – a pretentious notion to have about the might of the powers that wasted Israel and Judea so ruthlessly and finally destroyed their monarchies, exiling their people. It would seem to be a 'royal psalm', serving notice of an accession or celebrating its anniversary. 'This day have I begotten thee' has caused much confusion and needs to be read in terms like 'This very day have a launched you in power.' That the 'kiss' is an act of homage – whether on hand or foot or face – is clear enough also from, e.g., 1 Samuel 10.1. The 'kiss of peace' became a steady practice in the New Testament Church.

15 In the literal sense, there and then, the 'kiss' identified who was to be taken captive. Doing so, in the idiom of Psalm 2, did him homage in Judas' terms. Did not the Psalm intend to ensure that royal identity was understood in its proper right?

16 See below. In his 'Easter' poem there is no suggestion that George Herbert ever had Judas in mind. Yet might we not think so, since he wrote

> The crosse taught all wood to resound his name,
> Who bore the same?

The English Poems of George Herbert, ed. C. A. Patrides, London, 1974, p. 61.

17 Nor does the force of the argument assume that he could, while a keen sense of Judas' sympathies and where they lay is not in doubt. It is no part of the meaning of 'the divine in the human' in the Christian faith in the Incarnation of 'God in Christ' to conjecture some 'omniscience' pretending not to be. All is within the utter-human-ness of a vexing situation, learning and resolving as it went.

18 As did Hyam Maccoby, *op. cit.*, note 1, pp. 57–60. He reads the Acts version as recalling the 'curse' of Abel's 'blood' 'spilled' and 'crying from the ground'. Judas, it is inferred, is thus a 'sacrificer' analogous to false incrimination of Jews.

19 That perspective is evident enough in all the past tenses Jesus used about the completion of 'his work', the 'establishing' of the Church, and the retrospect of achievement. It read like a summary testament on the lines of post-Ascension faith. It even refers to Jesus himself (v. 3) as – grammatically – 'the absent person' to whom reference is made.

20 There are scholars who surmise that the very shape of the narratives turns on fulfilment of precedents – but not, surely, at risk to the history. Part of the reason for the strong concern to see 'fulfilment' of Scriptures was the re-assuring of Jewish actual or potential Christians still wrestling with old loyalties.

21 Edwin Muir: *Collected Poems*, London, 1968, p. 200.

22 William Temple: *Readings in St. John's Gospel*, London, 1947, p. 321. He translates *apolote* as 'destroyed' rather than 'lost', where the context has to do with Jesus' 'guardianship'. The way in which Judas' deed 'fulfils' Psalm 41.9, except in the barest, literal sense, is far to seek. Temple writes: 'He perished by his own quality from which no external guardianship could protect him.' What then of Jesus' long, caring companionship and his last acceptance of that 'kiss', despite the surprise with which *in situ* he greeted it?

7 Understanding Gethsemane

1 John is making a clear link between this agony and 'the Lord walking in the garden (Eden)' in Genesis, 'at the cool of the day', asking of the creature: 'Where art thou?' There could only have been 'a garden' in the grim 'place of execution' in the imagery of a discerning faith. While the Gospels are always reticent, never horror-breeding about the Cross, we do well to have its horror in mind.

2 Mark 10.45. Discussion is well nigh endless about 'the Son of Man'. Here we absorb the issues into the four points being made in this chapter where that debate has its implicit setting.

3 John 10.14–18 – in the 'good shepherd' context which, of course, conditions the meaning. John Donne's *Biathanatos* noted in Chapter 2 is ready to write – surely in ill-judged rhetoric – of 'Christian martyrdom having its source in the suicide of God incarnate'. Elsewhere he defends suicide with Jesus as exemplary of the case he makes. John Donne: *Selected Essays*, chosen by E. Simpson, ed. Helen Gardner, Oxford, 1967, pp. 26–40. Donne's phrasing betrays a bizarre theological mind, or was he being 'theatrical' as often in his preaching? Is there a similarly strange inference in G. W. Bowerstock in *Martyrdom and Rome*, Cambridge, 1995, pp. 14f., where he coincides the rise of martyr cults in Anatolia and adds: 'The coincidence (of timing) with the composition of the New Testament would suggest that stories (sic) of Jesus' life and death were related in one way or another to this extra-ordinary development'?

4 Revelation 7.17 – a quite incongruous phrase unless the imagery is understood. See below. Hebrews 5.8 makes a play on words: *emathen epathen*.

5 Why was the true 'neighbour' on the Jericho road a 'Samaritan'? The 'a certain man' formula for so many parables had no feel for Jewish separatism. 'The Temple Court of the Gentiles' had to be kept from being taken into a Jewish exclusion zone like the rest of the building. The welcome to the likes of Zaccheus and Matthew, as noted earlier, was unequivocal. He had a heart for late-comers in the employment league of those 'idle in the market-place'.

6 Exactly that *antilogion* of Hebrews 12.3 he 'endured' in the narrative of the Gospels as 'words of antipathy'.

7 See below, concerning a history yielding biography – a 'writing into life' where – as in poetry – *what* is said is told in *how* said, so that meaning is 'biographized'.

8 Jeremiah 11.18–23, 12.1–6, 15.10–21, 17.9–18, 18.18–23 and 20.7–12. Of him it was finely said: 'The Book of Jeremiah does not so much teach religious truth as present a religious personality. Prophecy had already taught its truths, its last effort was to reveal itself in a life.' James Hastings: *Dictionary of the Bible*, vol. 2, London, 1898, p. 576.

9 The famous passage in Jeremiah 7.1–16: 'Stand in the gate of the Lord's house . . . ' in which he disavows that Temple's worship and summons its denizens with their moral reproach, in a thrilling call to spiritual integrity. His personal courage is strikingly eloquent of the cost of his calling.

10 This sadly has often been the case, with preachers blandly likening YAHWEH to Abraham and going further in that He, 'the Lord of hosts', 'sacrificed His Son' as a 'substitute' immolated in a ritual. Nothing that makes God external to the Cross constitutes the Gospel nor tallies with Paul's – or any intelligible – meaning of the Cross. There was nothing 'ritualized' in Gethsemane and the 'Lamb language' is of another order.

11 It is wise to distinguish here and everywhere between this sense of the 'secular' as an entire disavowal of God as ever over human life, and what is denoted by the 'secular' state, i.e. a political pattern which no single faith dominates but which holds the ring for all 'believings' compatible with the due discipline of common good and public order. Such a state may well be deeply 'religious', but only in terms of citizen faith(s).

12 As in many other ways, the logic of the parables which the Synoptic Gospels carry – all absent from the Fourth – is enlarged into the Johannine Christology by a retrospective possession of their meaning as faith was fulfilled.

13 In this its capacity to be thus only 'negative', it anticipates what is beyond its own reach, namely grace. The theme is well personalized in Paul's experience and Letters. Justice relates to the consequences of wrongs. It does not reach into their guilt.

14 The urgently necessary phrase in expressing the Gospel. Cf. note 10 above.

15 The clear intention of John 1.1–14 is to relate 'the word' that lets creation be, and 'the Word' incarnate in Jesus as 'light' and 'life'.

16 Percy B. Shelley: *Poems and Prose*, London, 1977, 'On Christianity', p. 65.

17 Exactly the sense of the Greek word he uses in 1.18 *exegesato*.

18 The Greek of John 14.1 may be read as two indicatives or two imperatives, or one of either with the other. Whether informing or advising, they have to do with this complete nexus.

19 Notably that of Albert Schweitzer: *The Quest of the Historical Jesus*, Eng. trans.,

London, 1911. He saw in Jesus one who sought to precipitate into being the apocalyptic Kingdom of God and was broken in its failure, leaving behind an empowering legacy of exemplary courage and self-forfeiture.

8   The Suicidal in Contemporary Islam

1   Though officially there are only 'Israeli Defence Forces'. Zionism, proposing a purely innocent presence, neither needs nor owns an 'army'. Yisrael Yadin's now abandoned predilections for the Masada site were discussed in Chapter 4. Was it only 'the armoured corps' that took the 'pledge' there?

2   What is so awesome about suicide is that, while it is so 'individual' an act, departing from the unique body–soul identity, it is just that quality which makes all its sundry perpetrators a kindred. The point is taken further in Chapter 10. All that follows here argues a total disparity between the Judaic incidence and the Islamic.

3   'Anomaly' is too mild a word in this context, unless held to its derivation as what denies its own 'law', e.g. (as Darwin suggested) a 'bird' that cannot fly. The point was developed in Chapter 5 of a faith faithless to itself by a self-destroying zeal.

4   Cf. Surah 13.40, stressing that Muhammad's sole task is the *balagh* or 'word-mission', and noting that he 'may be caused to die' before seeing what he expects as promised, namely the 'heeding' of that *balagh*. *Mutawaffika* is the familiar Arabic verb for 'being called home in death. Cf. Surah 3.55 of Jesus. There are several other passages about Muhammad's stressful vigil with adversity, in 'deep trouble of heart'. See, e.g., Surah 18.6.

5   Biblical phrases for long-suffering, long delayed vindication in and by the self-expending fruits of ministry 'after many days'.

6   Through the deaths of Khadijah his wife and great succourer and of AbuTalib his always pagan uncle and protector, father of his cousin and son-in-law 'Ali.

7   Thus the Calendar tells the abiding priority of Mecca for the 'identity' of Islam, as does the Pilgrimage likewise. The Calendar might have started from Muhammad's birth date, or from the onset of revelations to him.

8   'Fugitive' here must not mislead. The Hijrah was often, but always wrongly, seen in the West as 'the flight'. All was calculated 'migration', yet from the Meccans' point of view Muhammad was 'on the loose' as one now out of their reach.

9   The point returns us, as in Note 4, to occasions in the Qur'an of Muhammad patient under duress, shouldering the burden of unwantedness. He knew what it was to have his audience drifting away from his pleas and he 'seeming as one calling from a long way off'. See Surahs 41.44, and 62.11. Cf. 40.41.

10 In that when tensions arose over doctrinal propriety or duly 'right' conduct under *Shari'ah*, the 'complainants' had to make political challenge to the regime, as with the Khawarij and the Shi'ah. The political laid its hand on theological dispute.

11 The New Testament Scripture, and its Canon, preceded all things Constantinian (though not the Creeds in their classic form). The 4th century imperial dimension of Christendom found neither place nor warrant in the

controlling Scripture. The contrast in Islam with its 'Medina squarely in its Qur'an' is complete.

12 'Tributary' in the sense that what Mecca had in word alone is now bound over to the circumstances in which it actually prevailed and in which it is dually narrated in the Qur'an. In that sense, Medina 'possesses' Mecca, yet only because Mecca possessed uniquely what Medina served to 'establish'. That respective Surahs needed to be identified is important, though the process by which it happened is obscure and some Surahs may be composite containing both periods. Notably Islam itself does *not* begin with arrival in Medina.

13 As a significant part of the 'Islam against Islam' due to be broached there in the necessary concern here for 'an Islam self-judged', controversial as the theme must be.

14 Ibn Khaldun: *Al-Muqaddimah*, trans. F. Rosenthal, New York, 1958, Vol. 1, p. 415.

15 As in Surah 3.19 (cf. 5.3).

16 *Shahadah* (witness) was the prime duty, the first of the duties of the believer just as *Iqra'* – 'Utter' – was the initial command to Muhammad in the onset of Quranic *tanzil*. The Qur'an (2.2) was not involved in 'dubiety'. While in Mecca, however, this declarative, definitive verbal, literal mission neither enjoyed nor sought physical enforcement.

17 How clear-cut and emphatic this entire distinction between *iman* and *kufr*, surrender to God and staying *mushrik* is explored in David E. Marshall: *God, Muhammad and the Unbelievers, A Quranic Study*, Richmond, 1999.

18 That there must be promise, as well as prejudice, concerning the self-defini-tion of Islam, in this Mecca/Medina 'before-and-after', which here bears on Chapter 11. See also: *Muhammad in the Qur'an*, London, 2001 and *The Tragic in Islam*, London, 2004, Chap. 3, pp. 63–87.

19 This transition is vividly mirrored in the change of temper in the Qur'an. The lyric celebrations of the natural order and the fervent appeals to faith give way to a greater asperity of tone and to the gathering legal and military elements of a growing 'establishment'. There is also a new sharpness about Jews and Christians as of failed expectations.

20 Arabic, Arab and Arabism will always be central in Islam, since its Prophet was Muhammad, Arabic its vital scriptural language and Arabs who launched it in the world. Yet there were long centuries in Europe when 'Turk' was the synonym for 'Muslim', as in the English Book of Common Prayer.

21 The not very inspired jingle was coined by Samuel Huntington in: *The Clash of Civilizations and the Remaking of World Order*, New York, 1996, which developed the case earlier made in a now famous article in *Foreign Affairs*, Summer, 1993, volume entitled '*The Clash of Civilizations?*' The piece has since been translated into some 26 languages. Mixing metaphors, he wrote: 'The fault lines of civilizations will be the battle lines of the future.' The phrase 'The West and the Rest' was used as the title of Roger Scruton's study, London, 2002.

22 The years of Ronald Reagan as President of the USA (1980–1988) are often hailed as deserving the credit for that collapse by his insistent invocation of the 'axis of evil' charge and 'the evil empire'. He would ask: 'Is nothing worth dying for?' in urging action (political and economic) to 'free millions of the

enslaved' under that 'empire'. A sort of warranted hate syndrome easily passed later to Islam as 'evil', in western eyes and mind-set.

23 See the analysis and discussion in: Loretta Napoleoni: *Modern Jihad: Tracing the Dollars behind the Terror Networks*, London, 2003. She writes: 'Fuelled by political violence, organized crime and common greed, the New Economy of Terror is today twice the size of the GNP and three times the size of the US money supply and still growing. At present its main engine is the Modern Jihad, and the socio-economic aspirations of the Muslim World,' pp. 203–204.

24 From the root meaning 'to aid towards victory', both ideas being present. 'Isa's disciples are so termed in Surahs 3.52 and 61.14. The twin ideas are of succour towards success in the enterprise. Without Yathribites favourable to him, Muhammad would have been at great risk on entering Yathrib.

25 See *Muhammad in the Qur'an*, London, 2001, Chap. 5, pp. 90–113.

26 Such as the Banu Quraizah and Banu Qanuqa' – who suffered despoliation and grievous punishment as unable – or unwilling – to assert their separation from an inter-Arab quarrel and whose resources the campaign against Mecca coveted.

27 Islam in its normal mind is well aware of *hudud*, 'bounds' that Allah has set and, as such, not to be crossed. Unprovoked aggression, harming children, making orphans and much else are among them. Yet there are points at which the very warrant that itself places these 'limits' can become precisely the factor in suspending their prohibiting range, if too zealously served. That 'zeal consumes' is no idle reality, among its 'parties' most of all.

28 For example, there have been fatwas among Chechians that to be killed by *the enemy* is not the only qualifying of a martyr, if his cause is genuinely *fi sabil Illah*: in October 2003, the Egyptian Shaikh 'Ali Jum'ah declared suiciding against Israeli oppression authentic martyrdom, as against *Ahl al-qital* 'people of violence and war'.

29 That it achieves this is all too evident. As argued earlier, 'terrorists' gain by being so described. Surmise and apprehension work indirectly for them. There were occasions, for example in the 2004 'siege' of Fallujah, when traps were set for US forces by deliberate atrocities, sure to demand unwise reactions of 'avenging'.

30 'The Days of Ignorance', i.e. uncouth wildness out of lack of truth, traditionally denote the time before the Qur'an came with enlightenment. There are radical Muslim writers who see this Muslim generation as still in that forlorn condition.

31 Ed. Satish Kuman, New Delhi, 2002, pp. 123–9. The writer further argued that global factors had now out-dated Muhammad's Medinan-style pattern and that now he, too, would commend non-violence. 'We cannot go back to the time of the Prophet: we have to bring him into our age.' He added tantalizingly: 'Do not judge Islam by Muslims, judge Muslims by Islam.' These sentiments reflect the Indian situation. For reflection on 'a partition of Islam' in the 1947 partition of India, see: *The Tragic in Islam*, London, 2004, Chapter 7, 154–77.

32 This highly individual assessment of final things, and these familiar images of 'books' and 'scales' and cumulative 'accounts', are studied in my *A Certain*

Sympathy of Scriptures: Biblical & Quranic, Brighton & Portland, 2004, pp. 94–108.

33 The evolution in the sense of the term in the Qur'an, the nuances in the meaning of 'trial', i.e. 'what tries', is clear at once via an Arabic Concordance to it. See also, e.g.: Fazlur Rahman: *Major Themes of the Qur'an*, Chicago, 1980, pp. 159f. and my *Muhammad in the Qur'an*, London, 2004, p. 91.

34 *Akbar*, as grammatically a comparative subdues all that would compete with it, so that to counter it is the nature of 'idolatry'. The more, then, is the quality of what 'greatness' connotes at stake in the meaning.

35 The instinct, that is, of a true worship that fears to think unworthily of Allah.

36 The precept Paul has for the Romans in 12.19 namely: 'Leave room for the judgement of God.'

37 There are three places where the Qur'an has this verdict of a wrong theology against its pagan hearers, i.e. Surah 6.91, 22.74 and 39.67. 'Esteem' here conveys the rich sense of 'weighing', 'valuing' and 'measuring' the *qadar* root has. With thought of Allah there is no room for culpable vagueness.

38 'Plural gods', using the *ilah* term which can be pluralized as Allah never can be. It is important to realize that Muhammad's message did not assert the existence of Allah but His *sole* existence.

39 On Al-Kawakibi, see: Khaldun S. Al-Husry: *Three Reformers: A Study of Arab Political Thought*, Beirut, 1966, pp. 55–112, and my *The Tragic in Islam*, London, 2004, pp. 135–47. He and his kin did not attack the Caliphate *per se*, they coveted to have it back where it belonged – in Arab hands. Yet they rebelled in the end against its *de facto* holder and – in the event – with non-Muslim aid and succour.

40 While rigorists may dream of 'Islamizing' Illinois or Holland, the subterfuge and violence it would imply meanwhile can only jeopardize bona fide believers in their will to 'belong' constructively and thus further embitter the situation in arousing suspicion and a climate of enmity.

41 The flexibility of 'readings' of the Qur'an is apparent, while *not* being offensive to its intended meaning, as a negative test, is no great hurdle for the ready minded. 'Perhaps they may reflect' is its own repeated hope concerning readers.

42 *The Times*, mid-November, 2004.

9   Suicides and Shares

1 See *Letters of Charles Dickens*, ed. Humphrey House *et al.*, 12 volumes, Oxford, 1962–2002, Vol. X, p. 346.

2 As when in *Dombey and Son*, he saw the world, in their eyes, as meant 'for Dombey to trade in'.

3 *Our Mutual Friend*, London, 1866, Book 1, Chapter 10. Penguin Classic ed., pp. 159–60.

4 The more so in that the novel's title was a late option out of several. While Dickens leaves hints of who it was meant for, his sympathies would surely allow us this guess too. The opening in Book 1, Chapter 1 is grimly graphic, with the boatman's brutal coarseness offset by his daughter's horror rowing

with him, the eyes of both searching the dark surface of the tide. Penguin Classics ed., p. 47.

5 Robert Browning: *Poetical Works*, Oxford, 1905, 'Apparent Failure', pp. 518–19. Browning was fond of taking themes for his verse from cuttings and notices in the daily press – as here and most notably in the chance origins of his masterpiece *The Ring and the Book*.

6 Matthew Arnold: *New Poems*, London, 1867, p. 65. In another edition, he omitted 'Empedocles on Etna', as 'an unprofitable example of the dialogue of the mind with itself'. *Complete Works*, ed. R. H. Super, Ann Arbor, 11 volumes, 1960–71, Vol. 1, p. 13.

7 *Ibid.*, p. 64.

8 Charles H. Sorley (1895–1915), son of a distinguished Cambridge philosopher, W. R. Sorley, never took up his Scholarship at University College, Oxford, but enlisted in the Suffolk Regiment in 1914, to die at Loos a year later, a Captain, aged 20. His *Marlborough and Other Poems*, Cambridge, 1916, brought him wide posthumous fame. 'Blue horizons far away/Do not give the rest we need.'

9 Ernest Hemingway: *Death in the Afternoon*, New York, 1932, where the theme centers on bull-fighting in the arena.

10 *For Whom the Bell Tolls*, New York, 1940. This, his longest novel, is set inside the Spanish Civil War and makes a noble plea for the defence of liberty as of universal relevance beyond immediate time and place and politics. A useful reckoning with Hemingway's literary style and its 'match to his mood' can be found in: John Atkins: *The Art of Ernest Hemingway: His Work and Personality*, London, 1952.

11 Ernest Hemingway: *To Have and to Have Not*, New York, 1937.

12 John K. M. McCaffery: *Ernest Hemingway: The Man and His Work*, a group of essays cited in John Atkins (note 10) p. 48. See critique p. 252 (ed.), and the citation p. 51.

13 *Diaries*, 1935–50, trans. A. E. Murch, New York, 1961. See p. 71.

14 Pavese had been a teacher in Levi's boyhood school. His suicide, also in Turin, affected Levi deeply, making the keener his apprehensions of dying likewise, while writing of it (in 1967): 'Nobody has yet been able to penetrate the reason and the roots (of it).' See Ian Thompson: *Primo Levi*, London, 2002, though elsewhere he could write of suicide as 'a legitimate bid for freedom', p. 532.

15 He had once read Herzl's *Der Judenstaat*, and kindled to it but he once declared himself 'physiologically incapable of hatred' (Thompson, note 14, p. 552) and misgivings troubled him around the 'once victim/now victor' aspects of Israel which ill-suited his Judaic conscience. His Jewishness belonged with Italy.

16 *I Sistema Periodico*, Turin, 1975, English translation: *The Periodic Table*, trans. R. Rosenthal, London, 1985. Under 'nitrogen' he noted with wry humour how the droppings of snakes go into lipstick manufacture, and how carbon is present in every substance associated with life.

17 *I Sommersi e i Salvati*, Turin, 1986, English translation, *The Drowned and the Saved*, trans. R. Rosenthal, London, 1988.

18 Thompson, *op. cit.*, p. 538.

19 It seems fair in context to echo 'the dyer's hand' of poetic imagery.

20 Virginia Woolf: *Moments of Being*, ed. J. Schuklind, London, 1976, p. 72. 'Putting it into words' somehow 'laid it to rest'. Yet a restlessness remained.

21 Virginia Woolf: *The Years*, London, 1969, p. 152. Account of her childhood experiences of abuse and rape at the hand of Gerald and George Duckworth can be found in Louise De Salvo: *Virginia Woolf, The Impact of Childhood Sexual Abuse in her Life and Work*, London, 1959. It made her call in question her right to exist, 'to be here', as somehow afraid and ashamed of her own body. There was the patriarchal despotism of her father, while her mother's extra-family solicitude for public acts of 'charity' made her seem inaccessible for the little/great aches of childhood in a large family of very disparate ages. There were also frequent illnesses. Despite ideal potential via books and celebrity aura for happiness, the father being a prestigious biographer, there was much anguish also.

22 In *Moments of Being*, she spoke in commentary on Palgrave's *Golden Treasury*, of 'poetry coming true'. 'The pen was on the scent'. *Op. cit.*, p. 90. See also p. 72 about capturing reality by putting it into words. See also: Alex Zwerdling: *Virginia Woolf and the Real World*, Berkeley, 1986. She writes of her overwhelming sense of significance in life in *The Letters of Virginia Woolf*, Vol. IV, p. 387 (6 vols. ed. N. Nicholson and J. Trautmann between 1975 and 1980).

23 Virginia Woolf: *Jacob's Room*, London, 1976, p. 182.

24 Cited in Lyndall Gordon: *Virginia Woolf, A Writer's Life*, Oxford, 1984, p. 5.

25 Virginia Woolf: *A Room of One's Own*, London, 1945, p. 15.

26 For a scene to the point see her *The Years*, London, 1937, and the beginning pages under '1880'.

27 This was the theme of *A Room of One's Own*, though she disliked the 'feminist' label. In his *My Early Beliefs*, 1947, p. 97, J. M. Keynes wrote of the Bloomsbury Group to which she belonged: 'We entirely repudiated a personal liability on us to obey general rules. We claimed the right to judge every individual case on its merits and the wisdom, experience and self-control to do so successfully.'

28 Virginia Woolf: *Three Guineas*, London, 1977, p. 142.

29 *Op. cit.*, p. 72.

30 Virginia Woolf: *Between the Acts*, London, 1953, p. 23.

31 *Moments of Being, op. cit.*, p. 311.

32 Virginia Woolf: *Collected Essays*, ed. Leonard Woolf, Vol. 2 (4 vols, 1966–7) p. 109.

33 *The Journals of Sylvia Plath*, ed. Karen V. Kukil, London, 2002, p. 151. Born in Boston in 1932 and dying at her own hand in London in 1963, and sharing the birthday of Dylan Thomas, her long and tragic fascination with suicide has vivid relevance here by the very reach of its exploration of the antecedents. (Subsequent citations in brackets.)

34 Michael Schmidt: *Lives of the Poets*, London, 1998, p. 929. A facility for daring metaphor hardly justifies this enthusiasm and Schmidt is not – it would seem – referring to the dissolution of human personality Plath's poems so grimly portray and analyze, or how any real acceptance of other mortals is felt as a threat to one's own autonomy.

35 Kukil. *Op. cit.* She was the Assistant Curator of Rare Books at Smith College. The *Journals* were in the care of Ted Hughes, her husband, and then of her

children, Frieda and Nicholas. Hughes guided the editor until his death in 1998. The task was completed the following year. The book with index reaches 732 pages, incorporates a few letters to friends and reaches from the date of entering Smith College until the final year of her life and carries only the briefest annotation of dates and phases.

36 Sylvia Plath: *Collected Poems*, ed. Ted Hughes, London, 1981, p. 193, 'Elm'.

37 The poems gathered in *Collected Poems*, comprised earlier collections to which she gave names that were frequently changed, while seeking or awaiting publication. Thus *The Colossus* and *Ariel* appeared between 1962 and 1965, *Crossing the Water* in 1971. *Three Women* was a verse play, written in 1962.

38 *Ibid.*, 'The Three Women', 'A poem for Three Voices', p. 179.

39 *Journals*, p. 46. 'the universal woman-man . . . '. She wanted to 'justify' what she called 'my bold, brave humanitarian faith' (p. 159) and was moved to yearn over the meaning of Dachau and Hiroshima, yet somehow stayed clueless in her self-absorption.

40 *Ibid.*, p. 150. 'Wearily' here tells its own story. The suicides of September 11, 2001 would have written: 'zealously', 'avidly', 'utterly', having no reservations to stay their hand from any 'weariness' about the world, no inhibitions around their 'Cause'. Indeed the word 'cause' had changed its whole meaning from being a 'factor' and become a set 'objective'. The contradiction, moreover, in this language – whether in Plath's despairing usage or theirs in aggressive resolve – is that nothing 'totalitarian' can absolve the private conscience of its vital 'jury' status and its veto. See below and *Servare Regnare*.

41 On the 'controversies' of the Hughes/Plath marriage see: Erica Wagner: *Ariel's Gift, Ted Hughes & Sylvia Plath and the Story of Birthday Letters*, London, 2000. It foundered after six years when he occasioned her separation from him. Was she too manipulative of emotions – his and hers – and frustrated by self-doubt in the ambition to be the perfect wife, mother, writer that her dream demanded? 'Ted is the ideal, the only possible person,' she wrote, three years into the marriage (*Journals*, p. 519) while he would come to see her as 'the jailor of her own murderer'.

42 *Journals*, p. 405.

43 As the king, Lear, invites his Cordelia in Shakespeare's *King Lear*, Scene 23, line 16. For 'mystery', in their dread case, they surely were, so far so that for long decades King Lear was only played with a changed and bearable ending such as audiences demanded. The tragic will not admit our will to inattention.

44 'The barnacle dead' was one of Sylvia Plath's stark images.

45 Theists, especially 'unitarians', will want – and need – to say that this 'beyond-us' is not exhausted in its 'towards-us' character. This caveat is right and necessary so long as what 'transcends' does not, in doing so, forfeit or withhold the other measure of 'omnipotence' as ever 'self-imparting'.

46 Paul, 2 Corinthians 4.5. To present this Christian theology is not to preclude other traditions from reaching towards a rationale of the divine/human theme, from within, if not despite, their readings of the world, of life and time.

10   Faith and the Bond with Life

1 William Shakespeare: *Hamlet*, Act 5, Scene 2, lines 299–301.

2 *Ibid.*, lines 296–7.

3 John Masefield: cited in A. P. Wavell, *Other Men's Flowers*, London, 1944, p. 44.

4 The Qur'an lays heavy stress on the mystery of birth, the care of parents for the time of infancy and, strikingly, the debts we must pay to orphans. All adult duty is thus reciprocal to the entrustedness in human rearing.

5 'Untimely', not in the sense of incidence, but of duration, in that suicide foreshortens the span for which birth otherwise allowed. It resembles people in a theatre leaving before the ending of the play or, better, its actors quitting the stage while the 'plot' still unfolds.

6 The Greek term used means the manumission of a slave who is being legally exempted from that status. The prayer is not for leniency but for liberation, and the 'Let . . . ' is truly 'dismissive'. The very term makes the point central here of life as 'indentured' service. However, this is so much more than the Socratic idea of some untethered farm animal taking its own 'leave to go'.

7 'For their content' is crucial here. 'Utility', 'the common good', or even 'common sense' may well devise their codes. Reason is capable of ethical structures but what of criteria and motivation, if these only have some force of logic?

8 Philip Larkin: *Collected Poems*, ed. Anthony Thwaite, London, 2003, p. 109.

9 'Compassionate' is the familiar and common translation of the second descriptive, *Al-Rahim*, in the Muslim *Bismillah*, qualifying the first *Al-Rahman*. If the Latin *compassio* means 'suffering with' the Islamic doctrine of Allah's total 'non-association' must exclude it – though it entirely fits the Christian sense of the 'Passion' of Jesus as within the being of God. Otherwise 'compassionate' must be broadly synonymous with 'merciful'.

10 It was in the nature of their Islam that faith required the murder of its foes. They never used missiles, or poisons, but only daggers or clubs or strangulation. The lofty mountain of Alamut, near to Qazvin, Persia, was the stronghold of 'the Old Man of the Mountain', and their most famous place-symbol. Much of their fiery tradition stemmed from Shi'ah (Nizari) enmity to Sunnis. By their lights Allah had two 'proofs' – the speaker and the silent one, i.e. the 'executor of the speaker's 'testament. In this way, did they formulate the relation of Medina to Mecca for their sectarian mind? Scholars warn that something of their legend may need suspicion from hostile Sunni sources, straining veracity.

11 Both Jalal-al-Din's family and the Assassins were also harassed by Seljuq Turks who, like the Mongols, came into Islam after subduing it.

12 The famous lines in John Donne's renowned sermon were current, as we noted earlier, even in Ernest Hemingway's universe of narrative range. The preacher's point, however, was not about the toll and pathos of civil war but about how the villager should know himself so 'involved in mankind' that he need not interrogate the tolling bell about the identity of the newly deceased. He too was kindredly mortal and mortally akin. This allows us always to ask who and where and why society's vulnerable are. In the one case being 'involved in mankind' makes 'sending to know' unnecessary: in the other imperative.

13 William Shakespeare: *The Merchant of Venice*, Act 4, Sc. 1, line 180, 'compul-

sion', like 'impulse', is used here in the sense of constraint, i.e. a strong sense of obligation. It should not be confused with the 'compulsion' of Surah 2. 256, translating *ikraha*, i.e. something 'forcible', and being also 'detestable'.

14   *First Epistle of John*, 4.19. The 'him' some versions have after 'We love . . . ' is not in the Greek.

15   The central point here is that the 'shepherd' descriptive of God passes over to the caring Church, as if having His 'Name' for their descriptive meant being characterized according to God. Judaic psalmody pioneered this image in Christianity of 'shepherding' as crucial to religious existence and 'office'. No analogy can contain truth without demerit (e.g. in non-sheep-rearing cultures or imagination is wanting. Yet 'Lord Chancellors' sit on 'woolsack'). The shepherd metaphor is absent from the Qur'an and in Arabic the root *ra'a* has more the sense of 'keeping', e.g. a pledge or a covenant. Yet, given the entire control and mastery a shepherd has, it altogether fits Islamic concepts of divine sovereignty, while having also patience and gentle solicitude therewith.

16   Giving the word 'ministry', the breadth and range it has here raised this issue of 'differential' between the two. In any event and duly understood, 'office' as 'ministry' in Christianity means no exclusion of the non-ordained from their integral role. Islam, with powerful 'authority-wielders', has its own form of this situation but with significant accent, via *Ijtihad* and 'consensus' on 'lay' status.

17   A familiar Methodist hymn of this prolific writer, drawing from Hebraic sources the analogy of the altar where 'the fire must never go out'. Only 'complete' at death could well also be a Muslim verdict (excluding suiciders.)

18   That 'ministry' belongs with both Church and State is an intriguing example of the vicissitudes of language usage. A *magisterium* may give itself airs, but a *ministerium* is more suited to modesty than arrogance.

19   The final verse belongs with the first in the unity of the psalm. '*All* the days of life' are somehow needed to test the lastingness of his assurance. The original sense of 'always being in the house of the Lord' is his comment on mortality.

20   Wolf Mankowitz: *The Extraordinary Mr. Poe, A Biography*, London, 1978, p. 23. This is not to argue that there are, or have been, no 'compassionate atheists'. It is feasible to draw a pursuit of common good from many case-makings of reason and desire. There will always remain Shylock's question: 'Upon what compulsion must I?' with the answer, from such passions, far to seek.

21   Throughout in Browning's major poems but most ardently in 'Saul' where David, playing his soothing music to the broken King, cannot believe that 'love so full in my nature, God's ultimate gift' is superior to God's love. Or doubt that 'His own love can compete with it,' so that 'here the parts shift' and 'the creature surpass the Creator – the end what began', Robert Browning: *Poetical Works*, Oxford, 1941, p. 231.

11   These Unbelieving Believers

1   Just as 'genocide' or 'deicide' were neologisms once.

2   In respect of subsidy paid to bereaved families, sometimes with their homes demolished in retribution, as tributary succour from 'supportive' states or private parties.

3   'Those who go astray' is the opening Surah's term for those who are off 'the

straight path'. 'Vagrancy' is thus the right word for the perceived licentious, lustful, 'godless' ways of the West and its corrosive intrusion into Muslim life and society.

4   It is the will that is so often lacking – given, on the one side, the self-sufficiency of Islam, an almost inassailable instinct to feel itself secure in its own finality having no reason to enquire outside itself; and, on the other, the impatience of the West, its proneness to hasty and superior verdicts that miss the deep diversities in Islam and the wealth of its cultures as poetry and arts could tell them. Revulsion needs to be checked by longer horizons. If, either way, some will is present, there *are* the mutual positives that could come to meet and reward it. See further.

5   John Milton: *Paradise Lost*, Book viii, line 296 has it: 'thy mansion waits thee, Adam rise . . . ' not, however, of some paradisial 'garden', but the intelligible earth, presented for human tenure, but only on the basis of mind and will responding to its capacities open to his purpose – nature as potential of 'dominion', humankind potential of its making real and actual.

6   John Milton, *ibid.*, Book v, lines 529–34.

7   As in writers like Ionesco, Camus, Beckett and other despairers in the quest for meaning, and the sundry sceptics about the 'games' of language usage, as well as the loss of nerve about religious doctrine and fear, or anxiety about the integrity of its institutions, the pervasive instinct in such quarters for 'not believing in belief'.

8   In that the mandate is not withdrawn. God does not 'weary of mankind'. Generations indeed pass but not their sequence.

9   The theme of humankind and the natural order – and its being kindredly read so, alike in the Bible and the Qur'an – is documented more fully from both in my: *A Certain Sympathy of Scriptures, Biblical & Quranic*, Brighton & Portland, 2004. The movement in the meaning of *fitnah*, the different shapes of 'trial', was noted in Chapter 8, note 33.

10 Sam Harris: *The End of Faith: Religion, Terror and the Future of Reason*, New York, 2004. He finds it 'difficult to imagine a set of beliefs more suggestive of mental illness than those that lie at the heart of many of our religious traditions'. Islam, it would seem, is the immediate phenomenon conducing to this verdict. So-called 'liberals' inside the wretched creeds only make matters worse, by palliating the credulity and drawing back towards sanity scriptures and doctrines that it were better to jettison altogether. They too are cowards with blood on their hands by attempting to rationalize the indefensible. This writer ignores whole stretches of Islamic culture and faith in the vehemence of his indictment. Nor does he register anything in Islam but the hidebound and the fixated.

11 Religions as 'licensed lunacies' has often been alleged by 20th century dismay at the jeopardy into which they throw society and culture, countering 'sweet reason' and 'gentle compassion'. These values, always needing the caring custody faith should bring, find themselves the more betrayed.

12 *Loc. cit.*, note 10. How, on Quranic ground, this might not be so, see below.

13 The hyphenated word seems right, in that 'renew' or 'reform' or 'revise' might imply 'alteration' and so deter its would-be 'loyalists'. 'Re-new' suggests finding what it first meant with the change belonging, not to it, but to the new

context. Reading both is, of course, the perennial issue, taking Islam again to Meccan 'witness' but with the present necessity to 'co-exist' amid diversity – a posture 7th century Meccan Islam could not conceive as 'Islamic', and, then and there, never faced.

14 Such as Sam Harris would seem to imply in so far despairing of (or excluding wilfully) any Muslim sanity so that on no account must they be allowed to become nuclear-armed or equipped with W.M.D.

15 '*Aql* (mind) and its verb-derivative *ta'qilun* ('you sound-minders sound-mindering') or *tatafakkarun* ('you with reflective wits, use them, please') are its steady appeal. To be sure, Surah 2.2 describes the Qur'an as 'a Book with nothing dubious therein', but this re-assurance need not mean that there is no occasion to 'give it your mind'.

16 How to discern between them is left to the reader, with a rider about the 'unstable' drawing wrong conclusions from what is allegorical. By the very nature of language, the two may well merge into each other.

17 All faiths have to face this liability to be custodians of texts however sacrosanct. It is a hazard inseparable from the very notion of 'scriptured revelation'. Islam has a uniquely sharp form of the situation, inasmuch as the script *is* the revelation. It is not – as elsewhere – *about* what is antecedently 'revelatory' in event, history and personality.

18 Harris: *The End of Faith: Religion, Terror and the Future of Reason, op. cit.*

19 This summary of Islam's essential 'relevance' to humankind at large is why despair or denigration of it must be banished from attitudes of mind or prejudice of discourse. The five 'elements' here are more thoroughly presented, via the Qur'an's own question, in my: *Am I Not Your Lord?*, London, 2003.

20 The sentence is nominal and so lacks a verb and reads literally 'no compulsion in religion'. Is the meaning a virtual prohibition' ('there ought not to be') or a statement of fact ('there is no compulsion'). It cannot be both, in that the second would make the first unnecessary – unless something like 'Let us not have' is meant. The root sense of *ikraha* is that which makes for the detestation of what inflicts it. Leaving you unfree makes religion hateful.

21 'Those in whose hearts there is a sickness' (*marad*) is its comment on unbelievers in Surahs 2.10, 5.52, 8.49, 9.125, 22.53, 24.50, 33.12, 47.20 and 29, and 74.31, sometimes statement, sometimes query. It is almost a refrain, a steady assumption of Islam about non-Islam. But does the 'disease' analogy admit of reproach or guilt, if it 'cannot be helped'? The diagnosis is readily reversible.

22 Both are brought together in Matthew 5.45–8, with the precept: 'Be ye inclusive (*teleios*) as your heavenly Father is.'

23 Some have seen the current diaspora as a form of *hijrah*. All turns on whether it 'binds' the Muslim to seek to 'Islamize' his haven politically or dwell in it faith-wise religiously.

Index of Names and Terms

Index of Names and Terms

Index of Names and Terms

Index of Themes

Index of Themes

death, vi, 20, 22, 23, 28, 34, 98, 105, 107, 120, 130
   death-dealing, vi., 28, 29, 123, 124
   death-wish, 5, 28, 57, 106, 114, 124
   singularity of, 25, 54, 96, 196
delusion, gift for, 111
democracy – dubious concept, 9
despair, human, vii, 31, 108, 109, 111, 112, 144, 162
   Masada style, 42, 43
destiny to die, 33, 43, 112
   in Samson, 37
destiny to live, 19, 21, 58
diaspora, of Muslims, 9, 102, 103, 139. 140
disciples of Jesus, dereliction of, 74f.
disdain for life, 28, 41f., 122
distrust of life, 109. 110, 116
divine/human, inter-meaning, 127, 128 *see also* creaturehood
dreamings, 115

economy, God's, our place in, 119 *see also khilafah*
ecstacy, in martyrdom, 81, 82, 88, 122
emulation, in suicide, 28
   on Masada, 41f.
eschatology, ethics of, in Islam, 98
Eucharist, Christian, 52
   origin in Passover, 67
evil, problem of, 141

faith, and coercion, 138, 139
faith, as freedom, 118
faith's root in history, 74
faith – role in truth, 128, 129, 138, 140
Father/Son relation in Christian theology, 80, 81, 82, 83, 85, 127, 128
'feminism', in V. Woolf, 112, 113
fictions, as fact, 112
fideocide, 130f., 138, 164
finality, in Islam, 101, 142

'garden' in John's Gospel, 73, 154, 165
God – 'character' of, 75, 82, 84, 99
   'good faith' of, 80, 83
   will of, 98, 99
'God in Christ', 70, 80, 81, 82, 83, 90, 118, 127, 128, 153
Gospels, the, 60f., 75, 76
   their *post-facto* witness, 74f.
   Synoptics and John, 80f.
gratitude, 13, 132 *see also shukr*
greeting, restrictive, 19, 139, 144, 145
grief, appeal to in suicide, 123

hagiology, 58, 59
heart, unhardening of, 89

heroism, 33, 123
history and faith, 74f., 77, 82, 83, 127, 128, 129, 133, 148, 155
   despair over, 112, 113, 114
   in the New Testament, 142, 155
hope/despair in Iscariot, 60f., 74
hostage to the ego, 115, 116
humanism, Semitic, 11 *see also* creaturehood/*khilafah*
human rights, 126

image, defining, in Islam, 90, 102 *see also* Hijrah
   false in suicide, 131f.
imagery to sustain compassion, 124, 125, 126 *see also* shepherd
   in John's Gospel, 73
immortality by dying, 30
Incarnation, the, 56, 76, 83, 128, 154
Indian Islam, 19th century experience, 102
individuality, accent on Islam, 20
infancy, charm of, 115
   debts of, 12
insanity (?) in suicide, 20, 52
intention, divine – in creation, 5, 10, 11, 140
intercourse, sexual, *see also* birth
interrogations, in persecution, 54, 59
intolerance, 92, 93
irony, in life and religion, 1, 30, 35, 52, 92, 101, 121
irony, in suicide, 121f.
Islam – basic issue in, 8, 87f.
   conscience in, vi, 9
   self-referent, 92f.
   suicide in, 1, 86f.
   suicide legitimated, 95, 96
   suicide un-Islamic, 3, 5, 100f., 123, 130f.
   two Islams?, 29
   as tolerant, 102

Jewry and Rome, 40f., 47 *see also* Josephus
Jewish Revolt, the, 28, 41
Judas, the significance, 56f., 84
   'and Satan', 69, 70
   tragedy of, 65, 66 *see also* Edwin Muir
Judaism, 47, 48 *see also* Zionism
   in Primo Levi, 109, 110
Judgement of God, subverted, 99, 145
justice, limits of, 82 *see also* redemption

'Kingdom of God', the, 61, 155
'kiss', of Iscariot, 60f., 153
   irony of, 65

'Lamb of God', the, 70, 75, 80
language, issues for, 135, 136, 167

Index of Themes

Index of Themes

Roman factors in suicidal martyrdom, 50f.

sacramental, the, 6, 13, 126
  lack of, 115, 116
sacrifice – ambivalent term, 32, 38, 70, 71,
    124, 147
Scriptures, in readership trust, 27, 94, 134,
    135, 136, 166
secular, the, 133, 155
self
  assessment incessant, 115
  consenting, 11
  dispossession, 118, 119
  estrangement, 112
  exiting, 9, 32, 35, 45, 110
  fulfillment, vi, 31, 132, 135
  homicide, 1, 22f., 86f., 98, 121, 124
  refusal, vi, 107, 108
  storage, vi
  unwanted, 110, 111
  vindication, 31f.
selfhood, sanctity of, 22, 96, 118, 119, 131,
    141, 142
  disavowal of, 86f. 96, 108
'shepherd' analogy the, 58, 126, 128, 129,
    163, 164
  role of, 118, see also society, a caring
'sending the Son', 77, 78, 79, 80, 82, 83,
    84
'signs' and sciences, 132
  and sentience, 13, 132, 133
'sin of the world', 70, 77, 79 see also vine-
    yard parable
society, a caring, 118
solipsism, 116
'something there' – sense of, 112
suffering, 27, 74, 80, 122
  the 'servant', 80, 83, 87
  for society, 92 see also redemption
Sufism, 126, 134
suicide
  an absolute, in quest of, 115, 116, 117
  antecedent factors in Islam, 86f., 92
  bravado and, 107
  constraints against, 121f., 125
  constraints for, 8, 24, 100f., 160
  enigma in, vi, 99, 106f., 117
  faith prompted, 86
  in families?, 109, 111
  fated?, 9, 108
  insanity assumed in, 20, 138, 139, 165
  Islamic incidence, current frequency, vii,
    8, 9, 86f., 117
  of Judas Iscariot, 7, 8, 60f., 68f., 150
  malignity in, vii, 41f., 86, 92, 96, 122
  pathology and, 95
  perspective on, vii, 108, 109
  pity for, 23, 24

pride in, 130 see also Eleazar
sophistication in, 93, 94, 96
tragedy of, 4, 23, 86f., 103, 104f.
treachery to life, 9, 24, 87
unfaith in, 100, 104f., 117
untimely dying in, 98, 122, 162
veto and question of, 5, 10f., 15, 16,
    22f., 96, 99
vicissitudes of life prompting, 105, 108,
    117
zealotry and, 40f., 86f., 150

Temple, the earth as, 13
Temple, Jerusalem, 44, 47, 48, 76, 155
  cleansing of, 62, 63
terrorism(s), 94, 134, 135, 165
theology, source of, 13, 73f.
'as thyself', meaning of, 23f.
tragedy, in appeal to life, 120, 123
transcendence, 112, 117, 123, 136, 137
  issue in, for language, 137
tribute to Caesar, 66
truth, credentials of, 128, 129, 139
truth/power equation, 29, 138

unbelieving unbelief, 8, 130f.

vengeance as suicide motive, 31, 34
vicarious, the – in life, 32, 80f. see also
    bearers of wrong
vineyard parable, the, 77, 78, 79, 81, 82, 83
violence, vii, 22, 35, 87, 95, 100f., 107,
    124, 138, 158
  Samson style, 23f.
  sources in Islam, 87, 88, 90, 95
vocabulary theological, 27, 136, 137
vocation to the future, 121, 122, 124 see
    also bonding with life
vocation, Messianic, 73f.
vulnerable religion, 7, 139, 140
  serving the vulnerable, 124, 125

wantedness of the world, 12 see also
    creation
West, the, 102, 158, 164
  Islamic attitude to, 6, 8, 93, 94, 95, 96,
    97, 131
  power superiority of, 96, 131
West/East divide, 102
West/Islam inter-relation, 131, 134
witness-*martur* dual meaning, 27, 52, 54,
    57
womanhood, 112, 113, 116
wonder, 12, 115 see also the sacramental
'the Word made flesh', 58, 76, 82, 90, 137
word and sacrament, 126
worlds, public and private, 112, 113
worship, divine, 123, 127, 128, 132, 137

Biblical References

Hebrew Bible		New Testament	
Genesis		**Matthew**	
3.8-9	154	5.45–48	19, 20, 166
9.5	17	10.23	56
Deuteronomy		11.12	62, 152
4.9	16	11.28–30	152
Judges		16.13f.	76
9.54	16	27.5	152
16.21–31	31, 32, 36, 37	**Mark**	
1 Samuel		8.27f.	76
10.1	153	10.45	154
31.5	16	14.26	85
2 Samuel		14.44	65
17.23	16	**Luke**	
1 Kings		2.20	122, 143, 144
16.18	16	9.18f.	76
Psalm		12.8	57
2.11	65, 153	14.26	54
23 all	128	16.16	62
41.5	71	22.28	66
63.3	127	22.48	65
119.109	19	22.53	62
Job		**John**	
17.15-16	16, 17	1.1–14	83, 84, 155
Isaiah		8.22	74
53 all	83	10.14–18	58, 74, 85, 154
Jeremiah		13.8	71
7.16	153	14.1f.	66, 84
11.18–23	155	17 all	69, 80
12.1–6	155	18.1	72
15.10–12	155	18.30	60
17.9–18	155	**Acts**	
18.18–23	155	1.18	152
20.7–12	155	**Romans**	
Hosea		7 all	81
3.5	150	8.31	90
13.9	47	12.19	100, 159
1 Maccabees		**2 Corinthians**	
2.29–38	46	4.5	119
		Philippians	
		1.23-24	21.145

Biblical References

Hebrews
5.8	75, 154
9.27	146
11.32	33
12.3	155

1 John
4.19	163

Revelation
1.9	53
7.17	154

Quranic References

Surah 1 all	2, 134, 141	13.40	156
Surah 2.2	157, 166	Surah 16.61	18
2.30	133, 143	16.70	18
2.87	77, 135		
2.106	146	Surah 19.13	18
2.193	95		
2.217	91	Surah 21.16	131
2.256	138		
		Surah 22.74	100, 136, 159
Surah 3.7	135		
3.19	2, 157	Surah 39.67	100, 136, 159
Surah 4.29	13, 18	Surah 40.41	156
Surah 5.30	18	Surah 41.44	156
5.32	17, 18		
5.105	19, 24	Surah 50.37	113
Surah 6.91	100, 136, 159	Surah 56.58	6
6.162	95		
		Surah 62.11	156
Surah 11.16	144		
		Surah 74.31	166
Surah 12.2	135		
		Surah 96 all	3
Surah 13.39	146		